MW01484589

RAV DOVBER PINSON

INNER
WORLDS

OF

JEWISH

PRAYER

A GUIDE TO DEVELOP AND DEEPEN YOUR PRAYER EXPERIENCE

RAV DOVBER PINSON   ב״ה

INNER WORLDS OF
JEWISH PRAYER

A GUIDE TO DEVELOP AND DEEPEN
THE PRAYER EXPERIENCE

 IYYUN PUBLISHING

Published by IYYUN Publishing
232 Bergen Street
Brooklyn, NY 11217

http:/www.iyyun.com

Iyyun Publishing books may be purchased for educational, business or sales promotional use. For information please contact: contact@IYYUN.com

cover and book design: RP Design and Development

pb ISBN 978-0-9890072-2-1

Pinson, DovBer 1971-
Inner Worlds of Jewish Prayer: A Guide to Develop and Deepen the Prayer Experience
1.Judaism 2. Spirituality 3. Philosophy

DEDICATION

THANK YOU

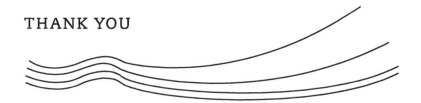

DR. HANNA AND DR. MORDECHAI WOSK
Vancouver, BC

MR. MORRIS & MRS. DANY SAFDIE
São Paulo, Brazil

MR. Y. LEVIN
New York

HA'TAMIM, MR. YONAH POLIS-SCHUTZ
La Jolla - Jerusalem

REB. EDEN PEARLSTEIN
Brooklyn, New York

MR. LENNY GROSS
New York

*To all those who contributed to this work,
may it be for a blessing.*

TABLE OF CONTENTS

INTRODUCTION

PRAYER IS A PHILOSOPHER'S BEST FRIEND AND WORST ENEMY—ABSTRACT, EXPERIENTIAL, AND ENIGMATIC; AS WELL AS IRRATIONAL, AFFECTIVE, AND ESOTERIC.

For everything that has been written about prayer, what seems to be most important, and most lacking, is an exploration and explanation of the actual inner experience of prayer.

Basic questions, such as:
  What is happening when I am praying?
  What is the appropriate mind-state for prayer?
  How does the body fit in to prayer?

What role do I play in my own prayer experience?
Are there techniques to enhance my experience of prayer?
How can I enter prayer fully?

These questions have been, for the most part, ignored.

There are many books that seek to elucidate the meaning of the prayers themselves, paying particular attention to the poetry, history, and theology of the actual texts that comprise the Seder/order of the Siddur/prayerbook.

It is specifically to enhance the reader's comprehension of the contextual breadth and depth of the liturgy that such books exist. This type of approach is effective in so much as it helps make the words of the prayers themselves more meaningful. This functions well on the intellectual level, the realm of ideas. But in today's cultural climate people are demanding more than just good ideas. In the digital age we are inundated with 'good ideas.' Everything we want or need to know on the level of information is available. What we are truly lacking, and that for which many people are yearning for is good, positive, uplifting and transformative experience. This requires an understanding of not only the prayers themselves, but of the inner process and practice of prayer as a spiritual act.

It is not enough for a majority of people these days to be shown a beautiful idea contained within a particular prayer. That bit of poetry, no matter how divinely inspired, does not provide the practitioner with enough experiential information or insight to animate that good idea, to embody it, and allow it to transform their very being as they are speaking it. That kind of understanding only comes from the realm of experience.

With this book, it is my intention to provide the traveler along the path of prayer with more than just informative signposts and mile markers, but with practical step-by-step wisdom on walking the path of meaningful and transformative prayer. In this way, one's experience of prayer may be transformed from an obligation to be discharged into an opportunity to be recharged.

PRESENCE

PRAYER:
A Path of Presence

THE PRIMARY OBSTRUCTION TO A DEEP AND FULFILLING PRAYER EXPERIENCE IS ONE OF PRESENCE. Whether it is in regards to one's own awareness and focus, or in relation to exactly Whose presence one is standing within during the act of prayer, the importance of presence is paramount.

It is quite difficult for most people to transition from one state of being into another, but that is exactly what is required of one who seeks to enter into a prayerful mode. One must shift from one state of mind into another in order to maximize the transformative potential within the experience of prayer.

This ability is not only present within the dynamics of prayer, but permeates all time-bound Mitzvos or spiritual practices. For instance, in order to fully access and appreciate Shabbos one must enter into a Shabbos state of mind or being. If one is in a weekday mode during Shabbos it will be much more difficult to acknowledge and appreciate the unique gift of Shabbos. Similarly, if one is mentally still at work while they are taking care of their child, they will most likely not be fully present in the moment and will hence miss out on the unique experience that such a moment has to offer. The same holds true for prayer.

One must be in a prayerful state to properly pray. One must be able to switch 'programs' so to speak in order to either leave behind the minutiae of their busy day, or to pack it all up and bring it along with them as they enter into prayer. With this understanding we can view prayer as both something that one does, as well as something that one actually is (i.e. 'prayerful').

In the context of formal structured prayer we pray three times a day — morning, afternoon and evening. With this three times daily prayer schedule an individual is asked to move into and out a state of prayerful presence numerous times throughout their day.

In the morning one makes the transition from the dream-state of sleep into the waking state through a series of blessings, songs and readings known as *Shacharis*/the morning prayers. In the afternoon one is required to take a break in the middle of the workday, with all of its demands and details, in order to enter into a quick yet potent prayer cycle called *Mincha*. In the evening, as one's tasks are coming to a close, the prayer of *Ma'ariv* comes to remind one of their relationship to the Divine before going off to sleep, the place from which the day emerged.

To further illustrate this dynamic let us look to the words of our sages.

Our sages tell us that upon entering the synagogue or place of worship we should, "walk in a measure of two doors before beginning to pray" *(Berachos, 8a)*.

In addition to the literal meaning of this teaching, which is not to stand by the exit-door when we pray, this teaching also suggests a deeper meaning.

Namely, that we need to leave behind one door/reality/state and enter into a new door/reality/state as we approach the act of prayer. We need to shift our awareness from one state to another.

But how do we do this?

How does one affect their awareness and improve their quality of presence before prayer? How does one incorporate and integrate such an idea into practice? Stated more philosophically, the question emerges as: "How does one transition from the phenomenal world of multiplicity to the essential world of unity, from the mundane to the sacred, from the surface to the secret of reality?"

Our sages hint at this dilemma when they state that, "The Sages of old would tarry for an hour before prayer, then they would pray for an hour, then they would tarry for an hour after prayer" *(Berachos, 32b)*.

Tradition teaches that the Sages would in fact meditate for an hour before prayer in order to prepare themselves to pray, as well as for an hour after praying so as to allow the ripples of their prayer to trickle down and settle into their psyche and soul before returning to their busy day.

The sages understood that one could not just jump into prayer. One needs to 'stretch' or 'warm- up' first, so that when one enters into their prayers they are fully awake and engaged. This kind of preparation for spiritual practice, which is an integral aspect of the practice itself, opens one up, calms one down, and activates a more receptive and relaxed state of being within the practitioner.

Simply put: The success of one's prayer is dependent upon one's preparations. In the words of a Chassidic Rebbe, "If you see that you are successful in the preparations for prayer, know that your prayers are already in the process of being answered" *(Pri Tzadik, Vayeshev, 3)*.

This is a prime example of exactly the sort of experiential approach to prayer that we seek to further explore.

WHAT IS PRAYER?

Before proceeding any further, we would be well served to outline some of the broad contours of what we are referring to when we say the word prayer.

This brief introduction is by no means exhaustive or definitive, but is merely meant to present some of the more paradigmatic aspects of prayer.

When one uses the somewhat generic word 'prayer' in the English vernacular they may likely be referring to a set order of religious services, the outpourings of an anxious heart, a serene end-of-day soul accounting, or some frantic version of foxhole mutterings. For our purposes in exploring the heights and depths of prayer as a transformative and spiritual practice we will pull from all of these associations, and many more.

At various times we all feel the need to pray, to reach out, to make contact with or acknowledge 'something' beyond us. In that moment we are attempting to sense that which is beneath or behind all of the mess, pain, confusion and apparent randomness of life.

But on an even deeper level, we recognize that aside from all of the specifics of one's life situation that is prompting them to 'pray', the initial impetus to pray ultimately originates from the fact that we all just want to sense a feeling of connection in our lives — a connection to our deeper selves, to our purpose, to our community, to the world around us, and ultimately to G-d.

Interestingly, the Hebrew letters that comprise the word *Tefilah*/prayer, when rearranged, spell the word

Pesilah/string or rope. Prayer can thus be understood as our way of throwing a rope to *Hashem*/G-d, or better yet, of grabbing onto the rope that Hashem is constantly throwing us. In reality, we are always bound as one with Hashem. Prayer just allows us to observe and experience this unity in a conscious way.

WHERE DOES PRAYER COME FROM?

There is a place deep inside our hearts wherein we all desperately desire some sense of profound connection beyond all the brokenness and alienation. It is from such a place that we aspire to make contact and communicate with something larger than ourselves, something more whole, intense, real and beautiful.

It is paradigmatically human to seek out, uncover or reveal such a place of perfection within this imperfect world, finding joy in the place of sadness, light in the place of darkness, and holiness in the place of foolishness.

We all deeply yearn for this. We all hope fervently that something will change, either inside of us or within the world itself. We all want more out of life and this inner hunger is the beginning of prayer. When we become aware of and reveal this inner aspiration, prayer occurs naturally and shifts begin to occur. From this raw and vulnerable place deep within, prayer is born.

In this way, prayer is like peeling an onion. You peel away layer by layer, going deeper and deeper. And as you do, you begin to tear up. You start to cry because as you are going deeper into the core, more of you is being revealed. All of the hidden layers of your psyche and soul — the memories, dreams, traumas, and fears that you harbor — are being exfoliated and begin to emerge. You are making a connection with your deeper self and at the same time allowing that deeper self to reach out and reveal that sense of connection with the Creator of the universe.

Walking the path of prayer is an often slow and sometimes heart wrenching *Avodah*/spiritual practice. We do not just chop open the onion to get to the core in one slice of the knife. Getting to the core without dealing with the multiple layers and veils that surround it is potentially more dangerous and deceptive than not embarking upon such a journey in the first place. This kind of instant gratification approach misses the point of the entire process, which is the revelation and reflection of the Infinite One within our finite lives. Rather, we slowly and arduously peel the proverbial onion layer by layer, prayer by prayer, word by word, breath by breath.

STANDING UPRIGHT:

Before one is able to walk the path of prayer, one must be able to stand firmly. You cannot walk if you cannot first stand. Prayer allows us to stand, and later, from that place of strength deep within, to move forward.

This is alluded to in the very name of the main section of our set prayers, the *Amidah*/standing prayer.

The Amidah is so central to the idea of prayer that it is referred to by our sages simply as *HaTefilah*/the prayer.

To stand means to be present — to encounter and engage.

In a sense, when one prays in the presence of the Most High one is standing up in a variety of ways. One is standing up to bear witness to the reality of the Creator of all Being and Source of all Blessing. One is standing up for themselves, for their needs, dreams, and desires. One is also standing up for others who are in need of help or healing. In prayer, one is essentially standing up for their belief in G-d, in themselves, and in the possibility of a better, healthier, happier and holier world.

Of course, one is also standing up in a different way — they are standing up to face and take responsibility for their own shortcomings, doubts, and misdeeds. In prayer, one stands up amidst the rubble of their own life, rising precisely from within their own brokenness, pain and hurt. And from there they are able to lament suffering while at the same time longing to connect with the Master and Life of the Universe in simple faith.

Hashem's presence is with us giving us the strength to move forward and to bridge the abyss of those longings — to heal, repair, transcend and become ever more holy and whole.

Clearly, the journey is perpetual. Once one gap is filled, we should long for more and more healing, wholeness and holiness. Every day we pray in the morning, afternoon and evening — always longing, sometimes reaching, and longing again.

A People Born in Prayer:

We have been speaking primarily of intrapersonal elements concerning one's process and practice of prayer, but our relationship to prayer is also founded upon our collective story.

Our collective history began as slaves in Egypt. Indeed, the Israelites were enslaved for a few hundred years before there was any sign of shift or salvation. During this period the Israelites just accepted their situation; they begrudgingly bore the load of their oppression. There were no prayers uttered. The people did not express their personal or collective suffering or yearning for change, for freedom, for something different.

In truth, these two things are linked: The Israelites' enslavement and their inability to pray. For it was not until they began to express their pain to Hashem that they were redeemed. This is reflected in the Torah's statement concerning the beginning of the Israelites' liberation, "and they groaned...and Hashem heard their groan" *(Shemos, 2:23-24)*. There is a profound connection between speech and salvation.

Only once there was a groan, a crying out, a reaching towards an alternate reality, was there a "hearing Above" — and so began the process of their redemption. Prayer is the path of liberation through acknowledgment and articulation.

The 'groan' or sigh was enough to relax the inner rigidity that had accumulated within the slaves during their years of abuse, both individual and collective.

This opening, the actual sigh, softened their heart and allowed them to sense their relationship with something greater, something outside their condition of slavery.

And slowly, as a result of that first guttural groan, that non-verbal and unselfconscious expression of pain and yearning for change, they were eventually redeemed from their bondage and taken out to walk with G-d towards their Promised Land. The opening below aroused an opening Above. As they softened, so in a manner of speaking did Hashem. And in response to their opening, Hashem began to open the way for their redemption.

THE REDEMPTIVE NATURE OF PRAYER:

The act of praying is redemptive. When we have the ability to express our hurt, desire and yearning, this itself is a form of inward redemption. The deepest exile is an exile of speech. To be human is to be a Medaber/speaking being. When we cannot express ourselves, we are in exile; we are, in a way, less human. Taking away the ability to speak robs people of their humanity. Sometimes this silence is externally imposed, and yet, often it is internally generated. In this situation, one is in a state of deep exile or stuckness.

According to the Zohar, the story of the Israelites going out of Egypt is the story of our collective redemption from a seemingly external, but ultimately internal enslavement — an exile and redemption of speech *(Zohar 2, 25b)*.

A slave cannot express or reveal who he really is or what he wants, for his conditioning is imposed upon him. Speech implies choice, for it is through language that we define our reality. Additionally, a slave cannot truly listen to another, nor can they hear the possibility that things may be different.

Even though Moshe/Moses was essentially above slavery (as he was born into the un-enslaved tribe of Levi and raised as an Egyptian prince), he still could not easily speak. At the Burning Bush Moshe says of himself, "I am not a man of words, and I have a hard [or heavy] mouth" *(Shemos, 4:10)*; as well as, "the people will not listen to my voice" *(ibid. 4:1)*. These statements are related. Moshe could not speak because the people were not yet open to listening. At the same time, the people were unable to listen because there was no one to speak for them. There was no opening.

In Egypt the slaves were forced to do *Avodas Perach/* harsh labor. The word *Perach* can be broken down into the two words, *Peh Rach/*weak mouth *(Sotah, 11b)*.

This symbolizes the fact that their faculty of speech was in exile.

The word Pharaoh can also be pronounced *Peh Ra/* negative mouth. This symbolizes the force of negativity that sought to keep the slaves stuck within their current situation, with their hearts hardened and not open to change.

The word *Pesach*/Passover can be divided into two words, *Peh Sach*/the mouth speaks. When we have 'a mouth that speaks', we can liberate ourselves from our own 'weak mouth' and 'negative mouth'.

Prayer is a means of release from our own personal exile. When we are troubled and are given the amazing gift from Above — to stand in prayer and pour out our hearts — the act itself is redemptive, healing, and cathartic.

We were not only born in prayer, we in fact birthed ourselves through prayer. Prayer can thus be seen as a spiritual midwife for one's ultimate dreams and desires to be born into the world. That is precisely the work of prayer: To move one's inner potential into the realm of the actual.

THE HUMAN NATURE OF PRAYER:

It is a human instinct to pray.

A person is ontologically an *Alul*/effect, which is caused by the Ultimate prime *Ilah*/cause. Every Alul is connected to and needs its Ilah, and hence it is natural to pray *(Maharal, Netzach Yisrael, 23)*. It is only natural for an Alul to be drawn to its Ilah.

In fact, prayer is understood as a defining factor of what makes us human. A human being is referred to as a *Ma'aveh*. The word Ma'aveh is from a linguistic root which means 'implores, asks, or prays' *(Rashi, Baba Kama, 2a)*.

Furthermore, the hidden substance of the human being is prayer. The word *Adam*, the generic word for 'human', reveals this reality beautifully when we apply the Kabbalistic technique of "filling out" a word.

In this technique one spells a given word by actually spelling out each letter. For instance: The word Adam is not just spelled with the three Hebrew letters—*Aleph, Dalet, Mem*—as it usually is. Instead each of the three letters is spelled out: Aleph is Aleph, Lamed, Pei. Dalet is Dalet, Lamed, Tof. And Mem, is Mem, Mem. When you subtract all the "original" letters from the word Adam (Aleph, Dalet, Mem), you get the word, *Mispalel*/praying (Lamed, Pei, Lamed, Tof, Mem). The inner nature of an Adam is a being that prays.

WHO ARE WE? WE ARE PRAYERS, PRAY-ERS.

To live means to dream, to aspire, to long for. Some long for power, others for love, but at their root, all yearnings are ultimately for *Yichud*/Unity. Without awareness this primal longing can easily manifest in cravings for consumption, be it for a new possession or a new relationship, coupled with the mistaken belief that if we were able to just attain this one desire, completion would be achieved. When we feed our desires with false perception, satisfaction is never attained and frustration only increases. To respond to this root desire of all desires in a healthy way means to constantly be in a state of prayer, reaching ever inwards toward the Source of all Life, and reaching out to connect oneself to all that is good and holy.

In prayer we come to recognize that our lives are being lived within the presence of the Creator. It is through prayer that we transform the abstract and intellectual understanding of Hashem into a living and loving truth. In this way, through prayer, we make Divine reality our reality.

KAVANAH, INTENTION:

It would be a severe oversight while attempting to provide a deeper and more experiential understanding of the practice and process of prayer if there were no mention of the issue of *Kavanah*/intention. This brief note will have to serve as a general introduction, but rest assured, we will be exploring the concept of Kavanah in much more depth throughout the body of this text.

To put it simply, Kavanah is what turns speech into prayer, action into worship. It is the 'how' and the 'why' of whatever one may be doing. Kavanah is the underlying purpose and passion that propels one's pursuits.

One's Kavanah is directly related to the quality of one's presence while immersed in a given action. To become aware of one's Kavanah prior to or while engaged in a particular undertaking is an essential goal of all Mitzvos, especially prayer.

Often to achieve such a state of sensitized awareness in the moment of one's doing or being, it is necessary to 'take a moment' or a breath, pause to focus the mind, maybe even sing a melody or contemplate a passage from the Torah or Psalms to activate the imagination or open the heart.

Kavanah is where the experiential and the contextual aspects of prayer come into dynamic interplay.

Regarding prayer there are two main areas in which Kavanah is fundamental:

A) The act of prayer itself as being a real attempt at communication and relationship with the living presence of Hashem, who hears and answers our prayers. Prayer is not mere monologue, but rather a space created for profound dialogue. Our prayers are heard, and it is also through prayer that we open ourselves to hear. Therefore, one must seek to initiate and maintain an immediate awareness of the presence of the Infinite One in order for genuine prayer to occur. In Reality, Hashem is always listening. But it is only during the time of our prayer that we generally decide to consciously acknowledge and encounter this Infinite Presence in our lives. It is on account of the quality of this Kavanah that one is able to enter fully into the spiritual practice of prayer.

B) The depth and meaning of the words one is saying during the act of prayer. This pertains particularly to one who is praying during the three set prayers of the day from the *Siddur*, which is comprised of the pre-written words of our sages, prophets and the Torah. It is an alchemical act to transform the written prayers of an-other into the living words of one's own heart, and it is only with Kavanah that this is possible. Regarding these two fundamental Kavanos, there is an old argument about which is the most important Kavanah to hold while praying: Is it to concentrate on the meaning of the words, or is it to stay connected to the awareness that you are praying in front of The Infinite One who hears all prayer?

Clearly, the most important Kavanah and the most basic intention to establish while praying is that one is standing in front of the *Shechinah*/the immanent presence of the Most High *(Rambam, Hilchos Tefilah, 4:16)*. Without this general Kavanah there is no prayer *(R. Chaim Brisker. Al Ha'Rambam, ibid, 4:1)*. Without this intention, not only has the *Gavrah*/person not fulfilled his or her own obligation to pray, but the *Cheftzah*/ thing of prayer itself did not even occur (Likutei Sichos 22, p. 117). Ultimately, in order to properly pray we need to be in a prayerful state of mind. We need the *Hergesh*/feeling of literally being in the presence of the *Shechinah*/the Divine Presence while speaking to Hashem.

And yet, it goes without saying that it is also extremely

important to know what you are saying while praying. The best approach would be to engage both intentions together *(Miteler Rebbe. Hakdamah, Shar Ha'emuna.)*

In fact, it would be most commendable to use the *Pirush*/meaning of the words to arouse one's awareness and focus one's concentration on the fact that one is standing in front of Hashem throughout the course of the prayer.

In this way, the *Pirush Hamilos*/meaning of the words is not a distraction. Rather, it enhances the general awareness of just Whose presence one is standing within as they begin to pray.

EVERY PRAYER IS AUTHENTIC:

There is a well-known and universally retold parable:

> *Once there was a powerful king who built himself a beautiful castle. In order to furnish the castle he divided it evenly in half and called upon two of his ministers and told them to each decorate one part of the castle. He told them that they have two months to finish the decorations, whereupon they will be rewarded for their work.*
> *One of them immediately set out to decorate his part of the castle with the finest gold, paintings and tapestries.*

He toiled for two months, night and day, and at the end of the two months, his half of the castle was magnificent. On the opposite side, the other fellow lazed around and did not get started on the project until a day before the two months were up.

The night before the grand opening a deep remorse set in and he was sick with worry for not obeying the king and wasting his time with frivolity. But what could be done? Just then, a genius idea came to him. He took some shiny potter's glaze and covered his entire part of the castle with it. The glaze acted as a mirror. He then took a curtain and hung it between his half of the castle and the other.

In great anticipation the day finally arrived and the king, accompanied by his entourage, came to inspect and marvel at what he hoped would be his beautifully decorated castle.

He was shown the first half (the side which had been labored over for months) and he was quite pleased. It was beautiful and magnificent. At this time the second half was still hidden behind the curtain. When the king asked to see the second half, the curtain was lifted and behold — a perfect mirror image of the first part was seen.

There are three possible endings to this tale:

A) The king punishes the second minister, for all he did was play a clever trick on the king. Of course if he does so, then it reflects badly on the king. It shows that he lacks a sense of humor and resourcefulness.

B) The king is pleased with his work and inspired by his ingenuity. He rewards him as he does the first minister.

C) The king cleverly rewards the minister through a similar use of mirrors. Instead of giving him actual coins as a reward, the king merely offers him a reflection of coins by placing them on the other side of the castle. Through the mirror it would appear as if he had placed the coins on his side.

The first option is obviously ruled out, as it reflects negatively on the king. We are left with the second two. The more well-known understanding of the tale supports the third option. As such, the story concludes with a clever king outsmarting a clever minister.

Yet, when Rebbe Nachman of Breslov told the tale he ended the story with option B — that the king is pleased with his work and rewards him accordingly.

What Reb Nachman is teaching us is that even if one feels inauthentic, like an impostor or charlatan, the KING still enjoys our work, our efforts, our practice. Maybe it is merely a mirror of generations past, or a miming of those who have reached higher levels, but it is our mirror, our ingenuity, our creativity, and we are indeed trying to see ourselves in its reflection.

Just because we did not put in the maximum amount of preparation or hard work — and of course we should — but even if we did not, we tried as best as we could at that moment, and Hashem rewards us accordingly.

PERCEPTION

1]

Prayer:
A Quest for Unity

IN HEBREW, THE WORD FOR PRAYER IS TEFILAH. This suggests that prayer is an act of *Tofel*/connecting and joining *(Unkalus, Berieshis, 30:8).* When we pray we reach out beyond ourselves, beyond the immediate, and connect with the Infinite Source of all life.

In English, the concept of prayer is used to describe various religious and/or psycho-spiritual states and activities such as, but not limited to, praise, petition, protest, confession, devotion, penitence, introspection and evaluation.

Prayer is likened to a blossoming tree with voluminous branches and plentiful fruit. This poetic image suggests that prayer is a multi-dimensional process that is fertile, gradual and rewarding. It is both an experience and an expression of our soul's deepest yearning to connect and communicate with that which is beyond and within us.

The above are just some of the potential pathways of prayer, but still the question remains:
What is prayer itself?
What is the essence of prayer?

MOVEMENT UPWARD AND INWARD:

There is a great debate between the celebrated codifiers of Jewish Law, the Rambam and Ramban, about whether daily prayer is required of us or not; whether we have to pray to fulfill an obligation, or whether we can pray as needed personally. And yet when discussing the actual experience of prayer, both sages agree that when we are praying we are in a state of profound elevation, but why? What is prayer and what is its objective?

On the most-simple level, prayer represents our consciousness moving upward, reaching out to the Transcendent One, by going inward, deeper into the Imminent Self.

As we move upward we are simultaneously moving deeper inward.

When we pray, not only do we acknowledge that there is an Other to whom we direct our prayers, but more importantly, that this Other is intimately aware of our existence, cares about our concerns and is worthy of our love and constant consideration.

THE LADDER OF PRAYER:

To illustrate this dynamic we will use the multi-dimensional image of *Yaakov's*/Jacob's Ladder. For as the Torah relates, Yaakov had a dream-vision in which he saw "a ladder set upon the earth, and the top of it reached all the way to the heavens. Upon it, the angels of G-d were going up and down" *(Bereishis, 28:12)*. In this short passage we are given an apt metaphor for the structure and process of prayer. The ladder is the structure of prayer (as we will explain shortly), and the movement up and down is the process and experience of prayer. Furthermore, the *Medrash (Tanchuma)* teaches that there were four steps on this ladder. These four rungs of the Ladder parallel the four main stages of the Morning Prayer service, which when taken all together, guide us along a spiritual journey of existential integration. At the outset of prayer we begin by standing on the first rung. Here, we sense a measure of distance and difference. Yet through the course of the prayers we climb the ladder upward, as it were, gradually feeling ever closer and more intimately connected with Hashem.

In short, the process works something like this:

1) We begin with a strong sense of awareness and appreciation for our body and the miraculous gift of a new day — *Birchas HaShachar*/the morning blessings.

2) Then we move on to integrate and elevate our emotions with thanks and praise — *Pesukei D'Zimrah*/the verses of praise.

3) Next we focus and direct our intellect towards the Infinite One Source of all being — *Kriyas Shema* /the reading of the Shema.

4) And finally we purify our desires, activate our true will and deepen our faith by moving into a more intimate embrace of the Infinite One —*Amidah*/the standing silent prayer.

Essentially, for this movement to take flight we need to ascertain that our body, our emotions, our intentions, and our desires are all aligned and activated.

PRAYER: A SERVICE OF THE HEART

Prayer is referred to as *Avodah She'ba'lev*/service of the heart *(Taanis, 2a)*. When we genuinely pray there is a deep movement inward and upward connecting us to our deepest, most vulnerable self and, in turn, connecting that self with the ultimate Source of all life.

Prayer is a service that emanates from and penetrates deep into our broken hearts when we are able to open up and express ourselves with total emotional involvement and honesty.

Prayer is analogous to the ancient offerings of the Holy Temple and thus, it requires fire. Not the physical fire of the sacrificial altar, but rather the internal flames of passion and desire.

There are times when the desire to pray is aroused spontaneously and feels like one of the most natural forms of human expression. And yet, at other times, it is difficult to pray and challenging to truly open up. The art of authentic prayer requires that we are

completely present and focused on the ultimate undertaking.

KAVANAH:

As mentioned previously, having Kavanah is essential to prayer. Kavanah is the soul of prayer. Prayer
without Kavanah is similar to "a body without a soul."
Another way to understand this is that prayer without
Kavanah is similar to inviting a guest over for dinner
and bringing out a plate, fork and knife, but forgetting
to serve the actual food. Kavanah is the nourishing
substance of prayer, the food on the plate, the soul in
the body.

The Hebrew word *Kavanah* can also refer to a window *(Daniel 6:11)*. For it is only with the right intention and focus that we are able to consciously open
up the window to our soul, our deepest self, and allow
who we truly are to be experienced and expressed.

In this way, a distinction can be made between the essence of prayer, a quest for unity and connection, and
the technique of prayer, the order of the prayers and
the requisite instructions and requirements. The technique of prayer is there to point us in the right direction so that we can truly reach out, connect and unify

with the Source of all life. But without the essence of prayer, the desire to connect and communicate, the techniques and directives are ultimately impotent. Language sets the coordinates, but there needs to be someone steering the ship, someone who is actively and intentionally praying the prayer, someone who is giving the words spirit, soul and meaning.

HONESTY IN PRAYER: WHO WE ARE AND WHAT WE DESIRE

Prayer offers us the opportunity to express our thoughts, feelings, needs and desires in front of our Creator, not merely as a hollow and meaningless monologue, but as a truly conscious and meaningful gesture of genuine dialogue. Prayer is the time we take and the space we make to hear the Creator speaking to and through us.

While standing in the midst of deep prayer we are filled with an overwhelming awareness that we are in the presence of the Infinite One. In turn, we find that the ego-walls of self-delusion and deception come tumbling down. Who we are and what we truly desire becomes increasingly clear when the garments and games of our surface-self are eliminated.

From one perspective, prayer is intended to petition the Creator for things that we cannot acquire on our own. But when seen from a deeper perspective we find that through the very act of asking, we are able to become more aware of what we really do want and need. We are able to reflect on our own desires through the lens of prayer.

When we pray and there is genuine openness and expression, we can no longer fool ourselves. When we reveal ourselves to the Creator, our life becomes increasingly more transparent. It is only when we have reached this place of honesty and humility that the deep inner work of self-improvement can truly begin.

For this reason prayer is called *Avodah*, meaning literally 'work' or service. The word Avodah shares its root with the Hebrew word *Ibud*, which means 'working over' or transforming. It is through the work of prayer that we can turn ourselves over and transform our very lives for the better. We can open ourselves up to experience as we express and examine our authentic selves.

This process is similar to a gardener working and turning over the soil in order to prepare it to receive and nurture the growth of new seeds. Our soul is the soil in G-d's garden and we are the gardeners. Our prayers are the seeds that we plant and our good deeds are the fruits of our labors.

This is serious internal work that demands full disclosure and honesty. It does not, however, need to be a daunting or depressing chore. On the contrary, "joy breaks down all barriers." When we enter into prayer with joy, faith, humility and holy chutzpah, we are demonstrating our intrinsic and intuitive connection with Hashem, openly communicating with and cleaving to our Source.

PRAYER AS UNITY:

As mentioned in relation to the ladder of prayer, at the peak of prayer we are given the spirit and strength to lay bare our deepest and most vulnerable self in the presence of The Most High.

And yet, beyond the paradigm of duality where we 'relate to' and 'connect with' an-other, the experience of prayer, if taken to its fullest expression, actually allows us to transcend the construct of dichotomous relationship altogether. Relationship implies inherent separation: two unique and individual entities coming close, but always remaining on some level apart and alone. The peak experience of prayer is when we attain unification with the Creator. When our personal "i" becomes realized within the embrace of the Infinite "I". In such an experience there is a melding of the "two" back into "One."

When we achieve this state of ultimate endlessness we transcend our limited and well-defined ego-self and slip into the limitless depths of the Infinite One. It is much like physical intimacy through which, when approached with the intention and integration of all of one's being, we are able to transcend the boundaries of separateness, to achieve a total melding of the two back into one. This state can only become fully realized when the four inter-penetrating stages of Yaakov's Ladder (i.e. our existential entirety) are activated and in alignment.

1) Our physical commitment is connected to
2) an emotional love, which leads us along the path of
3) a more fully developed and detailed understanding of the implications of that love,
4) which in turn gives birth to the fruits of union — a complete and absolute merging of the two into One.

To be effective in the pursuit of perpetual presence and purity we need our
1) Body,
2) Heart,
3) Mind and
4) Soul

to be properly oriented for the power of prayer to effectively take hold of our consciousness and creative capacity.

THE GIFT OF PRAYER:
A Chassidic Parable

Once there was a mighty king who announced that all his subjects could come and request whatever they wanted from him and their wishes would be granted. Some people came and asked for gold, some for silver, while some requested to be promoted to high-ranking positions. One humble and wise person asked to be granted the opportunity to speak with the king three times a day. Hearing his request and realizing that the wise man felt that conversation with the king was of greater value than any jewels or ranks of honor, the king decreed that access to the inner chamber should be granted. And as a token the humble and wise person could pass through any chamber of the palace on his way to the throne room and take whatever he liked (Toldos, Parshas Vaeschanan).

Prayer is the greatest gift of all. Along with the gift of prayer comes the promise that the King gives the wise person. Namely, that they are able to lift their eyes, turn inward and know that Hashem is there, patiently waiting and attentively listening. Prayer is the path we travel through the wilderness, into the courtyard of the castle, past the ballrooms of the palace and into the Holy of Holies — the inner chamber. The throne room is where we stand humbly in awe before The King.

Prayer is called "that which stands elevated from the universe" *(Berachos, 6b. Rashi)*. For the true power and purpose of prayer can lift a person to levels far beyond the earthly. Prayer can provide one with access to deeper, higher, more subtle perspectives, and ultimately, to the place of absolute unity.

According to the AriZal prayer is called "that which stands elevated from the universe" because through prayer we have the power to affect or initiate *Yechudim*/Unifications in the upper realms.

Additionally, prayer is considered beyond the universe because it is that which lifts us beyond our limitations. Prayer lifts us up and out of the trivialities of our life. Through prayer we seek to abandon our obsessions with over-indulgence and materialistic gain. During prayer we struggle to become spiritually elevated, refined and holy. Prayer allows us to align our individual self with the Essential Self — The Infinite One.

Through prayer we seek to enter into a world of perfection and wholeness. There are two paradigms of reality, one is *Hanhagas HaMishpat*/the way of justice, and the other is *Hanhagas HaYichud*/the way of unity. In simple terms this means that there is the world of linear causality, otherwise known as 'cause and effect.' And thus, what was put into motion in the past cannot be transformed or redeemed, only redressed. This is the world of strict Justice. Then there is the world of *Yichud*/unity, where there is no past or future, as it were, and everything is right now, in the eternal moment. In this world of Unity, where everything is all at once, we can access and alter the imprints and effects of our past on the future in our present moment. Through prayer we enter into the Palace of Presence and Unity.

2]

Guidebook to the Promised Land:
Making the Prayerbook more Meaningful

THE SIDDUR:

While discussing the general ideas and experiences of prayer it is necessary to discuss, at least in short, the *Siddur*/traditional prayer book.

All too often the uninitiated are handed a *Siddur*, literally translated as 'the order', as in the order of the prayers, and they are not at all sure what to do with it.

If they cannot read the Hebrew they stare blankly at the page. And even if they can, or if they happen to have a Siddur with a decent translation, the prayers can still sometimes seem very heavy, harsh, or archaic.

Many of the words sound like they are speaking from an altogether different age, and many of the phrases may seem repetitive and perhaps even uninspiring. This can be true for both the novice as well as the person who has been using the Siddur their whole life. So even while such a person may have the sense that the Siddur was formed and founded in great holiness and with *Ruach Ha'kodesh*/holy spirit, still that person may feel a lack of connection to the depth and meaning of the prayers.

PORTABLE TEMPLE:

If, through the experience of exile the Torah has become our portable homeland, then the Siddur is our very own personal and portable Temple. The core of the prayers, the Amidah, was composed and established only after the destruction of the Holy Temple. Prayer was meant to take the place of the Temple Sacrifices, which were no longer possible after national exile and loss of tribal land-based sovereignty. Prayer became our sages' response to the revelation that all of Israel would become "a nation of priests." Ceremony and temple ritual were no longer just for the actual *Kohanim*/priests. Prayer was the service that we could all perform, anywhere, at any time.

Since then the Siddur has been traveling with us from place to place throughout our many wanderings. Over time, it has accumulated the stardust of our history and mystery — our collective aspirations, struggles, hopes, dreams and dramas. Over the years it has been added to and edited in a creative process of communal collaboration. What we have today is the spiritual 'sheet music' of the sages, a set composition for the choir of collective consciousness to sing the song of our soul. The words we speak are the channels upon which the energy of creation, history and redemption flow. We are thus completing a cosmic circuitry — from Above to below, and from below back to Above.

To play/pray properly in such a spiritual symphony one must learn to 'read the notes' so to speak, and to practice the scales. But, as with music, learning which note to play and when does not a good musician make. One must also learn to play/pray with feeling and sensitivity, and at times, spontaneity.

While the core of the text may be essentially the same day in and day out, the personal involvement with and true potential for creativity in prayer comes from the presence each person is able to bring to the text. From this perspective it is possible to access inspiration, awareness and intention not only in the process of creating new or novel texts or spontaneous personal prayers, but also through accessing the archetypal code of ancient Divinely inspired poetry, dream-visions and heart-felt petitions of our ancestors and breathing new life into them. In other words, one must approach and enter into the *Keval* structure of the prayers and animate it with their own *Kavanah*/ devotion and purpose.

This can be likened to a marriage where we interact with the same person day in and day out, often repeating the same rhythms and patterns of our lives together; or to a musician who must perform the same songs over and over again, night after night, to expectant audiences. The songs and the schedules of our lives, for the most part, remain the same. What is potentially different is us — our consciousness, our perspective, our mood that we bring to the repetitive structures and experiences of our lives. It is, for the most part, up to us to keep things fresh, exciting and relevant. Each day the song remains the same, but the singer is different. A conscious awareness of the inner workings of this dynamic can open up new worlds of possibility in perceiving the potency of prayer or any other regular practice.

PATIENCE & FOCUS:

In addition to the over-arching general intention of prayer, which is the conscious awareness of Whose presence you are standing within, it is of course essential to make prayer more personal and meaningful — to seek to know on a deep level what, exactly, you are saying.

Towards this end, it would be a good idea to experiment with some form of active listening during prayer, to really try to hear the words you are saying — to listen as you speak. And thus as an added element to the Halachic requirement of carefully pronouncing the words of prayer, reflecting upon their sounds and vibrations will arouse a more focused intention, which will, in turn, give more immediacy and intensity to your prayers. This is true regardless of the language in which you are praying, whether you are praying in the traditional Hebrew or in your native tongue.

Another suggestion to further aid in developing and deepening your prayer experience, besides careful enunciation and active listening, would be to choose one particular passage or verse each day and spend some time focusing in on that one area.

In other words, every day before you pray choose a sentence or a section in the prayers that will be your focus and really meditate on it.

There were Chassidim, according to R. Yoseph Yitzchak of Chabad, who would make a mark each day in their Siddur so they would know that they prayed up until that particular point with the utmost focus and Kavanah. The next day they would attempt to move the mark a little forward. Each day you can add more focus, attention and intention to another part of the order of prayers.

PAUSE, REFLECT & SAY:

You will also find it beneficial for your concentration and Kavanah if, before reciting each blessing or passage, you take a moment to reflect on what it is you are about to say. Before you start a new blessing take a moment and think about what you are asking for or acknowledging, and then recite the blessing.

Within the blessings or prayers themselves you can,

and should, take a short pause after every two or three words to reflect and then continue. In fact there are works of *Musar* that suggest we should never utter more than three words in one breath during prayer *(Yesod Shoresh Ha'avodah, Shar 5:1)*. Between every two-three words pause for a brief moment, reflect on the meaning of the next two-three words and then recite them.

By focusing on individual passages in such a manner during the course of one's prayers one may come to discover what the Masters of Musar called a *Ta'am Tefilah*/a taste of prayer, or as the Chassidic teachers say in Yiddish, a *Geshmak In Davenen*/a relishing in prayer. Your entire session of prayer will be more heartfelt, meaningful, and personal if you choose to concentrate on one particular passage, word or phrase for an extended period of time.

Inhale/Reflect, Exhale/Express:

The Baal Shem Tov taught a radical method of prayer. What he suggested is that one should hold the intention of the meanings of the words only prior to their actual recitation. And then, when the words are being spoken one should 'enter' completely into the letters and sounds in order to feel the energy and vibration of the words filling and infusing you with light. In essence, one should not get carried away from the actual letters and words themselves by abstract intentions.

From this perspective, we should try to enter fully into every word we utter in prayer. Just allow yourself to simply be with every sound, movement, and vibration. Open yourself up to be fully present in each letter, each word, and let the light and energy fill and infuse your whole body.

A practical way for one to practice this profound yet simple method of prayer is to utilize the natural flow of breath — the inhale and exhale. Before one is about to recite an individual word or short phrase, inhale and reflect on the meaning of the word or words one is about to say, then hold and retain the breath. As one is exhaling, recite the words slowly and deeply with the outgoing breath.

This can be done within each word itself. For example, before you say the word *Baruch*, as you are inhaling pause a moment and know that you are about to say a word that means blessing, then slowly exhale the first letter: Baaaaaa. Then take another inhale and exhale the rest of the word: Rucccchh. The contemplation of what the word means transpires before the actual saying of the word. When in the act of saying the word itself, you are not thinking. You are just present with the vibrational energy of pure sound.

When it is difficult or too time consuming to pause at each letter or even at each word, one can pause before reciting every two-three words. As mentioned, there are many sources that suggest one should never recite more than two-three words at a time. Rather, one should pause and reflect on the meaning of the following two-three words of prayer, and then recite them. Pause, reflect and then recite another two-three words. What is unique about the Baal Shem's path is that when one actually does recite the two-three words following the inhalation and reflection one should let go of the mental activity of meaning-making and intention. Just be with the sounds and words of the prayers themselves.

For example, before reciting *Baruch Ata Hashem*, "You, G-d are the Source of Blessings," pause, inhale and think deeply about what these words mean. Hold that meaning in your mind and breathe into your lungs, then with one powerful exhale say the words Baruch Ata Hashem, entering them fully.

Sometimes, it would even be appropriate and beneficial to say the entire blessing in one powerful and extended exhale — especially if one is struggling with extraneous thoughts that are distracting your focus.

Before one would say a blessing, for example, inhale deeply and think about what the words of the blessing mean, and then in one long exhale recite the entire blessing.

The deeper we get into the prayers, the more the words lose their linearity and left-brain logical connotations. The more we enter into the words, letters, vibrations and sounds of the prayers, the more the rational content of the words recedes. The words, in effect, become the background noise. We slowly lose ourselves within the vibrations of the letters as the sounds morph into words, and the words themselves into a kind of musical mode, like a great symphony endlessly reverberating and resonating.

In this way, we are able to move from the world of *Asiyah*/the physical dimension, into the inner dimension of our emotions, the world of *Yetzirah*, as our affective awareness is stimulated and aroused by the ceaseless stringing together of the various sounds of the letters and words.

What began as the single sound of a letter becomes a word, and then many words and many sounds. There is an inner joy and pleasure that is generated by gently moving from one sound into the next, like the art of playing consecutive chords of music.

From this moving experience of having our emotions stirred up by the music of the letters we are able to move deeper and deeper into ourselves as we become more sensitized to the contemplative introspection of the world of *Beriah*/the dimension of mindfulness.

And finally, there is a complete collapse of all sound and noise, both external and internal. The mind is cleared of all thoughts, feelings and sensations. It is in this space that we are able to attain a motionless state of total oneness, the world of *Atzilus*/unity.

OPENING OF THE HEART:

Throughout history our sages, particularly the Kabbalists, have devised many meditative techniques to employ during the course of prayer. Some of them are simple and general suggestions of what to keep in mind during prayer, while others are quite technical and complex methods meant to super-impose deeper meaning onto the standard text. These individual intentions and points of focus are meant to activate the mind as well as to open the heart during prayer. But it must be stated that so long as these intentions remain in the headspace alone, objective and calculated, there is no genuine connection with the authentic essence of prayer. The purpose of Kavanah is to arouse the mind and the heart, to be objectively and subjectively identified with the depth of the prayers.

In this spirit, R. Mendel of Kotzk would never wear a scarf around his neck during prayer. He said that he did not want to cause even a symbolic separation between the mind and the heart. Perhaps if one finds oneself wearing a necktie during the prayers, a good idea would be to loosen the knot, which would also symbolically acknowledge the free flow of energy and awareness between the mind and the heart.

To reiterate this important point: Intellectual intention of the mind must lead to a heightened awareness of the heart. As mentioned, prayer is referred to as *Avodah She'ba'lev*/service of the heart. The numerical value of the word *Tefilah* is 515. When one adds four to this number, accounting for the four Hebrew letters that comprise the word Tefilah, the value is 519. The words *Avodas* (482) *Ha'Lev* (37), 'service of the heart', is also 519. Furthermore, the words *B'Kavanas Ha'Lev*/with intention of the heart, also equals 519. This series of *Gematriyos*/numerical equivalences serves to reinforce the idea that deep and authentic prayer is ultimately dependent on the state of the heart.

R. Shmuel of Shinava once complained to his teacher, Reb Simcha Bunim, that every time he prays he gets a headache from the intensity of his concentration and Kavanah. The Rebbe gently looked at him and said: *"Prayer is a Service of the Heart, not a labor of the mind."*

Kavanos are not meant to be merely mental exercises or mind games. There is a *Zeman Torah L'chud, Zeman Tefilah L'chud*/a time for Torah and a time for prayer. When in the midst of prayer, pray.

The Kavanos, if properly approached and integrated into one's organic practice, can help one deepen their prayer experience, not simply as an intellectual theory, but by truly opening one up to hidden wellsprings of intense emotion and engagement in the presence of Hashem.

Here is a simple exercise that exemplifies the difference between someone praying from their mind and someone praying from their heart: Pay attention when you say the words in the Amidah, *Ha'e-l HaGadal Ha'Gibor V'Hanora*, "God, the Great, the Mighty, and the Awesome." When you say these words, you can be thinking about the Creator's greatness, might and awesomeness in a very detached, philosophical and abstract way; or you can open yourself up to feel, live and breathe these words, trembling in awe and wonder before the Infinite One. When we say these words with our whole being, we can tangibly feel Hashem's greatness, might and awesomeness in its existential fullness. We are able to sense the greatness, might and awesomeness in our own life, and in all the intricate details and inner workings of creation.

THE SECRET IS SIMPLE:
Deep Peshat and Deep Sod are One

There are many mind expanding and consciousness altering Kavanos to be employed and entertained during the course of our prayers. Many times, however, people get so involved with the more esoteric allusions and associations that they forget the *Peshat*/ simple meanings of the words in the prayers.

In prayer we need to know that the *Peshat*/simple meanings and the *Sod*/secret meanings are inseparable. They are the body of the text and the soul of our prayers. Amazingly, the deeper we understand either one of them, the more we are able to realize that they are one and the same. The *Omek*/depth of the *Peshat* is in total alignment with the *Omek* of the *Sod*.

From the perspective of Absolute Unity there is only One, albeit reflected in multiplici-

ty. The deeper we go into the prayers themselves, the more we come to that realization.

Many times, the mere mental activity of studying and
meditating on the deeper Kavanos before praying in-
flames the heart and focuses the mind in order to pray
with inspiration and passionate feeling, even if during
the actual prayers one is not focusing on the Kavanos
themselves. This would be an effective form of preparation before prayer, as discussed previously. When a
person realizes the power of his prayer on the upper
worlds and its cosmic ripple effects into Ultimate Reality, i.e. the tremendous ramifications of his praying,
he will than pray with greater *Deveikus*/cleaving to
Divinity.

Early Chassidic Rebbes have suggested that this is the
reason one should study the deeper Kavanos before
prayer even if one does not maintain their intention
during one's actual praying.

CONNECTING WITH THE LETTERS OF THE PRAYERS:

As mentioned, there are times when a person may get
so intensely involved with the flow and motion of the
prayers that the linear, left side of the brain automat-

ically slows down and the individual enters, for a period of time, a totally open heart space wherein their connection with the Song of the Siddur is completely affective and non-rational.

They have thus achieved a state of Deveikus. At this point all the person wants to do is to hold on to the fire of the letters themselves, concentrating on and cleaving to the inner essence and quality of the Divine emanation that is present within the very energy of the words. They have stopped thinking, trying, or practicing. They are truly in a state of prayer.

This idea of entering into and holding on to the holy words themselves can occur gradually after a person has been praying for a long time with the Kavanos and already knows all of the deep secret meanings; or it can occur spontaneously for the novice, i.e. one who knows very little of the actual meanings of the words, but yet prays with great fervor and Deveikus, thereby making a quantum leap closer to Infinity.

A story is told of R. Hirsch of Rimnov who was a simpleton, almost an ignoramus, when he first met his great Rebbe, R. Mendel of Rimnov. The story goes that after the first time he saw his Rebbe he started praying with great excitement, passion and fervor. When the other students of R. Mendel saw the young lad praying with such *Hislahavus*/conflagration, they questioned him: "How do you pray with such excitement when you do not even know the proper meanings of the words you are saying?" He humbly replied: "Who needs meaning when you have the holy words themselves!"

When a person connects directly with the sacred letters themselves, they are connecting to the Source from which all Creation emerges. In Kabbalah it is taught that the world is being continually re-created through Hashem's resonant intonations of the letters of the *Aleph Beis*/the Hebrew Alphabet.

In Chassidic texts the anecdote is told: Once there was a simple Jew who was barely able to read. Every morning he would get up and say with an open heart: "Master of the universe, You know that I am a simple person and am unable to even read the words of the prayerbook, yet I do know the Aleph Beis. You surely know all the possible words and letter combinations, so I offer to You, Master of the Universe, all the letters of the Aleph Beis. Please Hashem, I pray that you will arrange these letters into their proper order." In great simplicity he was returning the letters to the Creator and asking Hashem to form the appropriate "words" that will in turn manifest as tangible blessings in his life.

From the deepest perspective, the moral of this story is actually achieved in all prayer. In our speech, directed as it is to the Infinite One, we are completing the cosmic circuitry and returning the letters and vibrations back to their Source in order that they will be reabsorbed and reformulated as a new expression of Divine flow and blessings in the world of Creation.

The preciousness of the words and letters themselves creates two ways of relating to the prayers. One approach is to pray very slowly, holding on to each and every word and letter, thereby pronouncing the letters clearly and carefully. The other approach is to say the prayers as quickly as possible — so long as each word and letter is pronounced properly of course.

The father of R. Yisrael of Ruzhin, otherwise known as the Ruzhiner, would draw out each word for a very long time. R. Aaron of Belz, on the other hand, would pray very fast. They were both deeply in love with the words of the prayers. The former, because of his great love for each letter and every word would not want to let them go — he cherished them and took his time with each one. The latter loved the words so much he could not wait to get to the next one, he could not get enough of them, and he ate them up as quickly as possible.

Total involvement in prayer is not only for the mind and the heart, but the full expression of prayer is also meant to be experienced with the entire body. Not only through the movements of the body during prayer, but more importantly, through the residual energetic effects on the body after prayer, which are generated by the 'positive' vibrations of the sounds and words of prayer.

This is a perfect example of how one can affect positive change through their bio-psychic feedback loop. By articulating and affirming holiness, joy, and blessing with one's whole mind and heart, one is able to positively impact their physical body.

Ultimately, Kavanah is about focus and alignment. When we verbally declare with our mouths what we feel in our hearts and know to be true, then we enter into a state of being where there is complete integration on all levels of self. This is the place where our bodies, our hearts, and our minds are all in sync with the articulated intentions and vibrations of our prayers.

Internal integration can ripple out and affect external integration. The reflection of our focused Kavanos is the unification of all of creation with its Creator. When we say the words of our prayers we are stimulating the sacred sounds and letters from which the heavens and the earth were created. The letters are thereby the conduits of consciousness and creativity through which the inner life force and spiritual structure of all of creation is animated. When we pray in the holy tongue, all of creation, which is the external manifestation of these letters, joins us in praise.

In effect, by returning the words to their Source we are thus returning all of creation back to the Creator, back into the Infinite Unity of Hashem, only to be recycled and returned back into the world in the form of a new expression of Divine Creativity and abundant blessing.

3]

Names of Hashem:
Names for the Nameless

THE NAMES OF HASHEM:

Names reveal meaning. A name is a definition. When we call someone or something by a name, we create a relationship with that person or thing and can thus interact with them/it appropriately. Once we define the subject or object we can more consciously relate. Being as we are lodged in a three-dimensional universe we need names, definitions, descriptions and discernment to help us navigate through space and time. This is all true when it comes to created reality, a "thing" that came into "being". But when it comes to the Creator, however, there is no possible description or definition. The Creator is Endless, Infinite, Formless and Transcendent.

While this is true, instinctively we still seek to foster a relationship and so we reach out in an attempt to encounter the Divine. Moreover, we affirm that a *Mitzvah* in general allows for this connection to be made. And more precisely, that prayer enables us to cultivate and nurture this relationship into full bloom.

But because the unified Essence of the Creator is unimaginable as content, the formless infinite light must manifest in various Attributes. These experiential Attributes then become the sacred names of G-d through which we are able to relate to and thereby form a connection with The Most High. Each name represents another aspect of our relationship to the One and of the One's revelation to us. Clearly there is only ONE, but these names represent various aspects of our relationship to that One.

All names are expressions of The One, although to us they appear as divergent masks and manifestations. Names such as Compassionate One and True Judge are merely the tangible wake left behind by the Will of the One couched in human terms that we can understand. They are finite templates to conceive of and contextualize the actions of the Infinite. Ultimately, these names reveal more about how we relate to Hashem and how Hashem relates to us, than they do about Hashem.

The *Medrash* tells us: "Hashem said to Moshe: You want to know My name? I am called by My deeds. When I judge My creatures, I am called "Judge". When I wage war, I am called "Master of War". When I tolerate the inequities of man, I am called "Merciful". When I have compassion on My world, I am called "Compassionate".

In the following pages some of the many names of Hashem will be explored. For the purpose of deepening the experience of prayer the focus will be only on the names that appear most often throughout the liturgy.

KEEP IN MIND:

The most elevated and transcendent name is the *Yud-Hei-Vav-Hei*. This is referred to as the Tetragrammaton, or the four-letter name. This name is understood as the unpronounceable name, meaning that we do not attempt to intone this name. In everyday conversation, when referring to G-d by this name we generally use the term "Hashem", which means simply — "The Name". During Prayer, on the other hand, we pronounce the four-letter name as "Ado-noi".

Whenever we see in the Siddur the appearance of the two letters *Yud-Yud* next to each other, with two strikes in between them, this is referring to the Tetragrammaton, the unpronounceable name, *Yud-Hei-Vav-Hei*, which is pronounced as Ado-noi. The reason for the two Yuds' is because they are an acronym. The first Yud is the first letter of the *Yud-Hei –Vav-Hei*, the name itself. And the second Yud is the final letter of the name Ado-noi, *Aleph –Dalet –Nun-Yud,* the way it is pronounced. We need to have both names in mind when reciting this name in our prayers.

THE NAMES OF HASHEM
A SHORT DESCRIPTION*:

for comprehensive description of all the names below, please see appendix 3

YUD-HEI-VAV-HEI :

The Infinite. The Transcendent. The Miraculous. Beyond and before the natural unfolding of reality. Experienced as the Awe of the Divine, Sacred, Infinite Light. The 'Personal G-d' as it were, of Israel and the Source of Revelation. Today this named is pronounced as Ado-noi.

ADO-NOI:

Divine Lord and Master of all Creation. Experienced as humility in the face of Divine majesty & royalty within creation. The name Yud-Hei-Vav-Hei is pronounced as Ado-noi. When pronouncing the name Yud-Hei-Vav-Hei as Ado-noi, meditate on the meaning of both names.

ELOKIM:

Initiator and Enforcer of Natural Law and the Order of Creation. The "Impersonal" aspect of G-d. G-d of creation. Experienced in the intellectual awareness of the masculine symmetry of creation. Observed as the prose and story line of creation.

SHECHINAH:

The feminine indwelling of the divine presence. Sensed emotionally as the poetry of creation and the harmonically interwoven details of all reality.

E-L:

Divine supernal kindness. Compassion beyond limitations. Experienced as the Divine kindness of the Creator that exceeds the "ways of the world".

ELOKA:

Divine kindness extended within the confines of created reality. Experienced as the Divine goodness present within the details of creation.

Y-AH:

Divine wisdom. Experienced as the wisdom within all creation, even within apparent meaningless suffering.

SHAD-AI:

Divine protection. Setter of limits. Experienced as the nurturing, shielding expression of the Divine, which also sets borders and secures boundaries.

TZ'VAKOS:

Divine leadership. Lord of Hosts. The orchestrator who conducts and cares about the details of all the celestial and angelic legions. Experienced as the collapse of the infinite within the details of finite existence.

IMPORTANT NOTE:

Each name above is written the way it would be pronounced in everyday conversation, which is different than the actual pronunciation of the name. Therefore the letter Hei, as in H, is replaced with a Kuf, as in K. So for example, Elo-Him is written as Elokim. However, in prayer, these names should be pronounced with their proper letters in place; i.e. with a Hei instead of a Kuf.

PREPARATION

1]

General Preparations:
Time/Space/Consciousness

THE PREREQUISITE OF PROPER PREPARATION FOR
PRAYER IS THE NEGATION OF ALL DISTRACTIONS,
BOTH EXTERNAL AND INTERNAL. Only then can
the process truly begin of filling the mind and heart
with the proper Kavanah. That is, first we need to
empty the vessel so that we can later fill it.

EXTERNAL DISTRACTIONS:

But before we can discuss the internal obstructions that may occur within the mind and heart, we must first address the possible external distractions that may exist due to the varying conditions of one's physical body or environment.

SPACE:

Overcoming external distractions begins with the conscious decision to pray in an environment that is conducive for concentration and self-expression. Simply put, this means that the place in which we pray is physically clean and that there are no overwhelming distractions such as excessive noise or even images displayed. Certainly this implies no negative images.

There should be a pleasant aroma in the room in which one has designated for prayer. This implies that the place should not emit any foul odors that may distract one from prayer *(Berachos 26a)*.

The place of prayer should not have stale air. Rather, it should feel open and fresh. The prophet Daniel prayed in a house with windows. Later on, the Talmudic sages *(Berachos, 34b)* suggested that the structure of a house dedicated for the purpose of prayer should have large windows so that one may look toward the heavens in order to arouse awe and humility *(Rashi)*. Also, as some commentators suggest *(R. Yonah)*, the fresh air and light clears and calms the mind to be able to focus and keep clear Kavanah. For this reason, among other more esoteric ideas, even a person who is blind is urged to pray in a place with windows.

The place where we regularly pray is called a "miniature temple" *(Megilah, 29a)*. This is the ideal context for prayer. Being, as it were, dedicated for the soul purpose of study and spirituality a house of prayer will intuitively evoke the mood of prayer and introspection when entered, especially when there is a *Minyan* - a group of ten or more joined together in prayer.

If for some reason one cannot pray regularly in a Shul, synagogue, or house of study, one should set aside a space within the home, or somewhere else secure and available as a *Makom Kavuah* / special place — for spiritual practice. This reserved place becomes our sacred space and the moment we enter into it we will feel charged and ready for prayer.

The place that you choose to pray in should be a stable flat surface, like a plateau. In addition, it should not be on top of a chair, or bed, or for that matter any high place *(Berachos, 10b)*.

BODY:

In addition to the proper environment, which is clean and has no distractions, we need to ensure that our body is fit and ready for prayer. This includes being dressed properly and appropriately, covering all parts of the body that are traditionally covered with presentable attire.

In conjunction with the verse in *Amos (4:12)*, which says, *Heichin Likras Elokecha*, "prepare to meet your G-d", we find that the sages would prepare themselves for prayer by getting dressed to pray *(Shabbos, 10a)*.

Beyond the normal dress, the Gemarah *(Berachos, 24b)* also mentions the wearing of a special belt, called a *Gartel*, to prepare for prayer *(Shabbos, 10a)*. Today there is the Chassidic custom or *Midas Chassidus* — a custom performed by those who are more scrupulous in their performance of Mitzvos — to wear a Gartel during prayer. The Gartel is a belt placed by the hips, symbolically creating a *Havdalah* / separation, between the upper and lower regions (natures) of the body. The ultimate purpose of the Gartel is not to separate, but to indirectly and paradoxically inspire a *Hamtaka* / sweetening — a coming together of the higher and lower selves. For truly, we cannot bring the two back into one until we are able to clearly distinguish and understand each individual aspect as unique and distinct.

We should also wash our hands before prayer *(Berachos 25a, 15a)*. Even when our hands are physically clean, we should still endeavor to ritually wash them in order to prepare for prayer. This is similar to the practice of the *Kohanim* / priests, who would wash their hands before entering into service at the Holy Temple.

In addition, before we begin to pray we should make sure that we relieve ourselves of any need to discharge any bodily fluids *(Ibid. 23a)*. We need to ensure that the body's needs for release do not end up hindering our ability to concentrate during prayer. Conversely, if you feel that during a lengthy prayer your hunger may encumber your focus, you may eat something light or take a drink before you begin your prayers for the purpose of good health.

MIKVAH:

There is a custom to immerse oneself in a *Mikvah*, a ritual bath of water, before prayer. The immersion in a ritual body of water represents a sense of nullification. *Tovel* is the Hebrew word that means to 'immerse'.

Tovel has the same letters as *Bitul* / nullification. Every time we enter a Mikvah with proper intention to Tovel we are enacting the practice of Bitul, which is the nullification of our separate sense of alienated ego, the small self. While moving from dry land to being under water, we are moving from a solid separate state of being to a fluid state of non-being.

In addition, and on many levels even more important than the physical immersion in a ritual bath, a Mikvah is the purification of our inner self, the purification of the heart. The truth is that many times a physical action can initiate and facilitate a mental, or inward, response. For example, often cleaning your room makes you feel more organized and psychologically 'put together'. In turn, the act of physically immersing in a Mikvah inspires us to reflect inwardly and purify spiritually.

MIND:

It is very important to make sure that our mind is in order and ready for prayer. Certainly, it goes without saying, one should not be intoxicated during prayer *(Eiruvin, 64a)*. We should try, as much as possible, to rid ourselves of all extraneous and distracting thoughts in order to create the proper context for our prayer.

One should imagine oneself standing in front of the *Shechinah*, the Divine Presence *(Rambam, Tefilah, 5:16)*.

In the *Shulchan Aruch*, the *Ramah* instructs us that prior to prayer we should set aside time to ponder and meditate on "the awesomeness of the Creator and the humbleness of man, and to banish all pleasures from the heart" *(Orach Chayim, 98:1)*. This meditation serves a dual purpose: it empties our minds of the deluge of egocentric thoughts, and it opens us up to experience the awesomeness of the Infinite One. It also makes us profoundly aware of "before Whom we are standing", transforming each word and phrase into a creative act of conscious communion.

Once a debate between the two holy brothers, Reb Zusha and Reb Elimelech ensued, which of the above two should be thought about first. Reb Elimelech, who was known throughout the world as the humblest of men, argued that we should first focus on the lowliness of man and then on the awesomeness of the Creator. While his brother, Reb Zusha, argued that we first should focus on the greatness of the Creator, and only then on the humbleness of man. They went to their teacher, the Maggid of Mezritch, for a ruling.

The Maggid responded that for the novice, there is a danger in starting out focusing on the lowliness of the human being. Such thoughts can bring a person down, leading to despair and depression. To begin with, one should first meditate on the awesomeness of the Creator and in due time ponder the lowliness of the human.

Correspondingly, in today's contemporary paradigm the focus should be more on the first part of this suggested contemplative recollection — the "awesomeness of the Creator" — and less, and only afterward, on the "humbleness of man." If a person meditates too extensively on his own lowliness, there is a danger that he may beat himself up to a point of not being able to pick himself back up again. Even when one does meditate on the "humbleness of man", the lowliness of the human being, it is best to do this in very general terms — i.e. the human being as a collective species and archetype — and not direct too much negative focus on oneself as an individual.

HEART:

Most importantly, whenever we are engaged in the service of the heart, we must first empty the heart of all distracting emotions and attachments so that the heart can truly awaken to a subtle sense of closeness to Hashem *(Chovos HaLevavos. Cheshbon H'nefesh 3)*.

Teshuvah / return and realignment, has the power to either hasten or delay our prayers from being answered *(Safer Chassidim, 612)*. Before we begin to pray we should aspire to awaken, at least on some level, an arousal for Teshuvah — to mend our ways and return to the inner essence of our being.

If we were not moved to Teshuvah before praying then, G-d willing, a genuine reflection on the essence of what we are doing in prayer — that we are, on a revealed level, standing in the presence of the Creator — should inevitably bring us to Teshuvah.

CHARITY:

A practical way to open the heart before prayer is by giving Tzedakah or 'charity' *(Baba Basra 10a)*. The act of sharing with another in need allows us to go beyond our own ego narrative, to expand and open ourselves to an 'other', which in turn opens us up to experience the immediacy of our dependence on the open hand of Hashem. Besides the opening of the heart that occurs with the giving of charity, observing the Mitzvah of Tzedakah right before prayer also rejuvenates our prayers with a renewed sense of aliveness and vitality. Since a poor and desperate person is despondent and considered as figuratively 'dead' *(Nedarim 64b)*, when you give genuine charity to that person and enliven him, this awakens a renewed life and vitality within him as well as within your own prayers.

PRAY BEFORE PRAYER:

In order to properly pray we need to be fully focused and engaged on all levels of our being. Our body, heart, mind, and soul need to be open and awake to experience and express genuine prayer. Sometimes, we enact all the appropriate preparations for prayer, but once we begin to pray we are not feeling it. We just cannot seem to truly enter into a deep state of prayer. When this occurs, a nice practice is to pray for the ability to be able to pray. Pray before praying. Pray that you have the strength, clarity, focus and intention to properly pray.

This pre-prayer prayer often bubbles up spontaneously. It is a prayer that simply rises up from the depths of your soul, unstructured and free. If nothing is coming up, then make that itself a prayer by saying, "You know Hashem, nothing is coming up, I feel so empty. I know I want to pray but I don't have the desire, I feel nothing. Please open up my heart, open up my mind and open up my mouth so that I may share myself with you through prayer."

This form of improvisational prayer can be very helpful to get into the head and heart space necessary to really open up and pray with all of your might.

The basic Kavanah for prayer, besides being aware of where we are standing and in front of whom we are praying, should be to make a good and thorough assessment of ourselves.

A Chassid once entered the room of the Rebbe Rashab of Chabad and bemoaned his troubles in meditation and holding the proper focus for prayer. The Rashab answered him that the meditation before prayer consists of three basic ingredients: a person needs to think of a; who he could be, b; what he ought to be and c; how he is in actuality.

2]

Settling the Mind for Prayer

"ONE SHOULD NOT BEGIN TO PRAY BEFORE AT-
TAINING KOVED ROSH" *(Berachos 30b)*. *Koved Rosh*
is humility *(Rashi, ibid)*. The literal meaning of these
words is, "heaviness of the head", which could also
mean serious-mindfulness, a state of mind where
thoughts "matter". Ideas and emotions begin to take
shape and substance. Choices have consequences.
Things get heavy. Our consciousness has become
conscious. Taking life seriously.

This kind of heaviness can, at times, weigh you down or depress you. Yet, through prayer, you are able to lighten up — both in the sense of light as in the opposite of heavy, as well as in the sense of light as the opposite of dark. Prayer both lightens your load and brings light to your life. This occurs when you are able to open up and let go in order to elevate your thoughts, your emotions and your whole life in defiance of depression and the 'gravity' of your situation.

Deep prayer allows us to float and soar above the stress and temporality of this life, into a state of communion and oneness, where things fall back into place and perspective. Through prayer we are able to check back in with what really matters.

Besides the literal meaning of heaviness, the word *Koved* can also be translated as 'cleaning'. Koved Rosh would then imply a cleaning up and clearing out of the head. Before we begin to pray we need to clear our minds and empty our hearts of all extraneous thoughts, feelings and sensations. Certainly we should not begin to pray when we are overwhelmed with feelings outside the intentions of prayer. Our sages tell us that we should not pray if we are feeling angry.

EMPTYING THE MIND:

The early *Chassidim*, or 'pious ones', would *Sho'im* / tarry, one hour prior to the beginning of prayer and for one hour after prayer *(Ibid. 32b)*. What does *Sho'im* mean? Literally *Sho'im* means to 'wait', the act of being still. They would settle their minds and quiet their thoughts, and only then commence to pray. The waiting was intended to quiet the constant inner chatter and to clear their thoughts of all distractions in preparation for prayer *(Rambam, Pirush HaMishnayos, Berachos 5:1)*.

This would be a very good and simple practice before prayer:

> Sit for a few moments, minimum.

> Settle yourself, relax your body and quiet your mind.

> Breathe deeply and consciously.

> From this place of calm and composure, begin your prayer.

FILLING THE MIND WITH
SELECTED THOUGHTS:

The purpose of settling the mind and emptying oneself of all distracting thoughts is to be able to pray
with a clear mind. Rabbeinu Nisan (on the Gemarah), however, writes that when the early pious ones
would Sho'im for an hour before prayers, they would
not only calm and clear their minds, they would also
meditate on the "Awesomeness of the Creator". Not
only would they empty and settle their minds, they
would also consciously choose a particular thought to
think about, a thought connected to the awesomeness
of the Infinite One. This exercise of directed free-will
in the realm of thought is a very effective and powerful practice.

This notion of filling the mind with selected thoughts
is also brought down in the code of Jewish Law *(Ramah, Siman 96)*.

Before praying, take at least a few moments to quiet
the deluge of random thoughts, settle the mind, collect yourself, and meditate on the awesomeness of the
Creator, the multi-faceted diamond of the moment,
and the spiritual journey you are about to take. Prayer
is the vehicle for that journey.

TORAH BEFORE PRAYER:

To facilitate this awareness, many have the custom to study *Kabbalah* and/or *Chassidus* before beginning to pray. Many study Torah that is related to the idea of the "awesomeness of the Creator" or the "humbleness of the human being." There are also those who have the custom to study Gemarah before prayers. Besides arousing one's love and awe of Hashem, this practice is also done as a mental practice to sharpen and focus the mind on holiness and spirituality.

The Baal Shem Tov teaches that before prayer we should exert ourselves with learning Torah or saying Tehilim so that we will be able to pray with expanded consciousness, negating all foreign thoughts. The exertion in Torah before prayer helps to insure that the mind is purified to pray. Although, he also teaches that a person should not overdo the learning and thus tire himself out completely, depleting himself of all energy and strength to pray. Set an amount of time dedicated to study and literally set an alarm clock, or have someone tell you when the time is up.

As a preparation for praying, take a few moments and think through an inspiring or challenging thought or verse from the Torah. You may also select a particular verse to say, chant, or sing to yourself over and over again. The repetition of a verse of Torah, besides containing innate spiritual powers of its own due to the letter combinations and subsequent vibrational fields, serves as an audible focal point. By repeating it over and over again, the verse begins to fill the mind with its content and sound, while simultaneously clearing the mind from all other extraneous thoughts and distractions. As a result your mind will become cleared, focused and ready to pray. Choose your thoughts consciously and carefully.

DIVESTING FROM THE PHYSICAL:

The word *Sho'im* — which means to wait, settle and quiet the mind — can also be turned deeper inward. Not simply to quite the mind, but to quite one's sense of self as a separate physical being.

The early pious ones would empty and silence themselves of all physical sensation and experience and they would, in turn, attain a measure of *Hispashtus Ha'Gashmiyus* / a divesting of all sense of materiality. They were literally in a state of mind over matter. When a person prays from this non-attached state their prayers are selfless and, in turn, redemptive, not just for him or herself personally, but for the very fabric of creation.

All in all, before you begin to pray you should aspire to settle the mind and select your thoughts. Take a few moments to think about what you are about to do. In front of whom you will be standing, and to whom you are about to pray. Think about your own self and soul. "What is going on with your life? Who could you be, who ought you to be, and how are you in actuality?"

SILENCE BEFORE PRAYER:

In order to enter into prayers with a settled mind it would be a good idea for you to not speak so much before praying. This is so that you are able to enter into a more self-reflective and meditative mood. Certainly you should not involve yourself in lengthy conversations before prayer. In general, we should try not to extend "formal" greetings before we pray *(Berachos, 14a)*.

With regards to the morning prayers this is especially pertinent, as the first words a person utters in the morning are the foundation of the words he or she will speak throughout the entire day. They are the seeds that slowly develop during the day and all subsequent words spoken are rooted in these first words. We must, therefore, be attentive to the words we do speak before praying in the morning.

In fact, in the place of any kind of small talk, one should aspire to enter into a prayer modality by practicing silence. It is silence that creates the appropriate internal environment for prayers to take flight. We need a healthy measure of stillness and inner and outer silence before we can truly open up and enter into a more expressive and receptive modality of prayer.

When the Master Prophet *Eliyahu*, 'Elijah', sent his student Geichazi on a mission to "revive the dead", he gave him his staff and told him, "Tie up your skirts, take my staff in your hand, and go. If you meet anyone on the way, do not greet him. And if anyone greets you, do not answer him" *(2 Melachim, 4:29)*. In other words, he was charged with a powerful mission and he was instructed to not greet or respond to any greetings prior to the completion of his mission. He needed to go in silence. Many years later we find similar instructions given by the AriZal to his students. When the Arizal would tell them to go meditate and perform certain *Yichudim* / sacred unifications, at the gravesites of the righteous, we find that he tells them to meditate and go with a particular Kavanah in mind and to not speak to any living being on the way.

Once a student was given a very powerful Yichud to meditate on in order to reach a deeper level of clarity in his life. When he did as he was told and nothing shifted for him, he went back to the AriZal to complain. The AriZal responded to him, "did you not bid good day to that person on your way?"

In summary, when you have done the appropriate preparations before praying and are ready to pray, it would be best if you entered directly into prayer with no separation between the preparations and the prayers themselves.

3]

Dealing with Foreign & Negative Thoughts

THERE IS THE POSSIBILITY THAT AS YOU ARE ABOUT TO PRAY AND YOU ARE ATTEMPTING TO SHARPEN YOUR FOCUS, YOUR MIND KEEPS WAN-DERING ELSEWHERE. Or it might be that you are in the middle of praying, trying to maintain your focus on what you are saying and doing, but your mind keeps drifting to other areas of interest. What could and should be done?

THIS TOO SHALL PASS:

The classic response to deal with intruding thoughts when they enter the mind is to push them aside. Deeper still, the *Shulchan Aruch* *(Siman 98:1)* rules that if a foreign thought enters the mind while praying you should, "wait a moment until the thought is nullified", so that you should not fight with the thought. Nor of course do you get involved with it more deeply or even entertain the thought, but simply pause and let the thought pass. In the words of the *Gra* of Vilna *(ad loc)* "stand still, unitl the thought moves on."

This is a much more gentle and effective way to clear the mind then pushing and fighting with your thoughts. The nature of your subconscious thoughts and fixations is that the more you resist them the more they persist. By pausing for a moment and letting the thought pass, you do not enter into a struggle with the thought, you simply let it dissolve on its own.

A disciple of the Maggid of Mezritz once asked his teacher what to do with intruding thoughts in prayer. The Maggid suggested that he travel to Karlin and visit his student R. Aaron of Karlin. It was quite a long journey to Karlin and when the disciple finally arrived he immediately preceded to the home of R. Aaron. Hungry and tired he knocked on the door of

R. Aaron, but to his surprise, though he saw the light still flickering in the study, R Aaron did not respond to the knock. He knocked harder and still R. Aaron did not answer. This went on the entire night and only in the morning, after many hours of knocking, did R. Aaron let him in. When he finally entered, before he had a chance to ask his question, R. Aaron told him, "You knocked, I heard you. But I was teaching you a lesson: You do not need to let in everyone who knocks."

GETTING TO KNOW YOURSELF:

Prayer is a time when we are alone with ourselves and in the conscious presence of the Master of the Universe. This is a good time for self-inspection and self-disclosure. This is an appropriate environment to observe our inner self, to examine where we are coming from, where we may be headed and what needs improvement and/or fixing. When standing in a state of prayer with the overwhelming awareness that you are in the presence of your Creator, all the walls of self-delusion come crumbling down. You cannot, nor do you want to, fool yourself any longer and you can finally be truly open and honest with yourself about your life and your shortcomings.

In general, intruding thoughts are called *Machsha-vas Zaros* / foreign thoughts. R. Mendel of Kotzk once quipped, "People call these thoughts "foreign thoughts" when in truth, these are a person's normal thoughts. Thoughts of prayer are what are, sadly, foreign to them". So the first step would be to be honest with yourself in order to recognize what stage of consciousness you are holding at, and what are your "natural" thoughts that come up. These thoughts indicate to a person what is really going on within and subconsciously point out what areas of their psycho-spiritual life they should work on refining, embracing and perfecting. In a sense, these "normal" thoughts reveal what needs *Tikkun* / repair.

Often, the best way to do this is to simply notice what grabs the mind as you are trying to concentrate on our prayers. If the mind continually wanders about, you can observe where it wanders. The mind of course wanders to the areas of our lives where we are holding or are being held. Clearly, it would be better and more beneficial to let go of these thoughts, since they are intruding on our ability to focus our consciousness on our prayers. Yet by noticing how these thoughts continue to creep in, you can discover what your concerns are and work to fix the trouble spots.

EVERY THOUGHT HAS A PURPOSE:

Noticing these thoughts opens us to what needs to be worked on and what we truly need to pray for. The *Mishnah* says, "Do not make your prayers set" *(Avos, 4:4)*. "Set", says the Baal Shem Tov, means "do not set a fixed agenda to your prayers". Before you begin to pray do not think, "I need to pray about this specific idea and nothing else". Rather, we need to be open in our prayers. Whatever pops up or comes to mind when praying is a sign of what is deeply troubling you. These are the immediate issues that need attention. Pray for them, pray for the wisdom and guidance to be able to deal with these issues.

It was once asked of the Baal Shem Tov, what one should do if he prayed without intention and his mind was occupied with 'foreign thoughts'? The Baal Shem Tov responded: "It is known that there is nowhere the Divine presence is not present, even in the midst of foreign thoughts." If one would decide to start over and begin his prayers again, it would demonstrate that Hashem's presence was not there the first time, which is heresy. Rather, one should meditate in their mind on the words of the prayers that were said without intention.

The depth of this principle is that nothing is random

and the Divine positive purpose-driven animating force is present everywhere and within everything. Even deeper, not only is Hashem present in an abstract way, but even the 'negative' thoughts a person has during prayer is also for a purpose and, in fact, we can learn something from them. They are teaching you something about yourself, revealing hidden 'sparks' that are seeking to be elevated.

We have, now become aware that these "foreign thoughts" tend to grab our attention more than our prayers. But we have also learned that by observing and becoming aware of them we may come to know who we are and what our inner situation really is. You still want to pray and yet you cannot pray without being distracted. You desire to enter into a place of infinite potential, but these splintered and distracting thoughts keep bubbling up, so what do you do with them?

DISCERNMENT & SEPARATION:

Introspection is in fact one of the fundamental purposes of prayer. The Hebrew word for prayer, *Tefilah*, shares its root with *Yefalel*, which means 'judgment', and with *Pallel*, which means to 'judge' *(Tehilim, 106:30, Targum. Sanherdrin, 44a.)*. "To Pray", *L'hispalel*, means to assess or judge oneself *(R. Hirsch, Bereishis, 20:7)*. Deep Tefilah or prayer is a simultaneous act of self-reflection and expression. It is a time to self-reflect in order to see where we are coming from and where we want to be headed. Observe what comes up that needs attention and improvement. By becoming aware of the thoughts that arise on their own while we pray, we may expand our awareness from beneath the surface of our subconscious mind to an expanded and elevated state of self-awareness. We may then aspire to repair and re-integrate each issue as it comes up. This is one of the foundational dimensions of prayer.

Tefilah is also rooted in the word *Phela*, which means to 'separate'. Prayer is a good time to discern and separate our positive and negative patterns and characteristics; as in to separate the good and beneficial Kavanos and attributes from the negative and destructive distractions.

OCCUPYING THE MIND:

It is important to understand that an occupied mind is not a mind that becomes distracted, at least not as easily. If, while you are trying to concentrate and engage in prayer, thoughts keep coming in, this shows that your mind and heart are not fully engaged in the experience of prayer. When a person prays with full intention no other thoughts can enter the mind.

Intellectual intentions are one path to ensure that little or no intruding thoughts enter the mind during praying. Since you become so fully engaged in the prayers through the mental exertion of maintaining the intentions, not just from a heart space but also from a mind space, there is no room for other thoughts or feelings to enter your mind. When a person is praying with the Kavanos of the AriZal for example, where exact intentions are prescribed for every detail of the prayers, then there is little to no room for extraneous thoughts.

Imagine yourself at your own wedding. At the peak moment of this beautiful ancient ritual you are standing under the Chuppa, at that very moment your mind is completely focused only on the immediate present. This is true in almost all moments of great joy or, Heaven forbid, in times of deep tragedy. It is beneficial to attempt to enter into a similar state of immediacy and intensity while praying. For, in truth, you are standing face to face within the presence of the Infinite One Creator, destroyer and sustainer of all that is, was and will be. This can and should be both terrifying and awe inspiring. This experience is related directly to the development of the inner quality known as *Yirah* / holy 'fear/awe'.

EMPTYING THE MIND BY
USING A CHOSEN PHRASE:

R. Yeshayah Halevi Horowitz, otherwise known as
the *Shaloh Ha'kodesh*, speaks of a tool to clear the mind
which involves the repetition of a phrase of Torah
three times. He writes that if a person is distracted by
extraneous thoughts before praying and he desires to
rid himself of these he should gently move his right
hand across his forehead three times and say each
time, *Lev Tahor*, "Create in me a pure heart O G-d
and renew within me an upright spirit" *(Tehilim, 51:12)*.

During the prayers, when you are in a place within
the liturgy that you cannot interrupt, you may utilize
this practice by meditating on the passage instead of
saying it aloud; thereby not actually 'interrupting' your
prayers.

Similarly, as mentioned, the repetition of a verse of
Torah, besides containing innate spiritual powers of
its own, serves as an audible focal point, and by repeating it over and over again, the verse fills the mind
with its content and sound, while simultaneously
clearing the mind from all other extraneous thoughts
and distractions.

Likewise, R. Moshe Cordovero, the *Ramak*, records

a teaching he heard from the "old man", *Eliyahu ha-Navi*, 'Elijah the prophet': If you are in the middle of your prayers and a negative thought comes to mind, such as jealously or hate, if it is in a place during the prayers that you can verbally interrupt, say the verse, "An eternal flame shall be kept burning on the altar, it must not be extinguished" *(Vayikra, 6;13)* over and over again and gently wipe your forehead while having the intension to wipe away these extraneous thoughts from your mind.

The codifiers of *Halacha* speak of a practice in which a person recites, "*Pi, Pi, Pi*", three times while moving his hand across his forehead, symbolically erasing the negative thoughts from his mind, and then spits lightly three times, symbolically releasing the thought.

BREAKING NEGATIVE PATTERNS OF THOUGHT:

If a person is trying to pray and their minds keep on slipping into negative thoughts — not only inappropriate thoughts unrelated to prayer, but actually negative thoughts such as anger, hate, or jealously — one way to break these thoughts is to pause and think of something more pertinent in your life, even if it is not directly related to prayer, such as your business or your relationships.

This is a very creative way to break a pattern of thoughts. Once the stream of thought is interrupted, now it will be easier for you to reengage your prayers.

VISUALIZATIONS:

"I have placed Hashem before me at all times" *(Tehilim 16: 8)*. While on a simple level this implies that one should sense Hashem's presence at all times, this verse in Psalms can also be understood literally — i.e. placing the letters of the Name of Hashem, the Yud-Hei-Vav-Hei, in front of us at all times. To actually visualize these four letters in front of you at all times. This visualization can assist in the eradication of unwanted and distracting thoughts.

If you find your mind roaming and drifting during your prayers imagine yourself disembodied, your soul outside your body and in the presence of Gan Eden, in front of the Throne of Glory. If you can bring this image up in your consciousness and secure a good visualization of this, it will certainly assist you in ridding yourself of unwanted and intruding thoughts.

You may want also to join the visualization or the repetition of a verse with a tune, a Nigun. While you are visualizing or meditatively repeating a verse or phrase to fill your mind, you may do so with a tune to help occupy, focus and direct your mind and heart.

LOOKING IN THE SIDDUR – SEEING THE WORDS ON THE PAGE:

The sacred words on the page, the words of the prayers themselves have tremendous power. When a person prays the words of the prayers he should visualize in his thoughts the word he is saying. If you find your attention drifting away from the prayers, optically focus on the words you are saying and visualize these words in your mind's eye. This, many write, is a proven practice to dispel all distracting thoughts, inspiring the person to have proper and focused intention.

The letters themselves are vessels of light and blessing, they have the power to hold our thoughts and dissolve all negative distractions.

BODY MOVEMENT:

There is a deep relationship between our bodies and our minds. The human is, in a sense, a bio-psychic feedback loop, with the mind effecting the body, and the body, in turn, effecting and influencing the mind. The human body is one organism and each part is interlinked with every other. The entire structure of the universe is called *Adam Gadol* / large man. The entire planet is one organism and nothing therein exists in isolation. Conversely, every human is referred to as *Olam Katan* / small world, indicating as well that we each contain a multitude of elements and weather patterns within us as a swirling symphony of creative energy.

When a person is stuck in a thought pattern they will continually find themselves drifting to other issues or ideas besides their prayers. For example, one may be constantly thinking about what they need to do at work, or about their relationship or finances.

What this person needs is a shift from one state of consciousness to another. The mere act of walking into a place of prayer can help facilitate this shift. Literally moving the body can help to inspire this shift in our mind.

Reb Pinchas of Koritz teaches that physical movement disperses negative, habitual, self-centered thoughts. A physical shift and movement triggers a mental shift and movement.

Overall, any movement breaks patterns. We may begin with a shift in the body's position and end up affecting a shift of mind set. The movement literally and figuratively takes you to another place. This is one of the inner reasons why the tradition is to *Shukel* / sway, moving to and fro during ones prayers. The rhythmic movement helps to focus the mind and maintain the Kavanah.

We may also at times use the body or hand movements to inspire or reveal an emotion.

CLAPPING HANDS:

If you find your mind wandering off and drifting during prayer, you may want to clap your hands to regain focus. Reb Nachman of Breslov teaches that clapping the hands breaks negative thought patterns. He teaches that we "clear the air" surrounding us when we clap our hands. When the air around us is pure we are more susceptible to pure thoughts. Our mind, as part of our bodies, is sensitive to and affected by our environment and surroundings. Our thoughts are apt to be more pure and clear in an environment of purity and clarity.

If you sense yourself wandering and straying from the focus of prayer, give a sharp clap with your hands. Besides the clearing and cleansing effect of the clap, you will notice that automatically your awareness will be directed towards the noise and simultaneously away from the distracting thoughts. You will distract the distraction. Your attention becomes focused with a sudden noise and then you can use that focus to re-direct it towards your prayers.

DEEP CALLS OUT TO DEEP:

Instead of using your hands, as in a clap, or your body, as in *Shukeling*, you may find that you can get a similar refocusing affect through using your voice. If you are praying alone, or in a less judgmental environment, you might try giving a sudden shout, scream, sigh or a cry to shift and sharpen your consciousness. In fact, there are some Chassidim, disciples of R. Aaron of Karlin, who regularly use their voices, as in shouting and screaming, to shock themselves into an immediate presence of the Divine during prayer.

Not as drastic or dramatic, but at times equally effective, a more subtle way to reengage your attention with your prayers can be done by quietly humming a *Nigun* / wordless melody, to yourself. A Nigun, as will be explored further on, has the capacity, says the Rebbe RaYatz of Chabad, to "eradicate all extraneous thoughts during prayer". A Nigun has the potency to clear the mind and empty it from all distracting thoughts. One of the words for song in Hebrew is *Zimrah*. The root word of Zimrah is *Zamer*, which means to prune. When we sing with intention we are removing the weeds that crowd the beds in the garden of consciousness. A Nigun, simply put, refocuses our attention and cuts away all distracting thoughts.

It may also help to take a deep breath before you recite a blessing and then try to recite the entire blessing in one breath, at least for the shorter blessings.

ELEVATION OF THOUGHTS:

The methods listed above are techniques used to rid one-self of distracting and/or intrusive thoughts. There is also another approach, the path of going deeper into these intrusive or distracting thoughts to strip them of their *Klipa* / hardened shell, in order to get to the subtle seed of light, beauty and holiness within the particular thought, and then to harness and channel the generated feelings and energies for the purpose of prayer and *Deveikus* / attachment and cleaving to Hashem.

Life becomes exponentially more meaningful and multi-dimensional when we are able to see that within everything there is a divine message. Each and every thought, feeling and experience is there to show us something, to teach us how we can better become more fully ourselves. When something comes up, we should be asking ourselves why? "Why am I seeing this?" Or, "Why am I experiencing that?" Within the answer to that question, which often appears in a still small voice from within our deepest self, lies the secret to unlock our dormant potentials for growth and inner development.

The technique goes like this: If a foreign thought comes to mind, instead of immediately pushing it aside or ignoring it, take a moment to look at it, listen to it, and realize that the reason you are having this particular thought, at this particular time, is because the inner desire— i.e. the inner spark of this thought/ feeling/experience — wants to return to its Source in holiness through you.

Everything, even the most intrusive or distracting thoughts or feelings are rooted in the Infinite Oneness of the Creator. We can actually play a pro-active role in the process of liberating the Divine from within the mundane by unraveling or cracking open the hardened shell of externality, which paradoxically protects and prevents the seed that is held within from fully blossoming before its time. This liberation, in turn, allows the Spark of Holiness to realign and return itself, as well as you, to a state of unity and purity in Hashem.

Assuming the thought revolves around a certain bodily and physical pleasure, one can expect that within the self-centered desire there is a spiritual Spark that yearns to be released and returned to its Source. For example, the desire to eat reflects an inner desire to elevate the energy contained within the food back to its source. As it says in *Tehilim (Psalms, 107:5)*, "Hungry as well as thirsty, my soul withers within me". In other words, my body feels hunger, but deeply it is my soul that seeks spiritual replenishment through the elevation of the food. The body's hunger is a manifestation of the soul's hunger.

Similarly with every aspect of life, thoughts included, there is the symptom and the cause. We are having certain thoughts, but why? In simple terms, these feelings and thoughts are surfacing at this moment in order for us to plant the 'seed' of these thoughts or feelings in the soil of holiness, so that we can discard and redeem the shell of these thoughts. In a sense, to re-root them in their supernal source from which they came, which is in the Infinite Unity of the Creator.

But how does one do this? How does one release the negative and reveal the positive quality of a desirous or self-centered thought?

The method of elevation is called *Ha'la'as Ha'midos* / the elevation of attributes. When a foreign thought enters one's consciousness, one should attempt to elevate and sublimate the thought.

Every thought, feeling and experience is rooted in a pure supernal source. Every feeling we experience can be traced to its root in one of the ten Sefiros. If a thought or desire for a physically beautiful object or person arises, one should contemplate the source of this desire. One should reflect and consider that the aesthetics and the beauty of this object, or person, are but manifestations of the divine animating force that created it to be so desirable. Therefore, one is able to redirect their desire in service of the Source of the beauty.

In more simple terms, every feeling or thought that arises carries with it both a Sensation and a Narrative. For example: You are feeling angry. There is the sensation of the body being angry — i.e. the heart races — and then there is the narrative, that which prompted the anger — i.e. you are angry because "this" or "that" has happened. Normally these two aspects of an experience register as one. In this method of "elevation", the idea would be to attempt to separate the sensation from the narrative. Separate the feeling of anger from the story you are telling yourself that validates the experience — the "I am angry because of such and such". The feeling itself is a feeling of being small, of humbling the ego, which in itself can be positive.

When feeling lust, the inner quality is a desire to connect — to connect with oneself, to connect with an 'other' and ultimately to connect with Hashem. So you must go deeper into the feeling or thought and strip the desire of its Kelipa, its negative story and narrative, and experience the purity of the feeling itself, which is both holy and noble.

The deepest level would be to move from a love that is directed towards one person, well formed and finite, to an infinite formless love towards Hashem and all of creation. Thereby, an exclusive and finite love can give birth to a truly inclusive and infinite love. One could practically explode with an infinitely holy emotion of burning love, by stripping away the earthly finite love to its core, which is a wildly passionate love for the Creator and thus, by extension, for all of Hashem's Creation.

The danger with this method — because it teaches one to go deeper into these thoughts, feelings or desires — is that if one does not have control over ones thoughts, and most people do not, what will happen is that the deeper one goes, the lower one will go, the darker one will go, the more entangled one will become with these thoughts. So instead of elevating these thoughts one will be lowering oneself deeper into the abyss of one's own chaotic subconscious. As the *Tanya* states with regard to elevating thoughts, "how can you elevate these thoughts on high when you yourself are bound by the below?"

Honesty is integral for any spiritual practice. For the majority of people, most of the time, their thoughts control them. Yet it also may be true that there are certain areas in life that one does have more control over. In most dimensions of life one may be struggling or battling and yet within one's life there may be certain aspects in which one is "like a *Tzadik*", or at least that one struggle less with. We all have weaknesses and strong points. We struggle in one area but may be very efficient in another. Each person has particular points within themselves wherein they may honestly state that with regards to those thoughts, desires or distractions, they are like a Tzadik.

When thoughts, feelings or desires arise to consciousness during prayer, be honest. Know your state of mind and heart, and see whether you feel inspired and awakened enough to attempt to practice the elevation of thoughts, but if not, let the thoughts go and utilize the other practices.

DEEPER KAVANAH AS A MEANS TO DISSIPATE NEGATIVE THOUGHTS:

A more subtle approach with regards to dealing with intruding thoughts was suggested by the wise Reb Bunim of Pshischah. He taught that one should not push aside or tangle with the thoughts, nor should one aspire to elevate them, rather, he advised that we can nullify negative thoughts through deeper Kavanah and analysis.

Let us imagine a person is in the middle of praying the *Shema* and a "foreign thought' about his "car" enters his mind. Now, instead of trying to push the thought aside, which never works, as the more one resists the more it persists, pause a moment and mindfully, objectively confront it, clarify its nature, and realize it is only a car. Of course, we are using "car" as an example in the form of a metaphor.

Whenever a person confronts and delve into his thoughts he will quickly realize, that there is nothing substantial there, they are just 'thoughts' and just as rapidly the thoughts will disappear on their own.

Most times, it is not the 'car' that is the problem or what is holding his attention, but rather everything he fantasizes about the 'car' — what it can do for him, how we will feel owning that car, and so forth. It is not the thoughts of the car itself that is the problem, and potentially damaging to his spiritual equilibrium, it is rather the fantasy, the narrative, attached to the car. The car itself is just a hunk of metal.

One can use his imagination and translate the 'car thought' to every negative, materialist, lewd or lustful thought that may enter the mind in prayer. A penetrating observation of the thought reveals that when the fantasy is stripped away, what remains is merely a 'car'.

EVERY DAY NEW STRUGGLES:

What worked yesterday as a practice to overcome, let go of, or elevate thoughts may not have the same effect today. Every day we encounter new foreign thoughts, feelings and desires. Life is a constant struggle for the *Beinoni* / intermediate man. Every day, every moment even, we grow to new heights and thus encounter new challenges.

Every day we struggle with new *Machshavas Zaros*. While it is correct that up to Ninety percent of our thoughts today were the same as yesterday, still everyday these very same thoughts have a nuanced twist.

Just as the AriZal teaches that there is no prayer from the time of creation until the time of redemption that is exactly the same. All prayers are distinct and unique. The same is true for foreign thoughts. The *Machshavas Zaros* of today are different than a day ago, even if only slightly.

Overall, anytime a thought, feeling or desire keeps on disturbing you, instead of simply getting upset and agitated, realize that everything in life is a messenger. There is a lesson to be learned, some positive quality to be gained, either by ignoring the thought and continuing to pray with even more Kavanah and focus, or by elevating the thought and liberating the latentspiritual energy within it. Either way, there is an aspect of redemption within the experience. Instead of engaging the distraction and becoming more upset, unsettled and unfocused, these intrusive thoughts can help you gain even greater *Koach* / strength, and Kavanah, focused intention.

WHAT DO YOU DO WHEN OTHER PEOPLE ARE DISTRACTING YOUR PRAYERS?

All the above methods and techniques can help a person when the distractions are coming from within, but what happens if when the distractions are outside of oneself? For instance, maybe when you began your prayers the space was quiet, clean and conducive for prayer, but now there is distracting conversation or commotion?   Imagine you are sitting in *Shul* or any space that is dedicated for prayer, and the person next to you is making noise, speaking, or fidgeting and you cannot move, and neither will your asking of the other to quiet down help the matter.

What do you do?

Remember, everything in life is a messenger. If you find yourself being disturbed by another person during prayer, know that this too is for your own good. Most probably you were not concentrating enough, otherwise you would not have even noticed these disturbances, and Heaven sent this person as a messenger to make you aware that you need to concentrate more intensely. Through their distraction, if you are able to respond appropriately, you will be aroused to pray with greater devotion and Kavanah until you will not hear any other distractions, even if they are happening right next to you.

Again, if you can move — do so, but if not, view these distractions as messengers to assist you in reaching a deeper level of concentration and Kavanah.

This method of viewing the distraction as a messenger to inspire deeper concentration can also be used with regards to negative internal thoughts, so long as these are not thoughts that you are consciously and continually entertaining. A person who has honestly prepared for prayer and feels that their mind and heart is clear to pray, and then when they are actually praying, "foreign thoughts" keep on creeping up, this individual may then view these thoughts as "divine messengers". These too are from Hashem, sent to the person to help him pray with even more Kavanah. Hashem is present even in our moments that feel distracting, beckoning us back to an awareness of acknowledgement and praise.

It may also be that these "foreign thoughts", if indeed they are foreign to your inner constitution, can be seen as a good sign. They may be an indication that you are truly focusing and praying, that your prayers are piercing the heavens and that is why you are experiencing a deluge of distracting thoughts. Upon approaching any new spiritual height or accomplishment, we are met with a series of obstacles and "enemies" to our spiritual development; in fact, the appearance of such obstacles is itself a sign of one's progress.

There is a parable from the Baal Shem Tov that can help us to better understand these internal dynamics:

Once there was a mighty king who had his palace protected by many guards and servants. These guards and servants were stationed throughout the palace so as to protect the king from any approaching threat to his sovereignty. These guards and servants did not however trouble themselves with people of little importance or strength. For even if these would be 'stormers of the palace' got to the king, nothing would happen, for they lacked the *Koach* / Strength and *Kavanah*, to pose any real threat. But when someone of any substance or significance approached the palace, perhaps a neighboring ruler or a mighty warrior, they would be put on high alert. For you see, the guards were plagued with anxiety that some other more qualified warrior would show up and take their place, making them obsolete, so when they noticed any other qualified warriors attempting to enter the palace and come before the king, they would place stumbling blocks in front of their path.

We learn from this story that if you are praying and you are honestly feeling more deeply connected and ever-closer to the Most High as you are approaching the Inner Chambers of the Heavenly Palace wherein dwells the Infinite and Eternal Sovereign of the Universe, and you begin to experience tremendous difficulty in continuing your prayers — either physically you begin to feel tired, or emotionally you become exhausted, or inwardly you feel overwhelmed by distracting thoughts — know that this difficulty may be due to the "guards/*Kelipa*/character armor" that do not want you to approach the "King". Take a deep breath and give yourself permission to disarm them, thereby deconstructing their rigid hold on your consciousness and rendering them obsolete.

These negative character traits and aspects of your smaller self may be likened to the devious guards from the Purim story who plot to kill the king, or to the magicians in Pharaoh's court from the Exodus story. In both cases, the guards and magicians can be seen as either scheming the downfall of a righteous ruler or upholding the illusion of undeserving authority. In both stories, it takes the concerted and Divinely guided efforts of a *Tzadik*, a qualified warrior, to break down their defenses and reveal their traitorous, self-serving aspirations.

Through this simple story, the Baal Shem Tov is subtly teaching us that if you experience these difficulties and obstacles in the midst of elevated prayer, it is time to muster up your last strength, gather yourself together and push yourself just that much further. In due time, all *Kelipos* will evaporate.

4]

Visualizations to Enter Prayer

DURING PRAYER IN GENERAL, AND MORE SPECIF-
ICALLY WHEN WE REACH THE PEAK OF PRAYER,
WE HAVE THE ABILITY TO INWARDLY ENTER THE
HOLY OF HOLIES, THE DEEPEST DEPTHS, WHICH
WILL BE EXPLORED LATER ON. And yet, in spite of
the fact that our body is physically turned towards the
place of the Holy of Holies in Jerusalem *(Orach Chayim,
Siman 94:1)*, our hearts are emotionally broken open so
that we may attempt to feel the even the slightest pres-
ence of the Infinite One, and our minds are focused

and clear enough to conceive of the Inconceivable — still our psyches may wander, our inner narrative and subconscious mind may not be fully engaged in prayer and thus may burp and bubble up various (seemingly) unrelated desires.

There are so many subtle levels of our psyches that scream out for attention. We need to actively engage them all in order to remain fully present in prayer. Towards this end various authentic visualizations and creative meditations will be offered. These awareness enhancing visualizations and practices will help one properly prepare for prayer, activating the recesses of one's mind and heart, while also reaching the deepest soul self.

ACTIVE IMAGINATION:

In general, the power of *Tziyur* / creative visualization, is a much more effective method of encountering and integrating higher wisdom than mere intellectual understanding. As the *Zohar* teaches, "the gate to holiness is through the power of imagination" *(Zohar 1.p. 103b)*.

Utilizing the *Chush of Dimyon* / sense of imagination, can tremendously enhance our praying experience.

Today we live in a time when our essential *Avodah* / Divine service, is the practice of prayer. Therefore we need to make sure that our praying is relevant, genuine, transformative and personal. When we sing *Az Yashir* / the Song of the Sea, for example — which was sung by the ecstatically awe-struck Israelites after the miraculous splitting of the Reed Sea — we need to be able to visualize in our own minds, the turbulent waters splitting right before us as if we ourselves are standing right this moment on that sandy shore and the rushing waters are parting and we are passing through. Everything we say in the prayers needs to be real. When we speak about going out of Egypt, we need to taste liberation and feel as if we are now going out of our Egypt. When we speak about being healed, we need to feel healthy and whole.

REDEMPTIVE IMAGINATION:

Our imaginations are where many of our *Klipos* reside and hide. *Klipa* is the outer husk or shell of our desires, fantasies and perverted perspectives of what is, or who we are.

Understood as rigid, condensed thought forms, and frigid static emotional patterns, Klipos hold us back from whom or where we would like to be. It is a function of prayer, and of the spiritual life in general, to break through these shells and husks of our desires, cravings, and neurosis in order to unleash the hidden potential of the seed of light that is waiting within the darkness of our desires to burst forth and bear fruit.

To yoke, discipline, and employ the chaotic and wild imagination in the creative consciousness of connecting to G-d while refining and becoming our deepest and truest self is a major *Tikkun* and our spiritual life will get a much needed, boost of momentum from the release of all the deep and dormant energy that resides in the untapped recesses of our imagination. Thus, in the process of harnessing our active imagination, there must also be a simultaneous purification, redemption and elevation of our imagination.

The following visualizations and practices can help facilitate this process of creating an inner awareness of openness and alignment.

DOORS OF PERCEPTION:

There is an art and science of spiritual/ritual preparation before entering into a new experience. The depth of one's prayer or focus is often directly related to their preparation. Our sages tell us that we should, "walk in a measure of Two Doors before beginning to pray" *(Berachos, 8a)*. Besides the literal meaning of not standing by the exit when we pray, this means, that we should leave behind one door, one room, one reality and enter into another parallel, simultaneous, interpenetrating world of infinite potential. Through Kavanah and prayer we are attempting to deepen and expand our sense of self and soul connection to Source in order to leave behind the 'constriction' of one-dimensional animal/ego/body identification and enter into a higher, deeper, more expansive world of spirit, subtlety and the sound of the still small voice.

It is preferable to pray in a Shul or synagogue that is further from our home than in the one that is close by, for then there is reward for every step taken to get there *(Sotah, 22a)*. This is not only an encouragement to walk for a Mitzvah, but the inner meaning is to show that in order to truly pray we need to, as it were, distance our self from the center of our personal necessities, our familiars, our "homes", our egos. We need to walk through the doors of perception, leaving behind our finite attachments, in order to enter into a proper perspective for authentic prayer. And through this movement, this exiting and entering, this dissolution and reemergence, we are able to shift our perspective from the self to the Self, from the many to the One, from "i" to "I".

PRAYING IN HEAVEN:

When we pray, our hearts and minds should be directed upward, as if we are standing in the presence of the Shechinah *(Sanhedrin, 22a)*. The Rambam writes that when we pray we should imagine ourselves as if "we are present in Heaven" *(Hilchas Tefilah, 5:4)*. We should envision ourselves as if we are literally standing in Heaven *(Rabbeinu Yonah, Berachos, 25a)*.

As an actual practice we can begin by becoming aware of our bodies, feeling your consciousness infusing every inch of your physical frame. Now imagine your awareness slowly rising upward, leaving your limitations behind and observing your body from above. Slowly you begin to rise upward into the sky, becoming lighter and lighter and floating higher and higher. As you feel yourself moving higher and higher you seem to escape the grip of gravity and you can feel yourself enter into a vast and empty space. You may even imagine yourself hovering all the way up above the skycap.

Often, as you are floating upward it is helpful to visualize the lightness of the body, for as you are drifting higher and higher you are becoming lighter and lighter. In this state you are able to sense a lessening of the denseness, coarseness or heaviness of the body. Thereby experiencing a subtle and gradual divestment from the gravity of the physical form.

Early Chassidic Rebbes teach us that when we feel that we have entered this vast, empty silent, humming space, we should attempt to expand our visual field so as to include the entire abyss that surrounds us and to not focus our attention too narrowly in any one direction. And when we feel secure in "that place", we have to tell ourselves to move even further beyond it, and then even higher, constantly moving upward and inward.

We need to overcome any internal fear, or perhaps frightening images that may appear in the inner screen of the mind, as they are the Klipos of each world or dimension we pass through that attempt to hold us back and keep us stuck in our predictable places of constriction. As we continue moving upward and inward we are able to more tangibly feel the subtle bond of unity that exists between Hashem and us.

A BEING OF LIGHT:

Imagining yourself as a being of light can help you "lessen your load" from the emotional and mental gravity that pulls on the denser aspects of your body and soul. Reb Chaim Vital speaks of a similar meditative practice where he writes that, "if you are praying, or desire to have proper intention, imagine that you are made of light and that you are surrounded by light from all sides and directions, and within the light is a throne of life…"

If you are in the middle of prayer and you find that your intention is not honed, you may want to "lift your eyes upwards, towards Heaven to awaken intention" *(Shulchan Aruch Ha'Rav, 95:3)*. A simple shifting of the head and eyes in the direction of 'the above' can refocus your intention. Remember, a physical movement facilitates and initiates a mental movement.

WE ARE WHERE OUR THOUGHTS ARE:

The power of creative visualization and thought is magnificent and immeasurable. In truth, everything essentially exists in our thoughts. We do not see things the way they are, but rather we see things the way we are. We are continually projecting our thoughts outward and seeing the external world from within a prism of our own internal perspective. Indeed, we can never know with our logical minds the thing-in-itself, i.e. the external world beyond its representation.

But, even deeper, in our personal subjective world, the objects we observe outside of ourselves do not, to us, exist independently of our minds that perceive them.

We are present wherever our thoughts are. In the words of the Baal Shem Tov: "In the place where a person's thoughts are, that is where they truly are." When we can imagine something in our minds eye, we are not simply being 'here' and thinking about something out 'there'; rather we are actually 'there.'

We find that when *Yaakov* was fleeing *Esav* he skipped over *Har Ha'moriah* / Mount Moriah, but then said: "Is it possible that I have passed over the place where my ancestors have prayed and I did not pray." Immediately, he had intention to return to that place and at once, miraculously, he found himself on Har Ha'moriah *(Chulin, 91a)*. The deeper meaning of this teaching is that once he thought about being there, he was there. He found himself instantaneously in that space he was thinking about.

We are where are thoughts are. If our thoughts are in 'heaven' we are in fact in heaven.

THREE LEVELS OF ATTACHMENT:

As noted earlier, the Early Pious Ones, would sit before each prayer for an hour, during which time they would experience a *Hispashtus Ha'Gashmiyus* / divestment of materiality *(Tur, Orach Chayim. 98)*, a spiritual state wherein they were internally isolated and detached from bodily sensations and able to enter into a place beyond the constrictions of the physical.

This practice of "divestment of materiality" does not mean that a person begins to forget about the body or the needs of the body, although it can mean that as well. But even more deeply this means that a person begins to function from a place of initial detachment and then holy re-attachment to the physical in a rectified and perfected manner.

There are three levels of attachment and non-attachment included within this process. The first station comes from the place of ego and self-centeredness. Here there is a tenacious bond between the self and its physical needs, appetites and desires. There is a strong reluctance to surrender anything in the way of satisfying the pleasure principle, or even denying the body for any period of time. This can be called Animal Consciousness.

Level two is where a person learns to be gradually less attached to the needs of the ego and of the physical appetites. This can result eventually, depending on how far it is taken, in a complete disassociation from the lusts and desires of the body. This person may still eat and engage in physical activities, but only for the purpose of sustaining the soul in this world or creating new life. At this level, the indulgence in physical pleasure s engaged only for the fulfillment of physical necessity. A person at this station becomes transcendent of self and begins to take on an attitude about life that is comfortable saying that, 'whatever happens is ok', and one relinquishes any form of ambition or desire. This can be called Angelic Consciousness.

But we are not meant to be angels, if we were, why would our souls descend into this earthly plane and not simply exist within the subtle realm of spirit? Rather, our purpose is to have an ego, a body, ambitions, and desires and to work to refine our egos, making them ever more transparent to the higher, deeper, selfless Self. This is referred to as Soul Consciousness.

The movement of divesting oneself from the lower ego-oriented relationship with the physical, where one needs this or that and cannot survive without it, and moving towards a co-creative consciousness as described in level three, must first pass through the transcendent station of level two. Only from a place of detachment are we able to re-attach ourselves to our soul, knowing deeply that the Divine purpose is ultimately fulfilled within the realm of the physical.

THE ESSENCE:

This is truly an Essence oriented consciousness, consisting of both an awareness of the fullness as well as the emptiness of everything in this world.

There is *Yesh* / Being, this is the first level of manifestation, definition, finite form, content, the 'black fire', Animal Consciousness.

There is *Ayin* / Non-being, this is the second level of emptiness, infinity, unmanifest, formless, 'the white fire', Angelic Consciousness.

And then there is *Atzmus* / Essence, this is the third level of integration and unity, which transcends and includes them both, the context, Torah, Soul Consciousness.

When we approach life from an egoic, *Yesh* perspective there will most likely manifest various degrees of unhealthy attachment. These can come in a plethora of shapes and sizes, from food to money to clothes to power to body image to honor to pride, and so forth.

When we empty ourselves of Yesh, as much as humanly possible, and enter the 'no-space' of Ayin we feel no attachments, we are unmoved, unconcerned, unambitious.

But then ultimately, when we are able to 'return to the world' from stage two, we can then reenter stage one in a rectified manner, from a place of non-attachment and equanimity so that we can reconnect to our story, our personality and the physical world in a spiritual way, because that is truly the Divine purpose.

PRAYING IN THE BEIS HAMIKDASH/ THE HOLY TEMPLE:

The famed Chassidic Rebbe, R. Elimelech of Lizensk, speaks of a visualization wherein the person creatively visualizes himself praying in the *Beis Hamikdash* / the Holy Temple *(Noam Elimelech, Lech Lecha)*. This visualization seems to have been a practice a few hundred years back and there are sources for it in both Chassidic and non-Chassidic texts *(Yesod Shoresh Ha'Avodah. Shar Ha'karbon, p.82)*.

Rabbi Yaakov Emdin in his Siddur calls the *Amidah* itself the "court of the sanctuary" *(Note: Tikunei Zohar. Hakdamah 3b)*. If possible try to imagine yourself present within the 'Holy of Holies,' the innermost chamber of the sanctuary. This is where you are at internally during prayer and this visualization serves to make you more aware of this truth.

Internally the 'Holy of Holies' within us is the deepest place of self, the highest level of our *Neshamah* / our soul, which we alone have access to. Before we enter into prayer we should try to go to that place within and allow ourselves to communicate freely from there.

When we enter the 'Holy of Holies' we are entering the essence of our very beingness — or better yet, our non-beingness — a place within that is beyond any sense of doing or achieving. Now imagine yourself there, in the 'Holy of Holies,' the most sacred space in the world, and the deepest place within you, and pray from that place.

Concerning the entry of the *Kohen Gadol* / High Priest, into the holy of holies on Yom Kippur, the holiest day of the year, the Torah says, "And there shall be no man in the Tent of Meeting when he goes in to make atonement in the holy place" *(Vayikra, 16:17)*. The Medrash asks *(Vayikra Rabba, 21:12)*, "Is not the

High Priest a man?" The Medrash then explains that when the High Priest entered into the Holy of Holies he was completely transformed, his face would glow with flames and he would take on the appearance of an angel.

Take a few moments before you begin to pray to flesh out this visualization and imagine yourself literally walking into the *Beis Ha'Mikdash* while simultaneously journeying inwards, into your own inner sanctuary — the deepest, quietest, safest space that is beyond emotion or expression. This visualization brings you into an encounter with the deepest truth of who you are and the deepest truth of reality.

PRAYING IN THE GARDEN OF EDEN:

The method of divesting oneself from attachment to the physical was later explored by R. Eliyahu ben Moshe Di Vidas, the 16th century moralist and kabbalist. In his work *Reishis Chochmah (Shar Hakedusah, Chap 4)*, he suggests that during our prayers we should imagine ourselves standing in Gan Eden, the Garden of Eden, in the presence of all the exalted souls of the *Tzadikim* / righteous people, of the past. Imagine yourself in the primordial paradise of Gan Eden in the presence of *Avraham* and *Sarah, Moshe Rabbeinu,*

Miriam, R. Akiva, Rashi, the *Arizal,* or the *Baal Shem Tov,* and that you are with them praying right now.

To make this more real you may also want to visualize a Tzadik or Tzadikim that you have personally known and physically seen.

When you can actively imagine yourself in the Garden you are thus in a space where there is no jealousy, lust, pride, anger, or ego. Empowered with this power of imagination, you will then be more likely to create this reality for yourself, and then you too, says the Magid of Mezritch *(Likutei Amarim, Os 262)*, will be able to pray without these negative feelings and thoughts.

What we see has a profound effect on our inner reality. By observing your teacher teaching Torah, not only will you understand the lesson better *(Eiruvin, 13b)* and tune in to the deeper wisdom that flows to the teacher as he is teaching *(D'rashos Ha'Ran, Derush 8)*, but the actual looking at the teacher draws down goodness and blessings *(Ya'aros D'Vash 1. Derush 12)*. This principle extends to the world of prayer as well *(Teshuvas Radbaz, 3:472)*. When we surround ourselves with our teachers or spiritual community our hearts and minds are more opened and we can be more receptive and open to pray. Not that we should actually look at human beings during our prayers, but rather, before praying, acknowledging or visualizing that they are there with you and knowing that you are surrounded by people you love and admire. If this cannot be done physically, the above mental visualization will suffice, as one visualizes being in the presence of Tzadikim in the place of *Gan Eden*.

It may also be beneficial to declare verbally before praying, "I hereby bind myself to all the tzadikim of the generations". This way you are both using your power of visualization coupled with the power of your voice. By vocalizing something you are able to make it more real.

These are two beautiful and powerful visualizations that a person can entertain during prayers — standing in the holy temple, or standing in paradise in the presence of a community of holy souls. These practices will greatly enhance your prayers. Another visualization that can be connected to prayer, but is also a worthwhile visualization throughout all hours of the day, will now be explored.

IMAGINE YOURSELF AS A PERFECT TZADIK:

In the above two forms of visualization you are actively imagining yourself in a scared place with holy people, but overall you are still separate from that reality, you are an observer, but still it is not you, it is not your reality. There is a deeper level wherein you attempt to visualize yourself as the Tzadik at the very moment that you are praying.

At 'the root of our soul', our *Shoresh Haneshama*, we are all Tzadikim, and we are all in a constant state of unity with the *Ohr Ein Sof* / the Infinite Light. In the words of R. Chaim Vital, "A person should turn his attention away from all physicality, sensory perception, bodily image and attachment in order to conjure up an image of his own ascension into the upper/inner worlds wherein he can receive the Light from the Source of his soul, from where his soul comes from…"

There is an "imperfect self" and the "perfect self". We are, in fact, both at once. There is a part of self that is still imperfect and we are constantly working towards its perfection. And there is a part of self that is, was, and always will be simply perfect. We are both perfect and imperfect at all times. We need to learn to imagine ourselves as a Tzadik and live from that place of perfection *(Tzav Ve'Ziruz 24. p. 340).* The Rebbe Maharash of Chabad says that every person should imagine themselves as a perfect Tzadik for at least fifteen minutes a day.

Every person has an inner image in their deeper sub-conscious that informs their life. If you believe deeply that you are a failure, you will continually fail. If you believe deeply that you deserve goodness and blessings, you will open yourself up to goodness and blessings. People who argue in favor of their own limitations, whether they feel themselves powerless because of past actions, low IQ, negative upbringing, or lack of education, will sure enough get to hold on to them, and the reverse is also true.

This is the case as well with our inner image of what type of person we think we are. In life you can either view yourself as a *Rasha* / bad person, and struggle in that image, or you can realize that there is a small Tzadik within you, a small measure of perfection and goodness, and aspire to live up to that image. Instead of subscribing to your "fantasy", which is not true, i.e. that you are a bad person, use your power of imagination, to access who you really are — a Tzadik.

Life is best served when we can envision ourselves at our best and brightest, as a tzadik, which we all potentially are.

Before we start praying we should meditate on this truth: Not only that we are in the place of holiness and in the presence of other Tzadikim, whether physically or mentally, but that deep within us there is this level of Tzadik and we are praying from that space.

To facilitate this awareness of the purity, perfection and potential of who we really are, it may be helpful for a person to recollect moments in their life that they may have felt very connected and in tune with their deepest selves and with Hashem. Visualize and think about that moment. How did you feel? What was your state of mind? Bring the potency of that previous peak experience into your prayer practice.

Another suggestion would be to bring up an image of yourself praying your deepest prayers, for example, praying the *Neila*, the 'closing prayer of Yom Kippur'. For many this is the most moving, stimulating and awe-inspiring prayer of the year. As the days of awe are coming to a close, many of us feel the intensity and holiness of the day and at those final moments truly open up. When you are about to pray you can aspire to awaken that memory and imagine that you are once again at that very moment, at the peak of Yom Kippur, and from that place begin to pray.

VISUALIZE SITTING IN THE PRESENCE OF THE SHECHINAH:

When we pray, we should attempt to feel as if we are

literally standing in the presence of the *Shechinah*.

Writing in the sixteenth century, Reb Eliezer Ezcari brings down an ancient practice in which a person, before he would begin to pray, would meditate on the light of the Shechinah that rests above a (righteous) person's head at all times and imagine themselves surrounded by the light of the Shechinah.

Here is the full quote: "And this is what we learned, 'The early Chassidim would settle one hour and then pray, in order to direct their hearts to Hashem.' And the commentators have explained that this means that they would redirect their thoughts from this world and attach their thoughts to the Master of everything, may He be blessed, with great awe and love. Meaning, for nine hours (each day) they would discontinue their studies and dedicate their time to the work of meditation and *Deveikus*. And they would imagine the light of the Shechinah (reflected as a dark blue color), hovering above their heads. (And then) as if it (the light) were flowing downward and infusing the entire space around them, they would sit in the light and tremble. And they would be joyous in their trembling."

Whether or not we can imagine the actual light of the Shechinah, it is still important that before entering into prayer we should imagine ourselves standing in the presence of Hashem.

On an even deeper level, we should take a moment and meditate on the fact that we are present in the midst of the Creator's glory that fills all of creation. In fact, there is great spiritual, mental and emotional value for a person to think and meditate at all times that he is present with Hashem and that the Creator is surrounding him from all sides.

In order to enter into a sacred space for prayer, meaning that special place within ourselves which is dedicated to openness and honesty about our true aspirations, desires and shortcomings, we need to first secure the "surroundings". In other words, before we enter into our most vulnerable space from which we will commune with Hashem, we must take the time to make sure that we are safe and feel protected so that we can truly let down our guards and defenses. To do this we need to create a protective *Ohr Makif* / surrounding light, so that we can enter this inner space feeling protected and open to being vulnerable.

A good meditation to do before entering into prayer would be to sense your *Ohr Makif*, to become conscious of this surrounding light, the presence of Hashem that surrounds you and protects you at all times.

FROM FORM TO LIGHT & BEYOND:

The feeling and sensation we are trying to achieve during prayer, and by extension throughout the entire day, is that we are in the presence of the Creator. But it is extremely challenging to think about the Infinite, Formless *Ein Sof* without creating, even subconsciously, some form or image. In fact, it is nearly impossible, besides within a deep and subtle inner awareness, to grasp onto and connect with Infinity without the mind, an inherently dualistic apparatus, structuring some form or image.

We want to pray, connect with, reach out to and feel an intimate personal relationship with Hashem, yet, how can we begin praying without some form or image in mind? An honest observation will reveal that most people do have some image of Hashem in mind when they pray. Maybe a child thinks of a King or mighty ruler, while a more mature person thinks of endless expansive Light, yet they are both (finite) images, and the Creator is Infinite and without form.

The objective is to train the mind to think more subtly. Developmentally speaking, to slowly train the mind to think in abstractions we may begin with an image and use the image as a stepping-stone towards the imageless. Although, for this practice to work, one must know full well that there truly is no image or form that can contain or fully represent the Infinite One. Essentially, we need to use the mind to transcend itself. Otherwise, the rational, concrete mind will continually place obstacles before us, drawing us back to the tangible.

The mentally and spiritually immature, while trying to conjure up a sensation of being in the presence of Hashem can begin with an image of himself standing in front of the most powerful ruler of the world. For instance, imagine speaking to the most powerful and yet loving person, but a billion times more powerful and more loving. Or visualize standing in front a majestic king, all-powerful and infinitely benevolent, who also happens to be your parent. This image will help the mind and heart grasp onto something so that the mind and heart slowly expands and widens, allowing your thoughts to grow stronger and more subtle, eventually morphing into an image of infinite light and love.

As the image of an earthly king slowly dissipates due to the inability of an earthly king's image to reflect the infinite power and love one is sensing in the midst of intense prayer and meditation, one must move beyond the image of a finite being to an image of pure light.

As this initial image fades, one begins to sense the presence of hundreds of shining bright lights dancing in front of them. Slowly, as one goes deeper and deeper, the various lights begin to merge into one great, awesome, indescribable light — a light of infinite proportions. A light like one has never seen before, billions of times brighter than looking straight at the sun; so much power, yet so gentle. The entire screen of their mind's eye is filled with this magnificent, beautiful, powerful, bright and loving light.

In the midst of this process, moving from a concrete image to a host of lights to a unified light, one simultaneously moves up the ladder of the Aleph Beis, starting at the end, from the final letter Tof, which is comprised of four hundred lights, moving all the way up to the one great light of the *Aleph*.

Then, as one arrives at a glimpse beyond the Aleph, beyond the first expression, before any sound or light, the Infinite becomes a possibility. From a strong tangible image one has traveled through the subtler worlds of lights, to one vast light, and beyond. Within the Beyond is a spark of prophetic insight, where the Infinite becomes revealed and one is able to sense the ineffable and unimaginable.

5]

Nigun:
Song Before & During Prayers

MUSIC, SOUND, VIBRATION IN GENERAL, AND MORE SPECIFICALLY A NIGUN, OR WORDLESS melody, has the capacity to clear the mind of all intruding thoughts, and to open the heart to be filled with proper Kavanah. There are two stages.

First, the Nigun can help clear and calm the mind. The subtle vibration of a wordless melody can gently and non-coercively direct and focus our attention while at the same time, allowing us to let go of our constant conceptualizing and inner chatter. We become our own sirens, seducing ourselves back down into the deeper layers of our psyches.

There is something physiological to this. Sustained, internally generated rhythm and vibration can help relax the body, and in turn, the mind. Much like the ebb and flow of the ocean or the rush and pulse of the wind can soothe our splintered psyches, even to the point of putting us to sleep. Which is actually one of the hidden points of prayer. To surrender our self to something which resembles a state of sleep and subconsciousness while still remaining awake and alert — like a lucid dream. This allows us a certain kind of 'behind the scenes' access to parts of ourselves that we are usually denied when we are in a normal waking state of self-conscious awareness, where our filters are generally set to functional and defensive. When we pray and meditate we are able to relax our filters to an altogether different setting — something closer to quantum. This is important, as discussed earlier, so that a person may enter into prayer free from attachments, tensions and distractions.

A Nigun can also help to clarify and intensify the actual intentions that we do seek to actualize. By giving our bodies and hearts something active and expressive to do, i.e. singing a Nigun, while we focus on the intentions of the prayers, we creatively occupy ourselves so as to not lose focus and intention. Also through the act of singing, which is primarily an act of the heart and soul rather than the mind and intellectual faculties, we are able to integrate the conceptual intentions even deeper into the core of our being. When a person meditates with his mind while his heart is joined in song, the Kavanah is that much more penetrating.

Singing opens us up figuratively and literally. It opens our mouths, our lungs, our diaphragms, our minds, our hearts and our bodies so that *Shefa* / flow, and *Bracha* / blessing, may stream more freely from, through, and to us. For, as the Zohar teaches, "there are chambers in Heaven which can only be opened through song" *(Tikunie Zohar, Tikkun 12)*. In fact, *Shira*, the Hebrew word for song and *Tefilah*, the Hebrew word for prayer have the same numerical value of 515.

There are songs directed towards the heart, and there are songs that come from the heart. Songs directed towards the heart are meditative and slow, introspective and reflective. Songs that come from the heart are often spontaneous and generally more joyous and free flowing. Nigunim that are sung as introductions to the prayers, in order to empty, calm and open the mind are traditionally contemplative, melancholy and slow tunes; whereas tunes that are traditionally sung during a prayer in order to inspire the heart and soul are generally exuberant expressions of the heart.

The Alter Rebbe was once asked why his disciples sing during prayers and he answered that it was an organic and spontaneous overflow of what the heart was feeling while in the presence of Hashem. Rabbi Yehudah HaChasid suggests that we sing during prayers in order to inspire us to reach higher heights and deeper depths of feeling and connection to Hashem.

Not only does a Nigun clarify and contextualize our intentions by opening the mind in order to listen to the heart, but through the act of singing a Nigun, more of the whole self is involved in the act of praying. The *Sefer Chereidim* writes that when you pray with your Whole Self, all your limbs shall pray, and all your powers and faculties of sight and hearing shall be engaged. Every part of your self should be engaged in your prayers.

There were Chassidim, in particular the *Kalisker* Chassidim of old, who would sing and dance fervently before beginning to pray in order to enter prayer in a rapturous mood of dance and animation.

When speaking of music and its intrinsic connection

to prayer, we are immediately reminded of a time when the holy Temple stood in Jerusalem. When instead of the set times of prayer, there were scheduled offerings where music was played. The tribe of Levi was in charge of the music and song and when an offering was being offered they would sing and play music.

There are perhaps four reasons, each one deeper than the next, for playing music in the Temple:

A] For the temple: The rational reason is simply to enhance the atmosphere of splendor and majesty through aesthetic engagement with the environment, as music is played in the courtyards of kings or at weddings.

B] For the priests: The music, which was received, written and performed in a state of spiritual joy and purity, serves to strengthen and support the Cohen or priest in maintaining his focus and Kavanah during the rituals.

C] For the person who is bringing the offering: To awaken, inspire and soften the heart of the person who is bringing the offering to do Teshuvah.

D] For the offerings themselves: Music, sound and

vibration serve as mediums, or vehicles, for any form of movement. The act of an offering is an act of elevation, of coming closer, of drawing near, and all elevations require music.

All these reasons apply to prayer. The Nigun helps the movement of our prayers, the Nigun inspires us and strengthens our Kavanah, as well as enhancing the environment of prayer. But the very basic reason to employ a song or Nigun before or during prayer is to clear the mind and open the heart. As a preliminary to prayer, a Nigun can also serve as a sort of audio Mikvah wherein the person fully immerses in the song and emerges in a transformed state — ready to pray.

Someone once complained to R. Yisrael of Ruzhin that his son in law wastes time before prayer. He said, "all he does is walk about and sing Nigunim". The Rebbe assured him that he has nothing to worry about and that singing Nigunim with passion and enthusiasm is as if being immersed in a Mikvah, wherein one is surrounded by a vibrational field of holiness and purity.

POSTURE

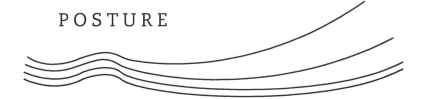

IDEAS EXPRESSED IN ACTION:

UP TO THIS POINT, SOME OF THE MORE INTER-
NAL EXPERIENCES AND INTENTIONS ON THE
PATHWAYS OF PRAYER HAVE BEEN EXPLORED.
Meditative processes and practices that can quite literally sharpen our minds and soften our hearts were
presented. But where is the body in all of these abstract ideas and intricate intentions?

Rooted as it is in the most basic and primordial functions and necessities of life itself, the body, in truth,
is the pathway to the most densely concealed layers
and levels of our very being. It is in our bodies, and in
our relationships to them, with all their needs and desires, that our most intimate and closely held beliefs
are played out.

It is in the realm of physicality that we express our
ideas in action. We bypass the ceaseless chatter of our
inner monologue and go through more direct and

subconscious channels of communication. How often does one really think about the way one eats or
sleeps? How rare to find one who moves through life
attuned and attentive to what one is or is not doing
and why. Part of the practice and process of prayer is
to realize the extent to which we act, speak and think
unconsciously and to bring awakening and awareness
to every level of our being and doing.

THE BODY:

Throughout history and geography the body has been
used, abused, refined and enjoyed in the pursuit of
self-realization and selfless devotion. From the more
aggressive and adversarial approaches such as fasting,
sleep deprivation and self-mortification, to the more
gentle and integrative avenues of dance and various
intentions for eating, the body has been the stage
upon which the cosmic struggle/dance of self and
other, sacred and profane, pleasure and pain has been
played out.

The body, indeed, is an instrument and avenue
through which we can approach and access the spiritual dimension. We need to include, however subtly,
the body in our praying, lest it become a distraction.
The positioning and movement of the body while engaged in the art/act of prayer is essential.

1]

Feet Together
at the Peak of Prayer:

WE LEARN ABOUT THE ROOTS OF PRAYER FROM
THE TANACH — THE TORAH, THE PROPHETS
and the Writings. From Avraham or Abraham petitioning The Most High to have mercy on Sedom,
to Yitzchak or Isaac meditating in the afternoon
field, to Chana pouring out her broken heart to The
Only One in a spontaneous surge of pain and faith.

We are offered many archetypal role models from the sacred texts. And from each one we learn something different. From Avraham we learn how to ask G-d for mercy and blessing on another's behalf. We learn from Yitzchak about the power of solitary seeking and sighing and singing in wide-open spaces during transitional times of the day. And from Chana we receive the gift of "silent and spontaneous prayer", as well as many traditional principles of how to pray.

Moshe Rabbeinu, in particular, was known for the frequency and intimacy with which he communicated "face to face" with the Infinite One Most High. Mimicking the modalities in which Moshe prayed, there are times when we sit and pray, exhibiting the mindset of being settled and focused. And then there are times when we stand, showing respect and veneration. There are times when we bow, demonstrating submission. And there are times when we jump upwards, indicating a desire to fly and defy our very physicality.

Yet at the peak of the prayers, which is when we pray the *Amidah* / the silent prayer, we stand with our feet securely together, as if bound, throughout the entire prayer.

Our sages tell us that we should pray with our feet together like the angels *(Berachos, 10b)*. The Jerusalem

Talmud adds that this is done to mimic angels and the priests in the Holy Temple *(Berachos, 1:1. Bach, Orach Chayim, 88)*.

All this symbolism is attempting to express the inner reason why we stand still with our feet together during the Amidah, which is because the peak of our prayer experience represents a space that is beyond all movement. Angels represent movement, as they are perpetually running and returning in a ceaseless flow of energy from one direction towards another, like the angels in Ezekiel's vision. When we have arrived at the apex of our prayers and entered into the innermost chamber, there is no movement left. We are already there. There is no "where" to go. We are beyond angelic.

On a more simple level, the idea of praying with our feet together shows our commitment to prayer and to what prayer offers us. It says, "we are here, and we are not running away". Feet together, symbolically bound as one, signifies that we have completely surrendered our sense of independent self and that we are totally bound up with the Eternal *(Rashba. Berachos, 10b)*.

The transformation of consciousness achieved through deep prayer reverberates throughout our entire being bringing into focus a total metamorphosis of polarity and priority. Our right-brain/intuitive/creative mind has crossed over and connected with the left-brain/linear/rational mind. Placing our feet together represents the inner negation of all dichotomy. When we place our feet together, we are symbolically gesturing that our right side – our expansive Divine transcendent inclination — as well as our left side – our contractive self-centered inclination — are now joined in unison while cleaving to Hashem *(Mabit, Shar HaTefilah, 7)*.

Feet, when they are not together, such as when one is walking or running, reflect movement, growth and progress, a non-acceptance of what is and a striving to reach more, to go further, to advance. Feet bound together represent the opposite — an acceptance of what is.

There is a custom that before we begin the Amidah we move backward three steps and forward three steps. This represents a simultaneous humbling and elevating of oneself in the presence of The Infinite One. It is at once a striving, a desiring, a retreating and a reaching. We step back to create that space in which the Divine can exist within the world, to 'let G-d in', as it were. And then we step up again to fill that void within ourselves as we approach the Ultimate Other as One. Finally, we stand still, which represents acceptance. In prayer there is this constant interplay between these two modalities of acceptance and non-acceptance, motion and stillness, song and silence, petition and praise.

In deep prayer there is no room for doubt. Be it self-doubt or doubt about how prayer works — only faith. Even with questions and confusions, only faith. Especially with questions and confusions, only faith. That is why we stand still, with our feet together, symbolizing that there is no longer a back and forth, a questioning and answering. Rather, we are praying from a place of *da'as* / knowing, through being as One.

2]

Swaying or *Being Still:*

THE IMAGE OF A PERSON WRAPPED IN A PRAYER
SHAWL SWAYING FERVENTLY BACK AND FORTH
with a book in his hands is practically an archetype
of prayer. There are various images that are conjured
up when one thinks of praying, and yet, the predomi-
nant image of praying is one of someone swaying. But
why? Why is swaying so integral to praying?

It is possible, that the original reason for swaying dates back to a time before the printing press. When, because of the lack of books, those who prayed or studied together would take turns looking into the text. One would move in close to see the words, while the other leaned back to allow him to get a better view. And that is how swaying developed. Still, even if this were historically the case, spiritually there is deep psycho-physical value and symbolic meaning attached to the actual movement of the body in the act of *Shukeling* / swaying.

Utilizing the body while deeply engaging the mind keeps one energized, focused and alert. Reb Chaim Volozioner writes that, "when a person sways they do not fall asleep". The movement not only keeps the person physically awake, but swaying can also serve to arouse us mentally. How many of us think more clearly when walking or doing something active? The same dynamic applies to swaying during prayer. The steady rhythmic motion of the body frees up and relaxes our tense mind, allowing us to sink deeply into the seat of our soul. This, in turn, helps us to listen to and feel what we are saying during prayer.

Essentially, the movement of the body helps to awaken the mind, which in turn opens the heart. This helps us loosen up and engage the whole self. The passion of our prayers then becomes all-inclusive. For not only is our mouth involved, but our entire body becomes involved in our prayer as well. As it says in the Book of Psalms, "All my bones will say, 'Hashem who is like You'" *(Tehilim, 35:10)*.

When we pray fully with our entire being, completely absorbed within every word, every letter, every sound, the meanings no longer simply reside in the mind or even in the heart. Rather, the whole body becomes a sonorous instrument. Our entire body becomes an orchestra playing the Creator's praise.

When we enter deeply into prayer we are in a place of no reservations, of not holding back, our entire being is present.

Reb Pinchas of Koritz teaches that the primordial light of creation, the Supernal Light that gives a person the ability to see from one end of the world to the next, is always present within this creation. However, because of all our idle chatter and hurtful words there is a metaphysical cloud that gets created from the breath of these negative utterances, a dense mist that covers over and obscures the light. When a person sways in prayer, the movement disperses and dismantles these clouds and the Supernal Light becomes revealed, as if one were waving their hand back and forth in a smoky room to clear a path of vision.

Overall it seems that all types of movement break-down Kelipa and help to create Kavanah.

Kelipa represents a condition of separation and all movement is a movement towards unity. *Kavanah* in prayer is the quality of inner connection to the meaning of the words, which are but the outer expression. When a person is praying the words but is lacking in Kavanah there is than a separation between the inner and outer. The movement of the body helps to break the barrier of separation and connects the person with the Kavanah.

In swaying itself there are two movements: swaying back and forth, and swaying from side to side.

SWAYING BACK AND FORTH:

When a person moves in and out, or back and forth, the movement represents a movement of coming closer and pulling away, drawing near and creating space. This is known as *Ratzu v' Shuv* / Running and Returning. We run towards Hashem and the expansive infinite heavens, and afterwards we must return to ourselves and to the finite world. This movement is symbolic of the paradoxical nature of prayer. A person feels themselves drawing closer to Hashem as they begin to pray and as their spiritual awareness expands, the further away they feel they are. Then, through their smallness and humility, they are able to feel close again, and as soon as you are aware of your coming closer, you are distant. For the closer you come to The Only One, the more you realize how far you really are, on a manifest level.

In the standard blessing formula we say, *Baruch Ata* - "blessed are You", or "You are the Source of blessing" - in a direct first person encounter. But then immediately we make the linguistic switch to Hashem, using indirect third person language. And this is emblematic of the constant back and forth movement. Mirroring this inward linguistic, the body as well moves in and out, back and forth, close and far.

ACCEPTANCE & RESISTANCE:

The forward movement, the bowing, represents submission and acceptance. The pulling back represents the opposite of submission — resistance, defiance, and non-acceptance.

In prayer we need both of these movements. Bowing forward, humbling ourselves, submitting to and fully accepting what is; as well as pulling back in petition, expressing confidence, holy chutzpah and non-acceptance.

In prayer we have the opportunity to realize that everything in our life is Divinely orchestrated. From the Creator's perspective, the perspective of absolute unity, creation is Perfect, and we humbly submit to that reality. And yet, the act of prayer itself, which is not only a gift that is given to us, but also a commandment that we fulfill, suggests a total non-acceptance of reality as it is. Such as when we pray for healing for someone who is sick, or for wealth in the place of poverty, or for peace in the place of war. We pray for change. We observe what is, and pray for what ought to be.

These sentiments are paradoxical and contradictory, and yet we strive to maintain both of them as we pray. Our human perspective relates to prayer as an agent of change. While from the Creator's perspective, prayer is viewed as a process through which we can develop the awareness of submission and acceptance.

Once, the Baal Shem Tov instructed his students to fervently pray for a harsh decree to be annulled. Reb Zeev Kitzes then said, "but Rebbe, Hashem is certainly a good father, and certainly what the Creator is doing is for our own good." "It is fortunate," said the Baal Shem, "that R. Zeev was not among the living during the times of Esther and Haman, for certainly he would have said the same about the decree of Haman."

The point is that whatever we have experienced or have been given in life is "perfect". For in truth, that is what The Creator wanted us to receive. And yet, Hashem also wants us to pray for and protest any dire situation or perceived lack. On the one hand we aspire to accept Hashem's will, and on the other hand, Hashem desires for us to be co-creators, and to sing a 'new song' to Hashem. So we pray with both of these perspectives in mind, as illustrated by our swaying back and forth during prayer. Bowing, or otherwise moving the body forward is an act of submission. It is a physical way of saying, "Hashem I accept that this is Your will." Alternatively, pulling the body back, or up to an erect position, is a posture of defiance or non-acceptance, which is the act of praying for "change" in our life.

Because we are able to entertain both of these perspectives simultaneously, all prayers are answered, either by the altered facts on the ground, or in the altered awareness of full acceptance which, when fully realized, alleviates all anxiety and sweetens all hardship.

These two perspectives, that "everything is perfect" and that "things must change", seem mutually exclusive, and yet, from the deepest, most radically non-dual paradigm, both of these perspectives are totally true.

From a place of *Yesh* – revealed finite existence, three dimensional reality — where we observe a person who is sick, poor or suffering, we demand and pray for change. And yet, from the higher *Ayin* – Divine No-thing-ness, Infinity — it is all perfect, everything just "is" and so we seek to accept it.

From the vantage point of Essence, both *Yesh* / finite being and *Ayin* / infinite non-being, are expressions of the One Divine Essence, this way, prayer as protest to change and prayer as full acceptance are both true at every moment.

Just as *Ahava* / love, and *Yirah* / awe, are normally two separate and opposing emotions, the former implying a feeling of closeness, the latter implying a sense of distance, yet in deep prayer they collapse as one, as will shortly be explained. The same holds true with the Yesh and Ayin perspective. When we pray for healing for example, we are acknowledging the Yesh reality that a person is sick, something is lacking and imperfect, and so we pray "Hashem heal us". And yet we conclude that very same blessing with the words, "Blessed are you Hashem…who heals (present tense) the sick." Which means that when we say these words we feel, and are in fact healed. This is the Ayin reality.

The peak of prayer is the Unity between these two, Yesh and Ayin. We open ourselves to the healing power of Hashem both now and in the future.

SWAYING SIDE-TO-SIDE:

As mentioned, there is also the swaying that is done from side to side — right to left, left to right.

This motion is much like the act of cradling, an act of *Ahavah* / love and nurturing. This motion is in contrast to the swaying front to back, which is an act of *Yirah* / fear and awe, indicating an awareness of nurturing.

When we sway from side to side we can feel ourselves being cradled by Hashem. In prayer there is the act of protest and the act of acceptance, which is the swaying of front to back. But sometimes in prayer we just want to feel safe and protected, that our life is in the hands of Hashem and that we are being held. The swaying side-to-side represents this state of mind.

DURING THE AMIDAH— THE PEAK OF PRAYER:

Whereas swaying throughout the course of the prayers is encouraged, during the Amidah swaying is strongly discouraged. When a person has reached the Amidah and scaled the peak of prayer there is no longer any room for any form of self-consciousness. In a state of Deveikus there is no mobility or movement.

"And the nation saw, they trembled (moved) and they stood from a distance" *(Shemos, 20:15)*. Normally the verse is understood to mean that because of what the people saw they trembled and then stood at a distance. However, it could also be understood to mean that they were "moved" (i.e. they trembled) because they were still at a distance. They were still observers. They saw, which represents that they were not in total Deveikus and thus there was still some room for movement.

Swaying, jumping, and moving about during prayer are all indications of pre-unity moments, where there is still separation as we are moving towards intimacy. When we have attained a measure of true Deveikus there is no longer any movement, for we have finally arrived. The Amidah is the place of prayer where we enter into an internal space of unity.

It is important to keep in mind that each person must do what is natural to them, whether they are moving in the earlier parts of prayer and not moving in the Amidah, or just the opposite *(Pri Megadim, 48. Mishna Berurah, 95;5)*.

The key is to set the coordinates with your Kavanah, but then to also let yourself cruise on auto-pilot, so to speak, so that you are accessing what is truly authentic to you at that moment. Otherwise if you are praying the Amidah and you are forcing yourself "not to move", that in itself is a movement, an aggressive and forced movement of the mind, and can be cause for distraction from prayer.

3]

Hands & Body Position:

ANOTHER QUESTION ABOUT POSTURE AND BODY MOVEMENT DURING PRAYER IS: WHAT SHOULD YOU DO WITH YOUR HANDS?

HANDS CLASPED, RIGHT HAND ABOVE THE LEFT:

"When there was trouble in the world Rav Kahana would remove his cloak and clasp his hands saying, 'like a servant before his master', and at times of peace he would dress and cover himself and enwrap..." *(Shabbos, 10a).*

From the above it seems that only in times of trouble should one clasp his hands. However, the Rambam learns from this that when we pray, both in times of distress and in times of peace we should clasp our hands, the right hand over the left, and place them both above the heart. This would indicate that the main difference in the 'times of distress' and 'times of peace', would be whether Rav Kahana was donning his cloak or not.

The placement of the right hand over the left is emblematic of the way a servant stands in front of his master. And in prayer we also stand in humble service to the Divine Presence in Creation. The AriZal, however, would also pray the Amidah with his right hand clasped above the left, over the heart. His reasoning, or Kavanah, was a little more esoteric. The right hand represents the Sefira of *Chesed* / loving kindness and boundless giving. The left hand represents *Din* / judgment and restriction. And so he would cover over and sublimate his *Din* / judgment and boundaries with *Chesed* / loving kindness and abundance.

While placing the right hand over the left, there is also a custom to place the thumb of the right hand within the grasp of the left hand. This symbolizes a more subtle dialectic between Chesed and Din. For, although the root of Din is embraced by Chesed, the fruit of Chesed is defined by the discipline of Din. This creates what is known as a dynamic tension, where the strength of each Sefira is leveraged against the other to create a safe and healthy resistance in order to grow.

BOTH HANDS UPON THE HEART:

A beautiful image is created by placing both hands upon the heart. The Chayit writes that by placing both hands upon ones heart in prayer we are forming a bow *(Pirush HaChayit, Ma'areches Elokus, 10. See also: Nefutzos Yehudah, Derush 24)*. The hands laying one over the other creates an image of a bow underneath. The hands are the bow and the arrow is the tongue. What pulls the bow back and thus releases the arrow forward with force is our Kavanah. When we are praying we are sending arrows Above to pierce the Heavens, and drawing the flow of *Shefa*, Divine Plenty, downwards into our lives.

Our Kavanah is the force that moves the arrow, the words are the arrows, the body is the bow.

HANDS LIFTED UPWARD:

The position of lifting your hands above your head

in prayer is a position that is mentioned in the Torah. We find that Avraham, who is the first person
recorded in the Torah to pray, says, "I have lifted my
hands to Hashem", which the Targum translates as, "I
have lifted my hands in prayer." The lifting of open
hands is symbolic of the act of receiving from Above.
You are standing here below in this world, poised to
receive the limitless abundance of Divine energy and
life from The Infinite One Most High.

The Sages teach that when a person spreads their
hands with the appropriate Kavanah it contains tremendous spiritual potential, and therefore should be
done with the utmost care and consciousness. The
Zohar speaks of the spiritual danger posed to a person
who lifts his hands above his head for no purpose or
without proper intention *(Zohar, Parshas Beshalach)*. Even
with the proper intentions, there are limitations as to
how long a person should stretch out his hands above
his head in this manner.

Stretching the hands above the head is no longer a
standard hand position during prayer. For the most
part the hands are not lifted above the head in prayer,
even if a person has the proper intention.

Yet, if while you are passionately and fervently praying and as you are immersed in your prayer, your

hands involuntarily fly upwards in a position of 're-ceiving from on High', "know, that this is a sign that your prayers have been answered and that in fact you are receiving from on High".

PALMS FACING DOWN:

Normally when people pray, if they do extend their arms, though not necessarily above their heads, their hands would most likely be facing upward with the palm of the hand facing up, indicating a process of re-ceiving. Yet, Reb Levi Yitzchak of Berditchov speaks of a different form of praying, where you are not pray-ing for your own self. You are not praying in order to receive healing, help, material support, or wisdom. But rather, you are praying for the "sake of heaven", so that Hashem receives "pleasure" and "sustenance" from your praying.

When a person prays for the self to receive, then he shall indeed put the palm of his hand facing upward as a vessel of receptivity. But when one is praying from a place of selflessness, then he should put his palm downward, as the Kohen does when he offers the Priestly Blessings. This is an act of transmitting and translating the flow of energy and awareness from the Above to below.

HEAD BETWEEN THE KNEES:

The Torah makes reference to a position where one sits and places the head between the knees. Eliyahu Ha'navi would pray in this manner *(Melachim 1 18:42)*. The Medrash says *(Rabbah, Vayikra, 31:4)* that he prayed in this position, with his head between his knees, so that his head, representing conscious intellect, would face the place of his *Milah* / the place of the covenant, representing subconscious vital life energy, so as to recall the Mitzvah of circumcision and be answered in that merit. It is also reminiscent of a circular pose, representing an image that speaks of regenerative inwardness and completion.

EMBODYING THE NAME SHAD-AI:
Shin –Dalet - Yud

The Name *Shad-ai* represents the notion of divine protection and nurturing, as mentioned earlier. It was once the custom that while in prayer, one would configure the body's position to reflect the three letters that make up this name.

The Name Shad-ai is comprised of three letters: Shin, Dalet, Yud.

Shin is a three-pronged letter- **שׁ**

Dalet is a vertical line attached above to a horizontal line- ד

Yud is the tiniest letter in the shape of a point, or a dot- י

SHIN: When a person throws up their hands to the heavens in praise and/or petition, this is the shape of the letter Shin. The head protruding in the middle with the two hands on either side creates a three-pronged image, representing the letter Shin.

DALET: When a person bows in prayers, such as at the beginning and the end of the Amidah, they create, with the position and angle of their body, the letter Dalet. The lower part of the body, the legs, is the vertical line of the Dalet, and the upper part of the body, from the torso up, when fully bowed at a 90-degree angle, becomes the horizontal line.

Alternatively, the Shaloh Ha'Kadosh suggests that the letter Dalet is formed in the body when the left hand is outstretched, as in a posture of receiving, and the right hand is gently resting on the side.

Interestingly enough, the letter Dalet also comes from the root word *Dal* / poor *(Shabbos 106a)*. By bowing to the Creator of the universe we are in fact showing that we are empty and humble. We are in need and we are ready to receive.

YUD: The position of the head facing the *Milah* is the letter Yud. The Yud is a point, so the body curling/spiraling up back into itself represents the ultimate compact point of consciousness. The infinite point contains within it the line and all further dimensionality. It is the infinitesimal dot — the little that holds much.

These three positions flow into each other quite nicely when put into a prayerful sequence. They are in fact a pattern we can put into motion in order to align ourselves with and tap into the cosmic inhale and exhale, expansion and contraction, and ebb and flow of life. You start fully open, extended and expanded with your spine straight, your head thrown back and your arms upraised to the heavens stretching and reaching for the infinite beyond. Then you bow respectfully as you come into contact with the Divine presence in creation.

You are still standing separate but have recognized the Immanent Reality. You then follow through this bodily intuitive logic and completely submit yourself, fully prostrated with your knees on the ground, bent over, with your head between your knees and your face in the direction of the Milah.

PROSTRATION:

There is also reference to the position of prostration during the prayers *(Berachos, 34b)*. In fact, the idea of prostrating oneself goes back to the Temple times *(Mishnah Tammid, 7:3)*, and it is possible that the root of the word Tefilah comes from the word *Nafal* / fell, as we find in the Torah, where Moshe falls on his face as an act in prayer *(Bamidbar, 14:5)*.

Though all these positions are mentioned by our holy sages in sacred texts, for the most part today in the impoverished state of the fourth exile, we only mimic the letter Dalet in our prayers when we bow. This may indicate how spiritually poor we really are right now as a people and planet. The Shin and the Yud have been left behind, both physically and psychically. We almost never fully prostrate ourselves (only on Yom Kippur), nor do we intentionally lift our hands above our heads in prayer.

One can only hope that these other two positions, and the letter energies they represent, will be re-integrated into our physical movements during prayer as well as within our consciousness.

Shin represents the ability to change and transform, as well as the ability to chew on ideas and properly digest exalted teachings and concepts as in the symbol of the tooth that Shin represents. Yud represents simple faith, as in the acknowledgement of and dependence on G-d's *Yad* / Hand, in all of creation.

4]

Eyes Open or Closed?

THROUGHOUT THE PRAYERS IT IS RECOMMEND-
ED BY OUR SAGES TO KEEP YOUR EYES OPEN AND
to look into the prayerbook, the Siddur. Besides help-
ing one to concentrate, the importance of looking inside the siddur is due largely to the fact that the Hebrew letters, both their form and vibration, are seen as
multi-dimensional meta-building blocks of creation.

Their particular sounds as well as their shapes contain limitless energy and information. As The Creator continually speaks the world into being, so it is that through prayer and Torah study we too are able to participate in this process, becoming partners in creation through our rectified speech.

As a sign of humility at the peak of the prayers — the Amidah — and in general during praying, our eyes should be directed downward. The question is whether they should still be open or closed?

EYES CLOSED:

The Zohar speaks of praying with one's eyes closed and many of the great sages throughout the ages would pray with their eyes closed. The AriZal would pray the Amidah and also listen to the repetition of the Amidah with his eyes closed.

Besides the deeper kabbalistic reasons to close the eyes, such as not to seem as if one is gazing upon the *Yichud* / unity, between masculine transcendence and feminine immanence, or to embody the quality of Rachel within *Malchus* who is called "beautiful but without eyes", closing one's eyes represents a 'taking leave of the physical', a *Bitul ha'Yesh* / nullification of what is. An integration of one's separate 'i' into the Infinite I. Closing the eyes is a form of dying to this world and entering a deeper and higher dimension, Inner Space. When we close off the world by shutting out our physical vision, we are moving away from a perceived world and entering into a world of transcendence and unity, a world of infinite potential. A world not of things as they appear, but of things as they truly are and should be.

Sight is also known as a sense that re-enforces dichotomy, duality and distance. You can only see something outside of you, something that is effectively not you. When we close our eyes, we are shutting off that sense of separateness. Hearing is the opposite. Physiologically, the act of hearing puts you at the center of what is being heard, thus the concept of surround sound. This is why we cover and close our eyes when we say the *She'ma*, a prayer that is all about listening and Unity.

Prayer, at its peak, can become a vehicle for genuine transcendence. "It is a miracle," said the Baal Shem Tov, "that a person who prays intensely remains alive and stable after their prayers".

Once there was a Chassidic Rebbe, known as the Saraph of Sterlisk. Every morning before his daily prayers he would say goodbye to his family, as if for the last time.

Since closing your eyes represents a movement away from this world and into an inner world, there are those who write that a person who prays with his eyes closed will merit to see the face of the Shechinah at the moment of death.

It is important, when considering such lofty and abstracted imagery to keep in mind that the point of prayer is not utter transcendence, where there is a total lift off, leaving at best, only a tenuous relationship with the physical. But rather, to begin firmly rooted in the body and to end again firmly rooted in this world.

This is demonstrated, as will be explored in the next section, in the ascending and descending stages of the Ladder of Prayer. Ultimately, the journey is the destination, with the goal being the graceful navigation of the perpetual back and forth between and beyond immanence and transcendence.

Ratzu / running, is the desire to attach oneself and to cleave to the Infinite One. This is the expansion, the expiring, the exhale, an upward movement. *Shuv* / returning, is the acknowledgement of the come down, the contraction, the inhale. The real *Derech* / way, to

Hashem, is to be an expert in both *Ratzu*/Running and *Shuv*/Returning. Ultimately we need to understand that the true purpose is in the here and now. We all need to climb the mountain to bring back the blessings from Above to this world below.

The numerical value of the word *Derech* is 224. The word *Baki* / expert, is numerically 112. When a person is a Baki in both Ratzu and Shuv it is thus twice 112, which is 224; meaning that they are proficient in both dimensions of the spiritual process and that they are on the right Derech.

EYES OPEN LOOKING IN THE SIDDUR:

While having the eyes closed during prayer may appear to be spiritually advantageous, for many the act of looking into the Siddur and seeing the words on the page helps them with their concentration and focus. For when their eyes are closed their mind seems to wander off elsewhere. In fact, since the "letters bring wisdom", many sages prayed all their prayers precisely with their eyes open and glued to the letters on the page.

EYES OPEN OR CLOSED:

Every person must choose the path that they feel is correct for them, eyes open or closed. If you feel that you cannot concentrate with your eyes closed, then read from the Siddur. Look down into the Siddur and do not move your eyes away from the holy letters. If your eyes are open, never look in front of you, outside the Siddur. Symbolically this is because the Shechinah is in front of you and it should not appear as if you are attempting to look at the Shechinah *(Zohar 3, p. 260b)*, as this would indicate a break in your perceived connection to and unity with G-d.

Whether people pray with their eyes open or closed, whether they feel they can concentrate better looking into the Siddur or filtering out all external stimuli, depends on their level of consciousness during the prayers. When a person is in a state of *Mochin D'Gadlus* / expansive mind, they can pray with their eyes closed. When, however, a person is in a state of *Mochin D'Katnus* / restricted mind, they may need to keep their eyes focused on the letters and words of the Siddur. Without getting into all the subtle distinctions between these two states, in a very broad working definition — *Mochin D'Gadlus* is when a person feels confident, alive, focused, and open with a quality of giving and a sense of the whole big picture, the total unity of creation, a *Chochmah* consciousness. On the other hand, *Mochin D'katnus* is when a person feels small, lethargic, distracted, and closed off with a quality of being judgmental and a sense of only fragmented details of the creation as a whole, a Binah consciousness.

Whenever a person is about to begin praying, or at any juncture during the prayers, he needs to be honest with himself in order to know where he is truly holding at that moment.

In conclusion it would do one well to follow the advice offered by the Magen Avraham, which is simply that whether a person prays with their eyes open looking into the Siddur or with their eyes closed "depends upon each person and what he feels will help him in his prayers" *(Orach Chayim. 93:2).*

PROCESS I:

The Structure of the Morning Prayers

1]

The Four Ascending Steps in the Morning Prayer

TIME OF BATTLE,
TIME OF TRANSFORMATION:

THE HOLY ZOHAR TEACHES, "THE HOUR OF PRAYER IS THE HOUR OF BATTLE" *(Zohar 3, p. 243a)*. This is a sobering perspective on the realities of spiritual development. From this perspective prayer can be understood as a meta-physical inner struggle to recognize, wrestle with, and refine our base, self-centered drives and desires, in an attempt to gradually and gently transform ourselves into a more subtle, spiritual, selfless state of being. One in which there is an authentic appreciation for the uniqueness of self, while at the same time maintaining a deep awareness of the universal inter-connectedness of every human being, and in fact, of all of creation.

Because of the gradual and non-linear nature of psycho-spiritual development this can be a difficult and demanding undertaking.

The word Avodah, which is another word for prayer, literally means work. Avodah originates from the root word Ibud, which can also translate as working over, transforming and changing. Whereas, the initial stages of this process are often accomplished with intense and arduous labor and struggle, as one progresses, the battle/dance/work of prayer becomes a peaceful battle, a synchronized dance of body and soul in which the soft light illuminates and integrates the wounded shadow and there is no longer any reason to lower oneself into the garments of the "enemy". For you will have reached the place of Hashem's unity, where there are no "enemies", nor are there any "garments", or even any others at all, only One, only this, only now.

How to use a Symbol:

Kabbalistic cosmology provides us with a symbolic map of reality.

The use of various symbols and metaphors — including words, sounds, colors, numbers and images — adds depth and detail to the meta-physical terrain, as well as offering us invaluable aid in deciphering the multi-dimensional topography of life.

The particular set of symbols that are employed provide a unique key to the map, which serves to unlock the inner secret and ecstatic song of the spiritual landscape, allowing us to more consciously and creatively navigate the territory. These symbols and stories have been crafted and collected throughout the last several thousand years. They are the contents of the archetypal collective memory script of our people's journeys through inner space, time, and soul.

Throughout the following pages, a series of these symbols and structures will be explored, paying particularly close attention to the four-fold model in order to animate and enliven some of the more poetic and developmental aspects of the spiritual practice of traditional prayer.

FOUR WORLDS:

There are Four-Inner Worlds of reality.

In descending order they are:
  Atzilus — Emanation
  Beriah — Creation
  Yetzirah — Formation
  Asiyah — Actualization

These four "worlds" can be viewed as four realms of consciousness and creative process. Effectively, they are a symbolic interface between the Creator and creation, as well as the world and us, through which we are able to observe and engage the world and ourselves, through awareness and action.

Alternatively *(Chayei Adam. Klal 20)*, the names of these four worlds are called as follows:

  Olam Ha'Elyon — The Most-High World
  Olam Ha'Malachim — The World of Angles
  Olam Ha'Galgalim — The World of Spheres
  Olam Ha'zeh — This World

Let us now explore the Four Worlds in greater depth, in ascending order.

Asiyah is the world of the physical, that which is observed within the quantifiable field. Asiyah is the world of action, of manifestation, of doing. On a cosmological level, Asiyah is the physical world as we know it, with all of its three-dimensions of time and space.

(Three-dimensional, element-earth, *Sefira -Malchus*, Lower *Hei*, 'Fruit')

Yetzirah is the world of pure emotion. On the level of cosmogenesis, Yetzirah is reality in process, in flux, in a state of emergence. This can be likened to a pattern, or painting, that has not yet fully solidified or been brought to completion. It is, in essence, a world in the process of becoming. If the world of *Asiyah* can be understood as the actual house, and the world of *Beriah* can be understood as the blueprint, then Yetzirah is the realm of the process of building, the harnessing of energies and resources, and the 'putting into motion' of ideas. At this subtler plane there is still a sense of time (process), but less of space (form).

(Two-dimensional, element-fire, *Sefira* –the six emotions: *Chesed, Gevurah, Tiferes, Netzach, Hod, Yesod,* the letter *Vav*, 'Branches and Trunk').

Beriah is the world of the mental faculties and the

intellect, the world of intelligence. On a cosmic level, Beriah is the dimension where reality is just beginning to emerge as a separate entity from the previous state of submergence in the absolute unity of Atzilus. Beriah is the world where the first signs of self-awareness are beginning to develop, and yet this existence is still without any defined shape or form.

(One-dimensional, element-water, *Sefira - Binah*, Upper *Hei*, 'Roots').

Atzilus is the world of Emanation, a state of 'nearness' to pure spirit, a world that is close enough to its Source, the Emanator, to have no sense of a separate or self-conscious existence of its own. It feels itself as a mere extension of its Source.

(Four-dimensional, element-wind, *Sefira - Chochmah*, the letter *Yud*, 'Seed').

LIGHT AND VESSEL:

Before moving on to a host of other Four-Fold symbol structures, it would be wise at this point to familiarize ourselves with two of the most important symbolic images in kabbalistic thought, that of the Light and Vessel.

These are two primary symbols that are used to illustrate some of the fundamental dynamics of the created universe and creative process. Light is the qualitative animating principle and Vessel is the quantitave form or substance that is animated. Light is consciousness. Vessel is physicality. Light is love. Vessel is restriction. Light is giving. Vessel is receiving. Light is the meaning of the words in prayer. Vessel is the words themselves. Light is intention. Vessel is the vehicle for intention. Light is inspiration. Vessel is action.

Even more subtly, the ego is the vessel for the light of the soul; that necessarily limited vehicle through which the limitless experiences and expresses itself. Light brings a vessel to life and, in turn, a vessel brings light down to earth.

In reality, these two concepts are not separate or opposed to each other; in fact, they are partners in creation. The objective of conscious co-creation is not to shatter the vessels through asceticism or ecstasy, but to elevate and integrate them through the development of the *Dirah BeTachtonim* / dwelling place below.

We are not meant to escape from the world, or to shun materiality, definition, or discernment. In fact, we are urged and encouraged to merge light and vessel into their proper alignment and supportive balance so as to safely, and sensitively manifest rectified desire and potential. At the deepest level, vessel is light. It is merely a matter of degrees — of density and directionality.

DYNAMICS OF LIGHT AND VESSEL
IN THE FOUR WORLDS:

In regards to the Model of the Four Worlds, Asiyah is the level of reality where the external vessel is most pronounced at the expense of the inner light. Atzilus is where the light is so overwhelming that it is as if the light and the vessel are one and unified. Light represents meaning, purpose and connection, while the vessel represents the opposite — a state of mind where there seems to be no Divine meaning, purpose or connection.

A simple analogy would be to experience the difference between a beloved child of yours falling asleep on your shoulder vs. someone whom you have never met falling asleep on your shoulder while riding the train. The weight of the child's head is around five pounds, and yet it feels weightless; whereas the weight of the adult head is around ten pounds, and yet it feels like twenty. The difference is that with your child's head you are feeling more "light" then "vessel". You feel love and connection with the child and thus the weightlessness. By contrast, with the person sitting next to you whom you have never met, you are experiencing your existential dis-connect from them and hence the perception of more vessel than light.

This is true with everything in life. When you are going through an experience and you are able to sense the purpose in the experience, you are sensing the Light. However, when you are going through an experience and there is no sense of meaning or significance, "Why me? Why now?" Then you are experiencing more vessel than light.

Whatever level you are praying from — whether in the world of Asiyah where you are sensing more vessel than light, more ego than transcendence; or Atzilus where light and vessel are seamlessly unified; or even beyond the paradigm of light and vessel altogether, in a place of simple unity — you must always make sure that you are genuinely praying from the level/world/perspective that is true to you at that very moment. Be honest with yourself. Acknowledge the world/level/perspective that you are at and be aware that the process and point of prayer is to take you to a deeper and higher place, to transport you from an Asiyah space to an Atzilus space and beyond; or even from an Atzilus space back down to the world of Asiyah, where you can actually do the necessary work to fix, heal and enjoy Hashem's creation.

FOUR LEVELS OF SOUL:

The four macrocosmic worlds mentioned above are also reflected in the microcosm of our own psyche.

These are the four levels of soul:
1] Nefesh
2] Ruach
3] Neshamah
4] Chaya

Each of these four levels of soul has a positive manifestation as well as a negative counterpart. They each contain within themselves an aspect that is from the side of *Kedusha* / holiness, connection and unity, as well as an equal and opposite aspect that is from the *Sitra Achra* / the other side, the opposite of holiness, fragmentation and disunity.

NEFESH:
> The densest expression of soul is Nefesh. It is our physical life force, the level of soul that animates our body and interfaces with our vital physical energy. It is the subtle bio-energy that connects our consciousness to the physical world. Nefesh is manifest in our ability to perpetuate action. It is a functional consciousness, which corresponds to the world of Asiyah.

RUACH:

A more subtle level of soul is Ruach. The word Ruach can be translated as breath, spirit, and wind. It is considered our emotional life force, the dimension of soul that gives rise and rhythm to our feelings and sentiments. Ruach is a fluid and emotional consciousness, which is analogous to the world of Yetzirah.

NESHAMAH:

The third level of soul is Neshamah, the power of objective intellect, a cognitive consciousness, which corresponds to the world of Beriah, the realm of intelligence.

CHAYAH:

The fourth level of soul is called Chayah, the living essence, our power of will and desire. It is a transcendent consciousness, corresponding to the world of Atzilus.

There is also a fifth level of soul that is called Yechidah, unique and unified.

YECHIDAH:

Yechidah, the fifth level of soul, has no counterpart or opposite aspect. From a deeper/higher perspective it is not considered part of the 'four' because it is not a level at all, rather it is our very essence, and essence has no division or separation.

MOVING BETWEEN WORLDS:

We begin life, and in microcosm every single day of our lives, on the embodied level of Asiyah/Nefesh — our soul has entered or returned to our body. Then we move into a world of formation and content — Yetzirah/Ruach. From there we move into a world of creation and context — Beriah/Neshamah. And then, we penetrate into the world of unity — Atzilus, where all the "lights and the vessels are one" — alive — Chayah, which is experienced and expressed as our inner most will to live life in connection with our Source.

In ascending order:

1] Physical Self –
   Asiyah/Action- *Nefesh*
2] Emotional Self –
   Yetzirah/Formation – *Ruach*
3] Intellectual Self –
   Beriah/Creation – *Neshamah*
4] Spiritual Self –
   Atzilus/Emanation- *Chayah*

THE FOUR SPACES:

The four-fold structure is also reflected within the four holy spaces of Jerusalem. From the outer to the inner they are:

1] *Har Ha'bayis* —
   The Holy Mountain
2] *Azara* —
   The Courtyard of the Temple Structure
3] *Kodesh* —
   The Outer Sanctuary
4] *Kodesh Kodeshim* —
   The Holy of Holies — The Inner Sanctuary

THE FOUR LETTERS IN THE NAME OF HASHEM AND THEIR "PERSONAE":

These four levels correspond to, and are a reflection of, the four letters within the name of Hashem:
Yud | Hei | Vav | Hei

The lowest letter, so to speak, is the *Lower Hei*. This is a 'full' letter, with both vertical and horizontal expansion. This represents the aspect of *Malchus*, the Divine expression within the functional and manifest physical universe, the broad and wide, multidimensional universe that is tangibly observable.

The next higher letter is the *Vav*, representing the Divine aspect of emotions. The Vav has the numerical equivalent of six. This is analogous to the six emotional *Sefiros*, the emotional attributes, as well as to the six days of creation.

The *Upper Hei* represents Divine intelligence. This is the womb of gestation, the chamber of inner purpose and higher meaning.

The highest letter is also the smallest, the *Yud*. It is the first primordial expression from within the Divine Nothingness, a small dot of a letter in which all other letters are contained — the infinitesimal point.

THE FOUR PATHS OF HASHEM'S NAME:

1]the Yud corresponds to Atzilus
2]the upper Hei corresponds to Beriah
3]the Vav corresponds to Yetzirah and
4]the final Hei corresponds to Asiyah

THE FOUR ELEMENTS/FOUR KELIPOS:

Corresponding to the inner, more intellectual, structure of the four-fold model is the outer, more physical, structure of the four-fold model. This is revealed as the four primary elements, the four fundamental building blocks of creation: earth, water, wind and fire.

There are multiple traditions of how to order the elements.

The four elements, from lower to higher, from the most reified and tangible to the subtlest and least tangible are:
1]Earth 2]Water 3]Wind 4]Fire

According to *The Gra* *(Bereishis, 1:6)*, there is also the way of viewing the elements from lower to higher:
1]Earth 2]Wind 3]Fire 4]Water

According to the *Sefer Yetzirah*:
1]Earth 2]Fire 3]Water 4]Wind

Parenthetically, these elements are reflected in the four basic types, the Inanimate, Vegetative, the Animal Kingdom and the Human Being:

1] That which appears as Inanimate corresponds to earth. This includes rocks, stones, gems, minerals, metals, mountains, sand. This is the world of the "still beings".

2] The Vegetative world corresponds to the element of water, for it is water that irrigates and causes vegetation to grow. This includes all plants, flowers, trees, bushes, mosses, algae, fruits, vegetables, weeds. This is the world of the "sprouting beings".

3] The Animal kingdom corresponds to wind. Wind moves about freely and unencumbered, this is symbolic of the animal's potential to roam freely and move about. This includes all beasts, fishes, birds, insects, amphibians. This is the world of the "living beings".

4] The Human being corresponds to the element of fire. Fire is the strongest symbol of life and vitality, and as fire reaches and leaps upwards, so too does the human being stand erect and reach and leap upwards in prayer, progress and the pursuit of justice. This is the world of "speaking beings".

These four elements — earth, water, wind and fire — are the foundational properties of the physical creation. They can also be viewed as sensory properties:

1] Dry — Earth 2] Cold — Water 3] Moist — Wind
4] Hot — Fire

Or as:

1] Solid – Earth 2] Liquid – Water 3] Gas – Wind
4] Energy –Fire

The world is called *Olam* from the Hebrew word *Helem*, which means 'concealment'. The physically manifest universe represents both the expression of the Creator's glory, as in the awe-inspiring beauty and inconceivably complex web, order and rhythm of nature, as well as the concealment of Hashem's Ultimate Unity. This is demonstrated when we look around at the world, we are able to see a multitude of seemingly separate and independent elements and entities: many people, many animals, many plants, many stones, and many ideas and agendas.

In this way, as elements of concealment, the four primary elements are also associated with the four primary *Kelipos* / concealments of essence, that do not allow the full expression of unified soul. These are:

1] Laziness and Depression — Earth
2] Insatiability and Misplaced Desire — Water
3] Mindlessness and Empty Chatter — Air
4] Anger and Haughtiness — Fire

CLIMBING THE LADDER OF PRAYER:

And now, armed with an arsenal of associative links and conceptual correspondences, we can now turn our discussion of the four-fold model to the primary topic at hand — prayer.

Prayer, as mentioned earlier, is analogous to the ladder in Yaakov's dream, which is planted firmly on the ground while at the same time reaching up into the loftiest heavens. This ladder is comprised of four rungs, representing four stages of ever expanding awareness, and four steps upwards and inwards throughout the course of the morning prayers. With each section of prayer, one attains a fuller and more expansive level of consciousness, a higher level of soul is revealed, and one enters a more integrated world.

Practically speaking, this means that there are also four sections of the morning prayers, with the fourth step being the peak of the trajectory, the *Amidah*. These four steps/stages/stations correspond to the four inner worlds of creation, which are analogous to the four levels of our soul and which in turn, are a reflection of the four letters in the name of Hashem.

THE FOUR ASCENDING STEPS OF THE
MORNING PRAYERS ARE AS FOLLOWS:

1) *Birchas HaShachar* / morning blessings and the recitation of the daily temple offerings: We begin each
day with a strong sense of independence and bodily
awareness.

2) *Pesukei D'Zimrah* / Psalms and songs of praise:
Gradually we move into a more expressive and emotional place.

3) *Kriyas Shema* / blessings and the recitation of the
Shema: Then we are able to enter into a more contemplative mental space.

4) *Amidah* / standing silent prayer: And finally we
merge into a totally transcendent and unitive space.

As we move through these ever-subtler worlds and
spheres of spirituality, it is imperative that we also
make a conscious and concerted effort to stay connected to, and not neglect, the body. This is necessary
to ensure that our praying does not become 'escapist'.
For ultimately, we are seeking to initiate an evolution
of awareness that is able to both expand and embrace,
to include and integrate all the previous levels in its
ascent. This is a paradigm that can be referred to as

one of inclusive transcendence. We are elevating the material into the spiritual and at the same time we are also bringing the spiritual down into the properly prepared and purified physical dimension. This process facilitates the conscious co-creation of what is known as the Dirah Betachtonim, the "Dwelling Place Below" for G-d, wherein we render, or better yet, reveal this mundane space that we inhabit as a fitting habitation for Hashem's presence.

FOUR LEVELS OF SONG:

There is yet another division of four that relates directly to prayer, and that is the structure of the four levels of song. In descending order they are:

1) *Shir Pashut* / a Simple (singular) Song. A melody.
2) *Shir Kaful* / a Double Song. A two-part harmony, the interval.
3) *Shir Meshulash* / a Triple Song. A three-part chord.
4) *Shir Merubah* / a Quadruple Song. A four-part harmony *(Tikkunei Zohar, Tikkun 21. Zohar 111, p. 227b).*

A visual of this image is as follows;

•

••

•••

••••

In total there is ten points, corresponding to the ten

Sefiros. The one point is the unified space of Keser, and more specifically *Chochmah*, the world of *Atzilus*/ Spirituality and Unity.

The two points are *Binah* and also *Da'as*, the world of *Beriah* / Intelligence.

The three points are the predominate emotions of *Chesed-Gevurah-Tiferes*, the world of *Yetzirah* / Emotions

And the four points are the lower, external Sefiros of *Netzach-Hod-Yesod-Malchus*, the world of *Asiyah* / the Body *(Tikkunei Zohar, Hakdamah, 3a)*.

Through prayer we are moving from multiplicity, from the four to the One, from inner and outer separation to unity, and from body to spirit.

At the outset of prayer, we are on the level of *Shir Merubah* / a quadruple song. At this level, there are "four" separate points to ourselves and our song. Our expression is not fully integrated and as we slowly climb the ladder of prayer we are moving from a splintered space to a more unified one.

In simple terms this means that our bodies may want and desire one thing, maybe to eat breakfast, whereas our emotions are focused elsewhere. Our minds are wandering in a third direction, whereas our spiritual-self really just wants to pray and connect.

By moving through the four stages of prayer we are unifying these disparate voices of self-expression, thereby harmonizing our song from four to three to two and finally to one song, sung in one voice.

The first stage in prayer is engaging the body. The world of Asiyah and the Sefiros related to actions and expression. This is the part of prayer called the *Birchas HaShachar* / the morning blessings. These are mostly related to the needs and necessities of the physical body, as in thanking Hashem for our healthy digestive system, or thanking Hashem for clothing us.

The second stage of prayer engages our emotions. They are aroused to feel a sense of closeness to Hashem. This is the world of Yetzirah, including the Sefiros of Emotions. This is the part of the prayers called *Pesukei De'Zimrah* / verses of praise, largely consisting of songs and Psalms chanted to arouse our emotions.

Once our emotions are involved we seek to engage our minds and intellect. This third stage in prayer is called *Kriyas Shema* / the reading of the Shema. Here we are entering into a more contemplative mental space. This is the inner world of *Beriah* / the world of intellect.

Once all three are engaged, body, heart and mind, we can move into a space of total harmony. We have attained, at least temporarily and inwardly, a level of unity. This is the fourth stage of prayer, the *Amidah*, the inner world of *Atzilus* / nearness and oneness.

CREATION – HUMAN BEING – CREATOR:

This movement from Four to One, from splintered self into unified self, from inner dichotomy into One voice, is a reflection of the external dichotomy and dualistic prism through which one views the world. In the course of the prayers one is unifying one's inner self as well as one's perspective on the external reality as well.

At the outset of the day, which represents the rudimentary spiritual development of man, one begins in a pronounced dualistic frame. There is the person, his inner world, there is the world around him, the outer world, and there is the Creator who creates both. Because each of these three appear quite clearly separate from each other, as it were, there is a subtle sense of

Four, the empty space that separates each one from the next.

In this world of Asiyah, there is a very clear awareness of the "I", the world, and the fact that I am now self-consciously speaking to the Creator.

Then, as one progresses and scales the ladder of spiritual development, he now enters the world of Yetzirah. There is still a clear Three — the I, the world, and the Creator — yet, in this reality these three are more deeply revealed as being interconnected. There is no inside without an outside, and no outside within an inner dimension, and both are created, sustained and enlivened by the Creator.

Going higher and deeper still, closer and more inward, slowly the external world around him begins to fade and the sensation is now just of Two — the "I" in communication with the Creator. This is the world of Beriah.

As the egoic separate sense of self and independence begins to dissolve even more, one slowly slips into the world of Atzilus, where the "Vessel" is one with the "Light" and the sensation is of being absorbed and within the Unity of Hashem.

FOUR PREPARATIONS FOR PRAYER:

As there are four stages within the morning prayers themselves, there are four stages of general preparation for the morning prayers. These are four physical and ritual actions, which serve to purify and prepare us — body, heart, mind and soul — to stand before the Infinite One in humble prayer. The four general preparations also correspond to the Four Worlds, as well as all the other four-fold models. They are:

1] Washing the hands and relieving oneself — *Asiyah*/Action
2] Wrapping oneself in a Talis — *Yetzirah*/Formation
3] Wrapping Tefilin of the hand — *Berirah*/Creation
4] Wrapping Tefilin of the head — *Atzilus*/Emanation

THE FOUR LEVELS REFLECTED IN SPIRITUAL ACTIVITY:

There are four basic emotions that are activated and aroused during prayers, often in ascending order. These qualities are:

1] Devotion
2] Gratitude
3] Love
4] Awe

Devotion- Birchas HaSchachar: One begins their prayers on the lowest rung, the world of Asiyah, the world of the body. This is reflected in the spiritual act of *Kabbalas Ol* / the 'acceptance of the yoke of Heaven'. This is an act of decisiveness, dedication and commitment to living a meaningful and spiritual life in submission to Hashem and the Torah, the Tree of Life. This is the aspect of Devotion. In fact, the mere act of beginning to pray is an act of Kabbalas Ol.

Gratitude- Pesukei D'Zimra: The next movement, parallel to the inner emotional world of Yetzirah is the place of praise and acknowledgement of the Creator's greatness, miracles, wonders, creations and Divine protection. This is the segment in the cycle of the morning prayers where we sing Hashem's praise, giving voice to the aspect of thankfulness and gratitude.

Love- Kriyas Shema: The next world and perspective is Beriah, creation, the seat of the intellect. This is the station of prayer where we focus our awareness on the absolute unity of G-d and declare our personal experience of this Ultimate Oneness. This contemplation upon the Unity of G-d has the power to generate the potential aspect of *Ahavah* / love. We say the first verse of the Shema and immediately speak about our love of Hashem. Love is the necessary 'strange attractor', to use a phrase borrowed from quantum physics, that which draws us inexplicably towards our essential goal, which is not just the conceptual unity of the Creator, but ultimately we are seeking to enter into that Unity and experience being absorbed within the unity of Hashem.

Awe- the Amidah: Finally, we reach the state of Atzilus, a point of total self-nullification, a dissolving of the separate 'i' into the Infinite I. This is a place of radical wonder and awe, Yirah. There is no more separation, we have become a part of the whole we sought to apprehend, acknowledge and approach. We are both speaking and being spoken to, we are listening — we are the word, which created the world, when spoken in silence.

Our prayers do not rise upward and are not fully embraced/embracing if they are not uttered with a sense of spiritual devotion and aroused emotion.

Each and every genuine expression of prayer also moves through these four general stages. It begins with an arousal, a spark, what is called *Re'usa*. Then it moves to *Machshava* / 'thought,' a Kavanah, to *Kol* / the 'voice,' and ultimately becomes a *Dibbur* / a word, 'speech'.

THE FOUR UPWARD RUNGS OF PRAYER IN GREATER DETAIL:

There are four ascending stages or stations of the Morning Prayer Service. Every morning as we awake we are like a new person. A new day is a new beginning. Being as we are a new person every day, we need to build ourselves up again, as it were, in order to establish ourselves as a full person.

Every day is a developmental microcosm of our life in general. We begin our life as infants on the soul level of *Nefesh* — instinctual and physical. Slowly, in our childhood we evolve into a place of *Ruach* — healthy and balanced emotions. Then at the age of Bar or Bas Mitzvah we expand our awareness into the level of the *Neshamah* — mindful maturity. Finally at a later stage in life, we are able to come into our own spirituality — the level of *Chayah*.

Similarly every day, we move and develop in the stages of the morning liturgy. First we start at the level of Nefesh, the world of Asiyah, acknowledging and sanctifying our physical self, thanking Hashem for all our bodily functions.

Then we move into the world of Ruach, becoming more human, feeling and expressing emotions verbally.

Next we enter into the world of Neshama, developing and directing our mind through contemplative thinking.

Finally we arrive at the world of Chayah, accessing and animating our deepest soul desires and inner yearnings.

This is ultimately not the place to fully explore the true depth and significance of these four movements, but we will offer a general overview so as to further develop and deepen our prayer experience.

FIRST SECTION: BIRCHAS HASACHAR — MORNING BLESSINGS:

The first segment of the morning prayers are called *Birchos Hashachar*. This initiatory stage of the sequence is comprised of two concepts. In the first, a person becomes aware of and acknowledges the Creator as the One who has provided for all his physical necessities, such as the gift of life, breath, strength, sight, food, clothes and shelter. Then, following the initial blessings of the morning, which also include the blessings for Torah study, one then continues with the recitation of the ritual sacrifices that were offered daily in the Temple. The order of the offerings represents our life essence, animal energy and physical self being offered up on the fiery altar of prayer.

The focus of both of these portions is on the level of *Nefesh*, the animating life energy, the physical self, the unique aspect of the soul, the material world, and the world of Asiyah or action. In this stage of awareness, a person acknowledges Hashem as the sole provider for all of his physical needs.

This acknowledgement occurs simultaneously on two levels of meaning at once. The first perspective is that of Hashem as the one who provides for all needs: The one who feeds the hungry, who liberates the captive, and returns the soul to its body every morning. Then the other, less obvious perspective is that of Hashem as the actual Creator of the need: The one who has created us in such a way that we lack, that we need, that we require help, food, protection, love. And not only do we lack on a general level, but each of us is ultimately defined by our own particular, individual needs. It is often not what we have that makes us who we are, but in fact, what we lack and what we strive for that shapes our potential perspectives and personalities.

When praying this portion of the prayers we should have a general Kavanah that we are actively directing and dedicating our physical self to the service of our soul through the acknowledgement of and cleaving to Hashem. This devotional Kavanah counters the Kelipa of laziness and depression, the element of earth. So in the place of feeling heavy, lethargic, down and unenthusiastic, we literally leap out of bed to offer up a spark of spiritual fire and passion, which enlivens and ignites our physical bodies in the service of Hashem. The most important aspect of this first movement in the prayer cycle is to 'just do it'. The first step is always the hardest, and once you have begun a process, you have momentum behind you; but to actually begin something takes a tiny miracle, a leap of faith so to speak.

The Zohar states that, "All feminine is sitting down". This first section of the prayers, represented by the lower Hei in Hashem's name, is the element of receptivity, the feminine / *Malchus*. It is at this initial stage of waking up that we seek to open ourselves up to connect and receive from the Source of all blessing. For this reason the bulk of this section of the prayers, including the recitation of the Temple sacrifices, is generally said sitting down.

This is the world of *Asiyah* / actualization, the lower Hei, the level of Nefesh, the element of Earth.

SECOND SECTION:
PISUKEI D'ZIMRAH —
VERSES OF PRAISE:

The next segment of the morning prayers, the second step on the ladder, is called *Pisukei D'zimrah*. In this portion of the prayers we thank and praise Hashem for the miracles of creation and for the wonders that Hashem has performed throughout our collective history. The objective of these songs is to generate and circulate Ruach, to arouse our feelings and emotions, to direct them towards Hashem and to enter into the consciousness of gratitude.

Zimrah means song and praise, but is also related to the word *Zamer /* to prune, to weed out, or to cut down. As we are singing to arouse our emotions, we are also weeding out or cutting down all Kelipos and negative emotions, in particular the feelings of insatiability and dissatisfaction.

GIVING VOICE TO THE INNER PRAISER:

In this phase of the prayer we are learning to allow the Psalmist and praiser within us to speak. There is and always will be a time to think, consider and contemplate. And there is even a time when questions can and definitely should be asked. But now, at this particular time, when we are in the middle of praying, we need to simply allow the inner part of ourselves that wishes to sing and praise the Infinite One to come forth and be heard.

To allow that inner voice of praise to shine forth sometimes an inner dialogue is required. We may need to tell our inquisitive, ever skeptical and over analytical mind that, "you had your turn to talk and voice your opinion and you will have another chance in the future, but now I would like for my simple hearted, emotional voice within me to do the speaking", or singing to be more exact.

Thanks and praise can be an opening for us to express our love, devotion and commitment to our personal relationship with Hashem. This part of the service is the place of subjectivity, a place of subtlety and sensitivity. This is the realm where a relationship with Hashem is possible.

By extension, the whole world is then elevated through our songs of praise. When we say, during the verses of praise for example, the words, "Praise Hashem, Praise Hashem sun and moon", we are not merely saying that the celestial bodies also utter praise. But rather we are speaking to them, to the very sun and the moon, and to all of nature, saying enthusiastically, "let us all sing Hashem's praise together". We are joining our deepest selves with nature and with all of creation to sing Hashem's praise in a cosmic symphony. When we say, *Ha'kal Yoduchah* / "All shall praise You", all of creation joins us, from the inanimate silent stone, to the tumultuous waters, to the living creatures — all of creation joins us in praising Hashem. Or, to put it differently, we actually join the rest of Creation, which is always in a state of praise. Humans are, in fact, the only aspect of Creation that is allowed the existential wiggle room, otherwise known as free-will, to slip out of a state of perpetual praise.

When praying this portion of the prayers we should have a general Kavanah that we are directing and dedicating our emotions, feelings and passions to Hashem. This Kavanah also counters the Kelipa of insatiability. By becoming aware of the self-centered nature of most of our desires and of the impossibility of filling spiritual emptiness with physical objects or experiences, we are gradually able to free ourselves from the perpetual cycle of never ending desire, expectation and suffering.

This is the world of Yetzirah, the elongated letter *Vav*, where an idea from the mind comes down into the heart space. This is the level of Ruach, the element of Water, where our emotions flow effortlessly and fluidly as a waterfall.

The Zohar says that, "All masculine is standing up". Vav is the element of assertive giving. For this reason, when we begin this section of the prayers we stand up. We stand up to recite the *Baruch She'amar* / "Blessed is the One who said…"

THIRD SECTION: KRIYAS SHEMA — BLESSINGS AND THE READING OF THE SHEMA:

Having dedicated our body and heart in service of the One, we continue to ascend the ladder of prayer into the world of the intellect, the world of Beriah, corresponding to the level of Neshama. This section of prayer is called *Kriyas Shema* / the blessings and recitation of the Shema.

The word *Shema* in Hebrew means to hear, listen, comprehend and understand. In this section of the morning prayers, we pray sitting down. The difference between standing and sitting is that standing indicates movement, excitement, and emotions; while sitting exhibits a sense of calm and stillness, of being collected and contemplative. At this point in the prayer we take all the previous awareness, excitement and inspiration experienced during the previous segments of the prayers and we internalize these aspects in focused meditation on Hashem's Unity.

The Shema is a place of pure objectivity. This is the

place of the impersonal and intellectual. At this level of prayer we are able to understand that we are here for a reason and that everything in our life, and life in general for that matter, was created, and is continuously being created, for a purpose.

This state of full intellectual awareness is similar to the Upper Hei of Hashem's Name, a letter that has both vertical and horizontal expansiveness. In the Lower Hei, this dimensionality is a physical property. But in the Upper Hei, this sense of breadth and width is representative of an intellectual depth and dimensionality.

While praying this part of the prayers, we should have a general intention that we are directing and dedicating our intellectual selves to Hashem and our divine purpose. This Kavanah counters the Kelipa of meaninglessness in general and mindless chatter in particular.

This is the element of air; expansive, uninhibited free movement, the level of Neshamah, free choice and objectivity.

"All feminine is sitting down". The upper Hei is the higher aspect of receptivity, the feminine, which receives lightning flashes of intuition and articulates understanding. Therefore we say the Shema sitting down.

It is only following the reading of the Shema, when we have directed our actions, emotions, and intellects to Hashem that we can now enter into the Holy of Holies, the inner most sacred chamber, the Amidah prayer.

FOURTH SECTION: THE AMIDAH- SILENT PRAYER:

The Amidah is the climactic and essential prayer of the Morning prayers, so much so that the sages in the Talmud simply refer to it as "the prayer". At this point we are ready to enter the world of *Atzilus* / emanation, nearness, unity, the reality of *Chayah*.

At this level of prayer there is a total nullification of the separate sense of the small 'i' within the Ultimate/ Infinite I of Hashem. Here we are like the small dot of the *Yud*, a miniscule dot of existence leaping up into the Infinite Unity of One. This station of the journey corresponds to the element of fire, for we are likened to a spark of fire that is leaping upward to its Source.

When praying this part of the morning prayers we should have the general Kavanah that we are dedicating and directing our whole self to Hashem, the Source of all life and reality. This Kavanah counters the Kelipa of anger. The root of anger is arrogance.

THE MORNING PRAYER CHART:

LETTER OF HASHEM'S NAME	Yud	Hei	Vav	Hei
MANIFESTATION OF HASHEM'S NAME	Av	Sag	Mah	Ban
WORLD	Atzilus	Beriah	Yetzirah	Asiyah
CAPACITY	Faith/Will/ Pleasure	Intellect	Emotion	Action
SOUL	Chaya	Neshamah	Ruach	Nefesh
CONSCIOUSNESS	Transcendental	Mental	Emotional	Factual
SPIRITUAL ACTIVITY	Awe	Love	Praise	Devotion
EXPRESSION	Arousal	Thought	Voice	Speech
ELEMENT	Fire	Air	Water	Earth
TYPE	Human	Animal	Vegetative	Inanimate
POSITION	Standing	Sitting	Standing	Sitting
BEIS HA-MIKDASH	Kodesh Kedashim	Kodesh	Har Ha'bayis	Azarah
SONG	Shir Pashut	Shir Kaful	Shir Meshulash	Shir Merubah
PRAYER UPWARDS	Amidah	Shema	Pisukei D'Zimra	Birchas Ha'Shachar
PRAYER DOWNWARDS	Tachnun	Ashrei	Shir Shel Yom	Ein Ke'lokeinu

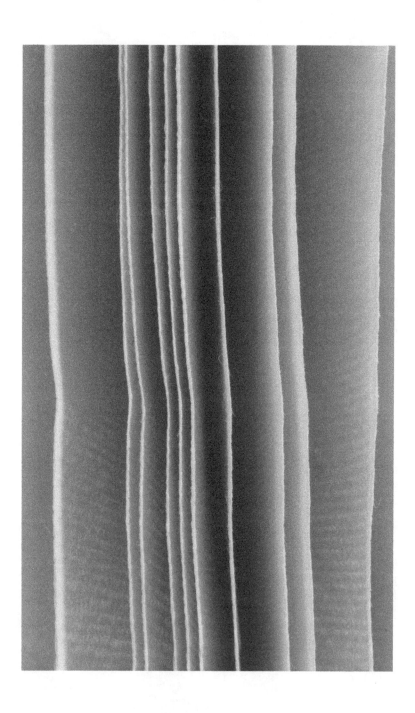

PEAK:

*The Fourth Rung
of the Ladder of Prayer:*
The Amidah

1]

The Redemption of Prayer

**BEFORE EXPLORING THE NATURE OF THE AMI-
DAH, THE MOST ESSENTIAL PRAYER, IN GREATER
DETAIL,** let us first venture to explore the transitional stages that lead up to the Amidah in the morning
prayers; as there is much to be learned about the nature of prayer from the liturgical process of prayer.

GEULAH L'TEFILAH —
FROM REDEMPTION TO PRAYER:

It is extremely important to juxtapose *Geulah* / redemption, with *Tefilah* / prayer *(Berachos, 4b)*. Functionally, this means that we conclude the blessings

after the Shema with the words, *Go'al Yisrael* / "Who Redeems Israel", and then right away begin the Amidah, which, as mentioned earlier, is referred to by the sages as simply "the prayer". In the Geulah prayer we speak about our collective past and the redemption from Egypt, the Tefilah prayer speaks about our hopes and dreams for the future. Simply, by joining the past to the future our prayers become ever more real, we can better imagine a brighter future based on our past history.

The Sages emphatically contend that we should begin the Amidah immediately after we say *Go'al Yisrael* and not to make any separation between Geulah and Tefilah. One should attempt to bring these two as close as possible, without even taking a breath in between Geulah and Tefilah. The Gemarah assures that if one joins Geulah to Tefillah, that person will not meet with any mishaps for the whole day *(Berachos, 9b)*. This can be perceived as a subtle hint into the inner dynamics of our psycho-spirituality. Meaning that if one is able fully integrate the concept of the union between redemption and prayer, which will be explored in a moment, then one's consciousness can potentially align itself in such a way as to view everything that happens as being for the ultimate good, and this thought itself, that everything is and will be good, creates that goodness.

King David expresses this conceptual progression, from redemption to prayer, in the book of Tehilim, Psalms. First comes the verse, *Hashem Tzuri Ve'goali* / "Hashem you are my Rock and redeemer" *(Tehilim 19:15)*. This represents the idea of redemption. And then immediately after, in Psalm 20, is the verse, *Y'ancah Hashem Be'eis Tzara* / "Answer me in a time of distress", representing the idea of prayer.

The juxtaposition of redemption and prayer represents, on a cosmological level, the union between *Yesod*, which is *Geulah*, and *Malchus*, which is *Tefilah*. This symbolic relationship is also seen as analogous to the masculine and feminine energetic interplay. This use of anthropomorphic imagery is not to be confused with literal biological man and woman. Rather, it is referring on a deeper level to a more elemental, archetypal and embodied poetic sense of self.

In this dynamic, *Yesod* / or redemption, is the giver — the letter Vav — that which is full already, straight, steady and in a constant state of giving. Whereas *Malchus* / or prayer, is the receiver — the Lower Hei — where there is desire, yearning, openness and receptivity.

In the Book of Ruth, Boaz is the embodiment of the male, the *Sod ha'Goel* / the secret of the redeemer. He is quoted as stating, "I am the Redeemer" *(Ruth, 3:12)*. Ruth on the other hand represents the archetypal female and embodies the *Sod ha'Tefilah* / the secret of prayer. As the Gemarah says, "What is the meaning of the name Ruth? [It is that]...she was privileged to be the ancestress of David, who *Rava* / saturated, the Holy One, blessed be He, with songs and hymns" *(Berachos, 7b)*. This is a subtle wordplay in the Hebrew that is lost in translation. But suffice it to say that in Hebrew the word *Rava* / saturated, is related to the word Ruth. The idea of praising The Most High with songs and hymns is the essence of prayer. And Ruth's name, as intuited by the Sages, embodies this very quality of prayer.

When Ruth — Malchus, the feminine — is elevated from a place of lack and is filled with light as she unites with Boaz — Yesod, the masculine — she then becomes the source of Rava, 'saturation'. Not only is Ruth then a proper *Mekabel* / receiver, but she becomes a beautiful *Mashpia* / giver, as well. Since the idea of Rava, 'saturation', expresses the idea of being filled to the extent of overflowing and filling others with a sense of fulfillment.

Often the idea of prayer indicates a need to be filled, which suggests the opposite of redemption or a lack of freedom. By bringing redemption to prayer, however, we thus transform our prayer from an expression of lack, need, or unfulfilled desire, into a conscious attempt to make the connection and to open a channel to the Infinite.

Before we begin the Amidah we say the words, *Go'al Yisrael* / "Who Redeems Israel". *Go'al* is not in the future tense, but rather in the present and past tense, indicating a redemption that has already been experienced. This hints to us that we should feel as though we have already been redeemed before we even set out to pray. We pray from a place of redemption.

Redemption represents a reality where you are no longer bound and limited by all the things you lack and are thus normally praying for. Once you feel yourself as already redeemed, as though you have everything you need, you are no longer a prisoner to your fears and desires and you can truly offer up a redemptive prayer.

Redemptive prayers are not necessarily prayers that seek to change or alter reality. But rather, they come from a place of acknowledgment and overflowing gratitude, thereby allowing you to realize that you already have all that you need. This may facilitate a situation in which one is able to receive that which they truly need through the perception and projection of themselves and reality as ultimately redeemed and already existing in a state of satisfied abundance. This allows them to remain open and available to receive even more of Hashem's blessings.

The redemption of prayer occurs when we no longer pray for the benefit of our own personal needs. We no longer need or lack anything. We have achieved a state of total acceptance. We are redeemed and rectified. And yet we pray — not for our own needs, but because the Creator wants us to have more. If there is a lack in our lives, even we do not feel it, it is a lack in the Shechinah, so to speak. If we are in a state of lack or exile, the Shechinah is in a state of lack and exile. Redemptive prayer is when we pray for the world, for the Shechinah, and not for the self alone, or even at all.

Deeply, we pray for health because Hashem wants us to be healthy. We pray for sustenance because Hashem wants us to be sustained. We pray for love because Hashem wants us to be loved and loving. These personal wants and needs are then transformed into something sublime and noble, as they are not coming from a place of ego, but rather from a place of transcendence. Therefore, by unifying Geulah and Tefilah we are bringing a sense of redemption to our prayers. Everything resonates and reflects itself back into rhythmic spirals of associative analogy. Prayer is the Shabbos of the weekday. The time spent in prayer is analogous to the consciousness of Shabbos manifesting within our weekday. On Shabbos we no longer rush, we live with an awareness that, "all our work has been done", everything is perfect and we are without worry and anxiety — it is a minor form of redemption, a taste of the world to come. Every day when we pray we are able to enter into our own personal Shabbos time and experience a timeless moment of truly redemptive consciousness.

2]

The Essence of Prayer

IN THE PREVIOUS CHAPTERS THE FIRST THREE
RUNGS OF THE MORNING PRAYERS WERE EX-
PLORED and the fourth rung upward, the Amidah,
was only touched upon. Now let us delve more deeply into the essential prayer, the Amidah, and by exploring the way this prayer is recited we will come to
a deeper understanding of what prayer is all about.
Instead of getting in to the content or words of the

prayer itself, the focus of this chapter will be more on the experiential process and over-arching perspective of the Amidah as a whole.

At this point, after having moved into and out of the first three ascending stages of prayer we have, as much as humanly possible, nullified ourselves as a separate independent "i" and we are, as much as humanly possible, now integrally identified with the Infinite I. It is only after we have properly directed and dedicated our physical, emotional, and intellectual abilities and dealt with the *Kelipos* / concealments, on each level that we can fully enter into the innermost chamber. We enter this deep space of unity through the Amidah. The Arizal speaks of the Amidah as being in the world of Atzilus, whereas the Ramak calls the Amidah the Seventh Gate. The Amidah is unanimously understood by the sages as the loftiest of all the prayers — the Holy of Holies.

The Amidah is the fourth rung on the ladder of prayer. Here we dwell in the world of *Atzilus* / emanation, where our soul is inseparable from the Unity of the Creator. The first three stages of prayer are about doing / *Asiyah*, feeling / *Yetzirah* and knowing /*Beriah*. The Amidah is about pure Being, and Being is stillness, acceptance and joy.

THE THREE STEPS:

Before beginning the Amidah we are instructed to take three steps backwards, followed immediately by three steps forward. These steps symbolize both our humility and acceptance of 'what is' in the presence of the Divine (stepping back), as well as our desire to be actively engaged in our own life story (stepping forward). We step back in order to create space for an Other, namely Hashem. This is an act of *Tzimtzum* / a contraction of self, in order to create space for soul. And then we courageously step up and move forward into the abyss in order to engage and interact with that Other, with G-d.

These physical steps help us to move mentally as well. We step back in humility and step forward in faith.

It is not enough to meditate and have Kavanah that you are entering into a world of Atzilus, but as much as possible you must truly try to enter into and experience that Unity. These three physical steps help us to "take that step", literally with our entire being, including our body.

Kavanah is not mere intention of the mind. The root word of Kavanah is *M'cha'ven*. We are not asked to be *M'chashev* / to think a Kavanah, but rather to *M'chav-*

en, whose root letters also mean to 'equalize'. Meaning that, to have Kavanah is to be like the Kavanah, to be equal to it. Not to think about Atzilus, but rather to be Atzilus.

Once, the Maggid of Mezritch was asked by a childhood friend, "why does it take you so long to pray?" The person told him that he too prays with all the Kabbalistic intentions of the AriZal and yet it takes him a much shorter time to get through the cycle of prayers. The Maggid asked him, "Since you are a merchant why do you need to travel to the market place to buy your goods? Why can't you just meditate and be there in your mind without having to actually schlep there?" The Maggid was alluding to the fact that there is a quantum leap between "being" there - actually entering into the space of a Kavana and merely "going" there - intellectually grasping the implied meaning of the Kavanos without fully entering into them or letting them enter into you.

Yet conversely, it is also true that, "a person is where his thoughts are". We learn from this that, although not initially ideal, the act of merely meditating on these Kavanos without fully entering into them can actually come to help a person really 'get there' by opening them up to what they are meditating on.

HASHEM, OPEN UP MY LIPS:

As mentioned earlier, the root of the word for Tefilah, prayer is *Tofel*, which means to 'join' or to connect. Prayer reveals our innermost desire to be at one with Hashem, just like the innermost desire of Hashem, however we are to understand this, is to be at one with us.

The deeper level of prayer is a method through which to reach and reveal our inherent connection and unity with Hashem that transcends duality. On this level of prayer our requests and petitions for Hashem's intercession are not for our own selfish desires to be fulfilled, but rather for Hashem's desire to be fulfilled through us. The practice of prayer is a spiritual exercise that allows us to connect and unite in a revealed way with the will of our Creator. Opening us up to align our desires with what Hashem desires for and wants from us.

The essential objective of prayer is thus fulfilled in the encounter itself.

As we are about to enter the Amidah we begin by saying, "Hashem, open my lips and my mouth shall speak Your praise." So even before we enter the prayers we make the request of Hashem, "please let my mouth be an instrument of Your Will." In other words, we are saying that, "I am at Your disposal". "What, Hashem, would you have me say?"

Instead of seeing yourself as someone standing before Hashem in supplication you should aspire to visualize yourself as being seen by Hashem. So as much as praying is a looking outside of oneself, turning to Hashem and asking for assistance; on a deeper level, prayer is a spiritual turning within, a reaffirmation and awareness of how deeply we already are part of Hashem — if we could only get our ego out of the way. This is precisely why we ask Hashem to open our lips at the peak of the prayers.

When we say, "Hashem open my lips," we are saying on a deep level, "Hashem speak through us". The Maggid of Mezritch teaches that the moment a person begins to utter these words with intention the Shechinah immediately rests upon that person and speaks these very words with and through them.

Ideally, as one approaches the Amidah — the height of prayer — there is a total *Bitul* / nullification and transparency of the small/separate self, or at least an increased awareness of the awesomeness of standing before the Immanent Presence of the Infinite One. At that moment we are rendered mute, we are speechless in wonder, and so we turn to Hashem, gather up some strength and say, "You, Hashem please open up my lips."

On a deep level, says the Maggid of Koznitz, if you are praying and are still saying the words by your own volition, you are still needing to consciously move your lips, know that you have not yet reached the true, deepest level of Deveikus and unity which prayer makes possible.

Another way of framing this state of reality is that on this level you, the individual I is no longer praying. Rather, prayer is occurring through you. The reason we pray in the plural, as in "heal us" or "sustain us" is because at the peak of our prayers there is no longer the sensation of a separate I who is praying. Rather, the world is praying through us and using our mouth as a mouthpiece to give voice to their prayers. When we pray for healing, all the sickness of the world is asking to be healed. We are simply the mouthpiece, articulating and revealing the inner cry of the world. The same is true when we pray for sustenance. Everything in the world that is lacking or deficient in sustenance, whether mineral, plant, animal or living being is praying for nourishment and harnessing our mouths to give voice to the needs of the world.

In this manner, we are not offering prayer for a specific person to be healed or a particular someone to receive nourishment. Instead, we open ourselves to pray on behalf of the whole, as a cog in the wheel of a much greater machine than only you and I as individuals are capable of becoming. The whole world is praying through us for the Divine Infinite flow of healing and nourishment to stream down into the world bringing the blessing of healing and nourishment to one and all. When we, as finite individuals pray in the form of imposing our desired outcomes on the Will of The Creator, we constrict the Divine infinite flow to that potential, as if the finite perspective we hold is capable of envisioning something beyond itself. In contrast, when the whole world prays through you, the prayer taps into the highest, infinite, most formless flow of healing, drawing down unlimited healing and blessing to all of creation.

PRAISE — REQUEST — THANKSGIVING:

The Amidah is divided into three groups. The first part is where we offer *Shevach* / praise, the third part we offer Hoda'ah, 'thanksgiving', and in the middle there are the requests / *Bakashos*. Praise and thanksgiving represents acceptance. This is the place of *Ayin* and *Bitul*. Requests occur in the place of non-acceptance — of *Yesh* / some-thingness. We need to sustain this delicate balance between *Ayin* and *Yesh* and on a deeper level, attempt to unify them as one. Meaning that, in the place of request, feel the Ayin; and in the place of praise, feel your own self-worth. Throughout the Amidah, and essentially throughout all expressions of prayer, we are perpetually moving into and out of the states of Yesh and Ayin — back and forth, forth and back, One inside the Other, the Other inside the One.

PERSONAL WITH NO EGO:

Although we pray in the Amidah for what may seem to be personal and perhaps even trivial human necessities such as wealth, strength, and confidence, which would seem to indicate the re-surfacing of our personal ego needs; on a deeper level, these requests are not mere requests which come from our selfish/small ego/self, but rather, they are articulate expressions of our spiritually transcendent higher-selves, as channeled by the sages.

This dynamic can be understood from multiple perspectives: 1] Physical/Individual and Physical/Collective. 2] Spiritual/Individual and Spiritual/Cosmic

PHYSICAL/INDIVIDUAL:

At this point in the development of prayer, our prayers are not an extension of the desires of our ego self, but rather they are an extension of the Will of the Infinite One. The innermost desire of the Creator is that all creatures should have what they need to survive. It is through these prayers of request that we are able to better understand what Hashem truly wants for us in order that we may live a meaningful and spiritual life in relationship with the Most High.

During the course of the Amidah, we ask the Creator to fulfill those very needs that have been revealed to be the most necessary areas of our lives in need of both fulfillment and rectification. These are the aspects of life most prone to corruption in the course of our acquisition of them, namely health, wealth, knowledge, food, success, salvation. It is very easy for one to become disconnected from The Source in the pursuit of the fulfillment of these particular needs. The danger being that we may confuse G-d's blessings with our own strength and cunning. That is why we pray for these specific things. So that we are able to stay connected and maintain the proper perspective as to where these basic necessities actually come from — from G-d.

We are not praying for food for its own sake, but so that we are physically satisfied and better able to spiritually serve Hashem. For without our most basic needs met it is often quite difficult to have the energy and state of mind to connect with anything more than the most immediate bio-survival instincts. We are able to move beyond this initial level of 'animal' consciousness when we are able to relate to and utilize one's health, wealth, wisdom and strength in rectified ways, as means of coming closer to Hashem and serving the greater good. This is accomplished through an elevation and integration of the physical drives and instincts into the spiritual calling of the Higher Self.

There is an experiential difference between throwing tantrums, demanding to have our needs met, and humbly asking for those most basic needs to be met in order that we may have the sustenance, strength and support to become more fully realized individuals for the sake of the greater good.

PHYSICAL –COLLECTIVE:

The prayers in the Amidah are not only prayers for oneself, but are also requests for the collective good, for the benefit of the whole world. We are not only asking for ourselves to be fed and provided for. It is not, or should not be, only the self-serving ego speaking. Rather, in this transcendent place of inter-connection, inter-dependency and unity, we also recognize that many others are in a state of lack, need and suffering — and we pray for them as well. This is why the prayers of the Amidah are phrased in the inclusive plural such as, "Hashem, please bless us with good health, heal us". The essence of the prayers are all about the collective receiving that which each one of us needs to survive and thrive as good and righteous people in the quest to make this world a better place. In fact, this is the mark of true transcendence: That during the peak of own inner spiritual journey, we still do not forget about or neglect the needs and perspectives of others.

SPIRITUAL/INDIVIDUAL AND SPIRITUAL/COSMIC:

SPIRITUAL — INDIVIDUAL:

Having elevated and transformed all of our bodily drives, energies and associations through the previous ascending stations of prayer, we may now speak the language of our soul. The desire for all things physical is merely a manifestation of the soul's yearning to elevate and unite with the Infinite One. The hunger for food, the requests for health, the quest for success, these are all tangible expressions of our soul's yearning to elevate the sparks within the food, within the body and within the world. Each and every soul has its own particular areas that need to be refined and wrestled with. This deep work can only be accomplished by one alone with Hashem's help — the Infinite One.

SPIRITUAL – COSMIC:

Every lack in this world is analogous to a lack, as it were, in the light of the Shechinah. The Shechinah is in exile when we are in exile *(Megilah, 29a)*. When we do not have what we need in order to maximize our spiritual potential, that is not only a deficiency in us, it is also representative of a lack of Godliness being expressed in this world. Hashem's presence cannot be felt throughout the entire creation when we are unable to access and utilize everything towards its intended spiritual purpose. Being that we are the "limbs of the Shechinah", by fulfilling our needs within a spiritual context the Shechinah can thus be more revealed and manifest within the world and within our lives.

On this level of prayer, we are not asking for our self-centered desires to be fulfilled. It is no longer our ego speaking. There is no longer a separate autonomous self that is expressing its needs and cravings. But rather, it is the soul expressing a transcendent desire for Divine revelation. Our deepest self is appealing to Hashem to grant us what we need so that the Divine presence can be more clearly actualized and manifest. Prayer, on a deep level, is simply a mechanism to bring down the Infinite Light into the finite creation that is our reality. Since, however, the Infinite Light does not settle upon empty vessels, we thus pray for the fulfillment of our materialistic needs, for those very blessings serve as the vessels that absorb the light of the *Ohr Ein Sof* / the Infinite Light. At this point, our needs are nothing less than an extension of a Divine desire to be fully present and to dwell within the lower worlds.

We are no longer praying for our own glory, but rather to fill the world with Hashem's glory. As King David says, "Not for our sake, Hashem, not for our sake, but for the sake of Your name, bestow glory" *(Tehillim, 115:1).*

BECOMING ONE WITH THE GIVER:

Not only are our prayers not about us and our selfish needs, but in deep prayer we actually become part of the 'giver', the resource, as it were, and we are no longer a mere 'receiver'. In deep prayer we enter into the natural Divine flow of giving, sustaining and creating.

Think of this in terms of a great reservoir of water, which, when the water overflows, naturally irrigates the surrounding fields. There are two ways to get the fields irrigated during a dry season. One way is to take a bucket and scoop up some water and water the fields. In this image the person is a receiver and, in a way, he is disturbing the natural flow of the water. Another way is to enter into the body of water itself and help push the water out. In this image, one is part of the giving nature of the water and is tapping into the natural flow of the water.

In deep prayer we enter into the pool of Divine plenty and become a conduit and facilitator for the blessings to stream outwards and downwards. We become part of the natural flow of giving and not merely a selfish receiver. Of course, as the Divine plenty flows outwards this brings blessings to all, us included.

3]

Silence & Sound in Prayer

WHEN WE REACH THE PEAK OF OUR PRAYERS
WE RECITE THE AMIDAH. But unlike the three previous levels of prayer, which were filled with ecstatic
song, enthusiastic praise and emphatically verbalized
exultation, the Amidah is meant to be recited quietly.
In fact, the Amidah is referred to as the "silent prayer"
(Yerushalmi, Berachos, 4:1).

There are two paradoxical dimensions at work in the
Amidah: The concept of voice and sound, and the
idea of quietness and silence.

VOICE & SOUND:

In the structured daily prayers of the liturgy we must say the prayer to fulfill our Halachic obligation to pray three times each day. It is not enough to meditate on the prayers or to just visualize them — they must be said.

There are many reasons to utilize the voice in the recitation of the Amidah and in prayer in general:

1] Words resonate within us in a very deep way. When we speak about something it becomes more real to us. So long as something is still in pure thought, it remains evasive and elusive — more ethereal. Only when thoughts "descend" into language do they become concretized and real.

2] The voice itself helps us to be more focused. "Voice arouses intention". The Hebrew word for 'voice', Kol, has the same numeric value as the word Sulam, 'ladder' — both equal 136. The sound of one's voice in heartfelt prayer becomes the ladder on which one can climb deeper and higher during the course of the prayers.

3] We pray audibly, not so that Hashem can hear us praying, but rather, we pray aloud to arouse our own hearts and to inspire us to better ourselves and improve our actions. Words, and even simple sound vibrations, have a tremendous effect on our psyche, whether calming, inspirational or aggravating. Certainly all the more so when those sounds are meaningful words said with devotion, intention and focus.

4] When we pronounce the words of prayer audibly we are then able to experience the prayers in our entire body, not just in the mind alone. The prayers become a full body vibrational experience when we use our mouth, lungs, tongue and lips in prayer.

5] Speech is a movement that is ultimately manifest in the realm of physical activity. Therefore its effects on the body are revealed through and associated with the world of 'action.' Although thinking, visualizing and contemplating are also physical activities that occur within the brain and do in fact register an effect on the inner workings and wiring of the brain, still these purely mental activities are relatively more subtle, and certainly less tangibly manifest than the act of speaking in a physically revealed way. And so, when our prayers are confined to the inner world of pure thought, the resultant answers to our prayers will also remain in the ethereal realm of pure thought.

Simply put, this could mean that the response to a purely meditative, non-verbal prayer is, potentially, a resultant shift in perspective, a shift in thought — but not necessarily manifest in the physical world of action. When we speak our prayers aloud however, we create the proper vibration and vessels to contain the influx of blessing that our prayers illicit to manifest within the world of Asiyah. Audible prayer creates the vessels to absorb and channel the blessings that are drawn down through prayer.

6] Language is a means to define and discern. Language is a way to contextualize and sift out a 'something' from the 'everything'. In prayer we use language and the voice, the very tools that normally cause separation, to resonate and reach towards an awareness of Unity.

QUIETNESS & SILENCE:

Voice is the generally accepted modality of structured prayer. In the Amidah however, which is the peak of the prayers, we also need to introduce the element of silence and quietness.

There are several reasons given as to why the Amidah should be said quietly:

1] On a simple level, the idea of praying quiet-ly demonstrates an understanding that Hashem hears all prayers, whether loud or quiet, and that one does not need to scream for Hashem to listen, as Hashem is present everywhere *(Berachos, 24b)*. A person who prays loudly is considered *M'Ketanei Emunah* / low in faith. Rashi (ibid) explains that the very act of praying in a loud voice suggests that the person does not have faith that Hashem will hear a prayer if it is prayed quietly, as if Hashem does not know our every thought and feeling.

2] There is also a technical reason why the Amidah is said quietly: If said aloud, the prayer may come to embarrass one who is confessing transgressions and praying for forgiveness, so the sages instituted that this prayer be said quietly *(Sotah, 32b)*.

3] On a deeper level, at this point of the prayers there is no room for self-expression. Therefore, the Ami-dah is prayed in a quiet voice. In fact the Ami-dah is referred to as *Tefilas Lachash* / the whispered prayer. When a person prays on this level there is total Bitul, nullification of the separate, small 'i'.

4] Unlike the first three stages of prayer, which are about doing, feeling and knowing, the Amidah is a state of being, and being is stillness. Elijah the prophet, hears a voice telling him to, "Go forth and stand on the mountain before Hashem. And behold, Hashem is passing. A great and powerful wind is crushing the mountains and breaking the stones before Hashem, but Hashem is not in the wind. And after the wind, there came an earthquake, but Hashem is not in the earthquake. And after the earthquake came a fire, but Hashem is not in the fire. And finally, after the fire came a *Kol d'Mammah Dakkah* / a still small voice, or a 'sound of subtle stillness' *(Melachim 1. 19. 11:12)*. This is the state of being in which we encounter and become one with Hashem. Prayer represents a level that is beyond speech.

5] The mouth, as well as the power of language itself, are both represented by *Malchus*. Prayer is the pinnacle of language that manifests through the mouth. Therefore, prayer is also associated with Malchus. Malchus is merely a reflection of the higher Sefiros *(Zohar 1, p. 209b-210a)* and is, by definition, always in a state of lack. Thus the voice of Malchus cries out quietly, at least until the time of Moshiach when Malchus will be fully realized and vocalized. When the world will reach its full potential and perfection, then as a correlate the Amidah will be recited "with voice," and not quietly.

6] Whispering is the appropriate mood of communication during the Amidah since this is a timeless moment of Intimate Unity. In the language of the holy Zohar the Amidah is a time in which, "everything is silent above and still below with the kisses of desire" *(2:128b, Tikunei Zohar, 10)*. Not only is the Amidah supposed to be said quietly so that no one else around can hear such a private and vulnerable exchange, but according to the Zohar *(1:210a, Netzutzei Ohros, Chida)*, it should be said so quietly that not even the person himself can hear himself praying.

7] The Amidah takes place in the super-subtle world of Atzilus. In the lower "three worlds" — Asiyah, Yetzirah, Beriah — which are "outside" of Unity, in order to connect with the Source there needs to be an "outward" expression. In these previous worlds/stages/perspectives a person is attempting to connect with something that is perceived of as being outside of them and thus, expression is externalized. When we enter the world of Unity, Atzilus, however, then speech is no longer expressed "outward", but rather speech is re-directed inward. This is represented by the prayer of Chanah, "Who was speaking to her heart, and only her lips moved, but her voice was not heard" *(Shmuel 1, 1:13)*. When the Divine is only perceived as outside of oneself, it is necessary to express outward speech, but when a person also feels the spark of the Divine within, and moreover, a sense of total unity with the Creator, then the speech is directed inward in a quiet, thin, fragile voice.

On Shabbos we read in the Siddur:
"By the mouth of the upright, You are praised. By the lips of the righteous, You are blessed. By the tongue of the pious, You are sanctified. Within the inners of the holy, You are exalted."

These four levels correspond to the four worlds. The outermost expression, which is on the first rung, Asiyah, is an expression of the mouth. A deeper level, Yetzirah is with the lips. Deeper, and more inward, Beriah, is with the tongue. Yet, the highest level, Atzilus, Ayin, is an exaltation that is experienced deep within. It cannot be expressed by the mouth, nor the lips, nor even the tongue, but only felt in a tangible, resonant silence.

Ultimately, the deepest, highest, most inclusive, transcendental level is Essence — a reality that is beyond and inclusive of both sound, Yesh, and silence, Ayin; being and non-being, fullness and emptiness. Today we need the absence of sound to enter into and access a deeper space, and it is silence that allows us to transcend and glimpse beyond the veil of the material Yesh. In the future, the Amidah will be said loudly with a strong voice, and yet, the sound will not be of Yesh only. Rather, a sound within a silence, a fullness within an emptiness.

DYNAMICS OF SILENCE & SOUND:

As the Jewish people, who had just emerged from their bondage in Egypt, faced the abyss of the sea in front of them, with the advancing Egyptians pursuing them from the rear, "Moshe said unto the people: Fear not, stand and see the salvation of Hashem... Hashem shall fight for you, and you shall *Tachrishun* / Hold your peace" *(Shemos, 14:12-14)*. The people were told to stand still and observe, and Hashem would fight their battles and they would hold their peace.

The word *Tachrishun*, which is translated as, "hold your peace", is not a precise, or totally accurate, translation. There is a subtle nuance that is lost in translation. A more careful translation would be, 'murmuring', as in a low quite noise. This is similar to what it says about Chana who was praying and "only her lips moved, but her voice was not heard". The process of prayer seeks to transport us to a place of Essence, of simultaneous sound and silence; or at least to catapult us, in rapid fluctuating succession, into and out of the consciousness of sound and silence. Reflective of this multi-layered modality is the paradoxically "silent/audible prayer" — the Amidah. A prayer we say with voice, but with a low voice.

SOUND & SILENCE: YESH — AYIN:

At a very deep level of prayer, which is when we recite the Amidah, we have to be connected with the Essence of being, which is comprised of both silence and sound.

Sound is Yesh —
something, creation, manifestation, the effect.

Silence is Ayin —
no-thing, the Source, the cause, the tangible hush that precedes the sound of creation. Underneath the ever unfolding incessant noise and manifestation, the Yesh/existence, there is the ever present hum of the Ayin, the silence.

The world was, and continues to be, created through the "ten utterances". As the Torah tells us, "G-d said let there be light, and there was light"; this is one of the utterances. Sound, which is an outward movement or manifestation from the Unity of the Creator is, in essence, a spiritual vibration that manifests as an outward expression in the form of physicality. Essentially sound is the very essence of the created world, of manifest reality.

The world "as is" comes from the reality of Divine sound, Divine expression. The world in "potential" is the place of Ayin — the silence that precedes the sound. Any change in reality, any alteration from the current condition, "as is", to an alternative reality, comes from the Divine Ayin, emptiness, silence. The silence, the Ayin is not the void of things, rather the space through with and upon which all things evolve. Silence is the space where creation occurs, everything comes from and through the silence.

"I lift my eyes to the mountains, (and say) *M'Ayin*, "From where", will my salvation come?" *(Tehilim, 121:1)*. The answer is in the question itself, salvation comes from Ayin, from the No-place of limitless potential.

When we want to effect change in our lives, to move from a situation "as is" to something else, we need to enter into the place of Ayin. This means moving from a place of Yesh, something defined, into the place of total surrender, humility, and nullification of any ego or expectation. We are thus able to move from reality 'as is', to reality in potential. It is this very place of infinite potential that is the womb of growth, change, healing and miracle.

PRAYING FROM THE PLACE OF YESH AND AYIN:

Yet the Amidah is not simply a silent, meditative prayer. It is, in fact, said in a quiet voice. Voice is articulation, manifestation, reality 'as is'. The Amidah is thus a unique blend of silent prayer and speech, but said in a low, almost inaudible, voice. Speech is the world of Yesh, something. Silence is the world of Ayin, no-thing. While in the world of Yesh, speech you sense the need for change, to change from illness to healing, from desperation to empowerment. But in the world of Yesh there is no possibility to change because one is in a place of being a 'something'.

When we pray the Amidah we do not scream and get caught up in the sounds of creation. We do not demand change from a place of Yesh, because from a place of Yesh there is no possibility for change.

Conversely in the place of Ayin/No-thing/Silence, while there is the potential for anything — because in this state truly anything is possible — there is no desire to change. This is because when a person fully enters the world of Ayin, they experientially become

Ayin, and thus they are no longer connected to any memories or aspirations, narrative, or story, that exists on the plane of Yesh. Resultantly there is the sense of total acceptance, submission and humility. While there is the potential to change, there is no desire to change anything; everything is "perfect" to a person who is truly in a state of Ayin.

This is the paradoxical nature of the Amidah. It is an audible prayer, not silent and meditative. This is an acknowledgement of the world 'as is'. But we speak the prayer in a low voice as a sign of humility, nullification, and Ayin, no-thingness. We 'speak' the 'silent' prayer, our speech is coming from and going into the silence of the Ayin. It is from within the simultaneous experience of both of these states, in and out from Ayin to Yesh that we are able to draw down from the place of Ayin a new reality into our Yesh.

PROCESS II:

Structure of the morning prayers:

The Four Descending Steps in the Morning Prayers

The Four Descending Steps in the Morning Prayers

UP UNTIL THIS POINT, THE FOUR ASCENDING STEPS IN THE CYCLE OF THE MORNING PRAYERS HAVE BEEN EXPLORED. But the morning prayers are actually divided into two sections of four. Four sections "going up", and four sections "coming down". These four descending stages allow us to integrate the transcendent energy of our prayers into our day-to-day lives.

The purpose of the process of prayer is to run up "there", up the mountain, and then to return down "here", back to the immanent and immediate world and all its concerns, in order to bring down the higher expansive awareness back into everyday waking life. This is referred to as, *"Aliyah L'tzorech Yeridah"* / "Ascent for the sake of Descent", as Reb DovBer of Chabad coined it.

The Choze of Lublin said that following the morning prayers one is on the highest level possible, having scaled inwardly to the height of Atzilus, and then drawing down all the way into the world of Asiyah. Essentially, by bringing down the high one experienced while in the high, one is able to elevate his low or normal awareness; and now the individual is both high and low together. One is Above while Below, and Below while Above. This is the beautiful and potent paradox of deep prayer.

The four descending stages in the structure of the morning prayers are as follows:
1] *Tachanun* — "The small confession", the world of Atzilus/Emanation
2] *Ashrei/Uva L'Tzion* — the world of Beriah/Creation
3] *Shir Shel Yom* — "Song of the day", the world of Yetzirah/Formation
4] *Ein Ke'lokeinu* — the world of Asiyah/ Actualization

Tachanun, also known as the "small confession", is where we confess our transgressions, mistakes and shortcomings, not only for ourselves, but also for the community as a whole. This prayer functions within the most subtle and unified world of Atzilus and transcendence, being as it is beyond the ego. We open ourselves up to feel the gravity of another person's pain, sin and mistakes. This prayer corresponds to the Amidah.

The *Ashrei* and *U'va Letziyon* prayers function as an intellectual reminder and reinforcement of the fruits of the experience and process of prayer. These prayers serve as a refresher course in the basic ideas and perspectives that we have cultivated and should be walking away with from the prayer experience. It is during this stage that we recite the *Kedusha* in the language that we understand. We also pray for Hashem to open our hearts to Torah wisdom. These prayers function in the world of Beriah, creation, the intellect. These prayers correspond to the Shema.

Shir Shel Yom / The Song of the Day, provides us with an expressive and emotive opportunity as we leave the mountain behind and approach the world. When you sing a prayer it is as if you have prayed it twice. There is something deep and evocative about melody and rhythm that opens us up to ideas and experiences, allowing them to sink in and embed themselves within the subtler levels of our psyches and souls. The *Shir Shel Yom* functions within the world of Yetzirah, the world of the emotions. This prayer corresponds to the *Pesukei D'Zimra*.

Ein Ke'lokeinu and the reciting of the incense ritual function within the world of Asiyah. The simple awareness of Hashem and the recitation of the incense offering represent the elevation of the physical into the service of the spiritual. This corresponds to Birchas Hashachar and the recitation of the offerings.

Between each successive section of the prayers there is a *Kaddish*. The Kaddish serves as the bridge between worlds and elevates the lower world into the higher, as well as bringing the higher world back into the lower.

THE FOUR DESCENDING RUNGS OF PRAYER IN GREATER DETAIL:

First Section:
TACHANUN — THE SMALL CONFESSION:

Tachanun exists within the world of Atzilus, emanation, unity, closeness and nearness. Tachanun parallels the Amidah, and as the Amidah it too is said quietly, suggesting an inwardness and less duality.

During the recitation of Tachanun, the penitential prayer, we confess that, "We have transgressed...we have stolen...". Reading through the text of Tachanun it becomes obvious that not every transgression mentioned has been committed by each person reciting the passage. And yet we all say the entire passage, and we say it daily. There are a number of interpretations for this apparent inconsistency. One reason is that, although on a surface level, we may not have stolen or cheated, for example, on a more subtle level we may have. Our sages have explained that publicly shaming another human being is tantamount to murder, being arrogant is comparable to idolatry, missing a chance to be fully present in life is stealing from ourselves, and that every time we speak words not of Torah, truth and meaning, we are speaking idle words.

Besides this more nuanced, subtle interpretation as mentioned above, there is also another explanation of why we all need to say these prayers daily. And that is because during this prayer, as we confess our transgressions and mistakes in the plural, we are functioning as a "We". We have stepped outside of our own small individual ego issues and stepped up to the experience of collective accountability and responsibility.

In the world of Atzilus we have, at least in principle,

transcended the personal 'i' and become submerged and identified with the larger I and, by extension, the entire community. We recite Tachanun in the plural-"we have transgressed, we have cheated…" Even if we as a singular individual have not committed these actions, we still say this prayer and identify ourselves with the whole. By doing so, we declare our inter-connectedness with others and we become aware that until the difficulties and challenges of others have not yet been fully resolved, we will not, and cannot, feel completely at peace ourselves.

During the recitation of the Tachnun prayer we gently strike our hand against our chest in the region of the heart. The simple reason is that most negative behavior is not rooted in the realm of the intellect, but is rooted rather in the desires and passions of the (lower) heart. The symbolic act of repeatedly striking one's heart identifies and acknowledges the source of one's negative actions within the realm of unrectified appetites, desires and emotions.

On a deeper level, consistent with the themes of compassion, ego-transcendence and feeling another person's pain as your own, gently tapping the heart represents a softening of the heart. This is analogous to the tiny drops of rain that over time will wear away the hardest stone. In this instance, the rock is your heart and the agent of erosion is your tears and your prayers.

For every time we act in a hurtful, negative, or self-destructive manner there is a 'closing of the heart'. The deepest, most vulnerable levels of our heart become rigid and covered over with defensive layers of unconscious character armor. To combat this reflexive reaction to pain and shame, the prophet encourages us all to, "Pour out your heart like water, in the presence of Hashem" *(Eicha, 2:19)*. Ultimately, we will reach the time of our individual and collective redemption when, as the prophet tells us, Hashem will "give you a new heart...and remove the heart of stone from your flesh..." *(Yechezkel, 36:26)*.

Second Section:
ASHREI – U'VAH LE'TZIYON:

This segment of the morning prayers, the second of the descending steps, is comprised of three elements. First we recite Ashrei, chapter 145 of Tehilim, then Chapter 20 of Tehilim, and finally the *U'Va L'tziyon* prayer. These all relate to the world of Beriah — the world of the intellect, and parallels the ascending prayer of the Shema.

Tehilim 145 speaks of Hashem's closeness and compassion that is shown to all creatures and all of creation. As the verse states clearly, Hashem's compassion rests "on all His works". This chapter in Tehilim is unique in that it follows an Alphabetic acrostic order, with each verse beginning with the next successive letter of the Hebrew Aleph Beis, except for the omission of the letter *Nun*.

Beriah, creation, occurs through Divine utterances, as depicted in the opening lines of the Torah. From a place of Oneness and Unity there begins a gradual process of separation, a movement outward. This represents a spiritual vibration, which gives rise to a physical vibration, the energy of matter. At this stage of the prayers we are beginning to individuate again. After every peak experience, we have the opportunity to re-create ourselves. And as the initial creation occurred through speech, vibration and intention, so too does any subsequent renewal of creation. We are coming down from the proverbial mountain and these portions of prayer re-enforce the spiritual imprint that we have accessed and downloaded during our transcendent and Unitive experience of the Amidah and Tachanun. Being that this stage of prayer is within the world of Beriah, it is appropriate to become aware of the creative process of Divine manifestation.

Next we recite Chapter 20 of Tehilim. This chapter is customarily recited in times of danger or distress, particular with regards to childbirth, when a woman is in labor. There are nine verses in this chapter corresponding to the nine months of pregnancy. There are also seventy words, which correspond to the seventy cries of the 'Great Mother' while giving birth.

In this vivid metaphor the mother is the Shechinah and the baby she gives birth to is Moshiach. This is referring to a cosmically creative act — the birth of a new redeemed, perfected world. In general, the entire exile is likened to a pregnancy, with redemption representing our collective birth. Parenthetically, right before the actual giving birth, there are the most intense and powerful contractions and pains. From that great Tzimtzum and contraction gushes forth new life and light. This is true on a microcosmic and macrocosmic level. That is why in this segment of prayers we first say chapter 20 of Tehilim and only afterwards do we recite the next prayer, "U'vah L'tziyon, "And the Redeemer shall come to Zion". First there are the pangs of birth and then the actual birth.

Originally this prayer was instituted for the benefit of the latecomers and therefore this prayer is actually a condensed form of the entire morning prayers. Our sages enacted this prayer to add verses of Torah study to our prayers. And being that by this point the entire congregation is present, it is a concentrated period of study that involves the entire community. In the U'vah L'Tziyon we recite the *Kedusha*, the sanctification of Hashem's name, in Aramaic, which was the common language at the time of the prayer's construction and canonization. This represents a familiar and personal approach to our relationship with the Most High as represented by Divine speech in the language that we understand. We also pray for Hashem to open our hearts to Torah wisdom.

This station of the morning prayers corresponds to the Shema. As the blessings of the Shema conclude with "The redeemer of Israel" the final passage of this segment begins with "And the Redeemer shall come to Zion", and in both these segments of prayer the Kedusha is recited.

Third Section
SHIR SHEL YOM-THE SONG OF THE DAY:

The essential recitation of this section of the morning prayers is the Song of the Day. The concept and practice of the Song of the Day comes from the times of the Holy Temple in Jerusalem. In those ancient times when the Temple stood and sacrifices were being offered daily the Levites would sing a different Psalm each day of the week in order to highlight and tap into the special energy of that particular beat in the rhythm of the week. To parallel this practice we too sing a different chapter in Tehilim each day of the week. In fact, the Tehilim we sing are the same chapters of Tehilim sung by the Levites in the Holy Temple in Jerusalem.

This segment of the morning prayers is within the world of Yetzirah, the emotional universe of song and expression. These Psalms correspond to the ascending section of Pesukei D'Zimra, verses of praise, where we recite chapters of Tehilim.

Fourth Section:
EIN KE'LOKEINU:

The fourth step back down into the physical world of Asiyah begins with the words, "Look to Hashem, be strong and of good courage, and look to Hashem" *(Tehilim, 27:14)*. "Rav Chama bar Chanina said: If a person sees that he has prayed and was not answered, let him pray again, as it is written, "Look to Hashem, be strong and of good courage, and look to Hashem" *(Berachos, 32b)*. Sometimes prayers go unanswered for long periods of time. Sometimes prayers are answered in ways that are unexpected, or even hidden from our perception. This introductory formula reminds us that we should ultimately trust in Hashem for all of our needs and never stop praying. But in the meantime we also need to strengthen and prepare ourselves to deal with reality. Asiyah is the place of commitment, dedication and doing.

The essential passage in this segment of prayer, which follows the introductory statement mentioned above, is the "*Ein Ke'lokeinu* / "There is none like our G-d." Ein Ke'lokeinu perfectly expresses the consciousness of Asiyah. This prayer states in no uncertain terms that, "This is our G-d, This is our Savior, This is our Master...." There is no subtle or complex theology or poetry in this prayer. It is straightforward and declarative. Due to the density of the Kelipos in the physical world, there needs to be a very clear affirmation that there is "none like our G-d", as if there were any parities or any genuine other than The One. This is indicative of reality in the realm of Asiyah.

Next we recite the passage that speaks of offering the incense in the Holy Temple. This is analogous to the first ascending section of the morning prayers, where we also mentioned the incense offering along with the other daily sacrifices. The incense represents the ultimate elevation of even the seemingly foul or impure. This symbolism stems from the fact that there is known to have been eleven plants included in the recipe of the incense. Ten of these plants produced aromatically beautiful and musky smells to intoxicate the olfactory, but one of these plants produced a terrible smell, and yet this foul smelling spice is integral to the spiritual makeup of the holy incense. This is similar to the idea that a community is not complete without a 'sinner' present. We are all necessary. We all have the capacity to be that sinner, that foul smelling scent. We are all included in the offering of self-to-soul; the elevation of even the lowest, foul smelling scent up into a realm of *Kedusha* / holiness.

We conclude with a prayer for peace. Peace is security and proper boundaries. Peace is harmony and balance. Peace is reciprocal and creative.

The return journey back from the peak of prayer insures that we are able to integrate and absorb the full depth of the experience. This step by step 'retracing' is a conscious descent through the four previous realms in reverse, which allows us to take the time to gather up all of our loose ends, so to speak, and check in with ourselves to make sure that our soul is safe and secure back in the body, here and now.

It may occur that after praying with great intensity, focus, devotion and expansiveness, a person may find that they have become more easily irritated and impatient with all the people or things that they now deem petty or beneath them. This is the ever-present danger of accessing enlightened or exalted states of consciousness. If one is not careful, the experience of being in a heightened mood of ecstasy may potentially result in toxic feelings of agitation and anger with others who are, on the surface, seemingly less spiritually in-tune. We need to be very aware of these negative sentiments that may arise. They can cause tremendous harm and damage to our prayers, our loved ones, our neighbors/co-workers and ourselves. And so we need to take the time at the end of the prayers as we descend back through the four worlds to put ourselves back together in proper alignment, with our speech, thoughts and actions oriented in a conscious and compassionate manner.

As we have opened up our body, heart, mind and soul through the process of praying, we also need to make sure to seal off the experience so that all the blessing and divine influx that has been circulating through us during our prayers remain intact within our vessel and do not spill out in unconscious and/or condescending ways.

THE ALEINU, THE "AFTER PRAYER" "PRAYER:

The final seal/imprint of our prayer experience is the *Aleinu*, a very ancient prayer. The AriZal taught that the Aleinu contains within it greater praise then the entire cycle of prayers.

Aleinu sets and secures the placement and position of our prayers so that none of the energy that we have tapped into and stirred up is lost or becomes a source of anything unholy. For example, the Aleinu seeks to insure that our vibrant rapture does not devolve into haughtiness or anger; or that our great outpouring of love and cleaving does not give way to any unwanted or misdirected passions or desires.

Deep prayer seeks to activate emotions within us that are potent and vital. When directed towards goodness, respect and life they are potentially revelatory and transformative. But there is a thin, sometimes imperceptible, line between holiness and the *Sitra Achra* / other side. If one is not careful, these very same strong emotions can be the fuel that ignites improper offerings. To use a Torah reference, these ecstatic emotions, when not contained or misguided, can turn into "alien fire", as offered by the sons of Aaron in the Temple in the desert. These fires are often self-destructive and traumatic and, by extension, hurtful to others.

The greater the possibility for holiness, for life, for connection and productivity, the greater is the potential for the unholy, for 'death', disunity and destruction. Through the process of prayer we are being birthed anew, building ourselves up from a Nefesh to a Chaya level. Birth is one of the wonders of creation. The Creator alone holds the key to birth *(Taanis, 2a)*. We mimic the Creator when we literally create new life. The joy, the euphoria, the unbridled emotions, the love that flows freely at childbirth are tremendous. And yet, the mother is rendered *Tamei* / impure, right at childbirth. And this is precisely because of the magnitude of the *Kedusha* / holiness, life, and creation that is revealed at birth. The immediate moment following a tremendous experience is in fact an existential vacuum where Kelipa can take hold.

This is a very important understanding concerning the spiritual, mental, emotional, and physical reality in relationship to the Kedusha/Kelipa dynamic. Once Kedusha is present and it is then 'over', as it were, the potential for Kelipa is much stronger. This is similar to the phenomenon of something like Post-Partum Depression. When a 'high' is extremely high, the potential for a correspondingly low 'low' is present. Prayer is much the same. The more intense one's prayers, the higher and deeper one reaches through their prayers, the greater the danger that the emotions aroused will be misdirected once the actual high of the prayer is over. Aleinu, which speaks about Hashem's presence and unity within this world, ensures that the emotions are directed positively.

BOWING OUT:

On the other hand, the Aleinu also serves as a "bowing out"; much like a servant would bow before leaving the room of his master. We bow one last time in the Alienu and then leave the room, the inner-space of prayer. Alternatively, the Alienu is a prayer that we say "after prayer" to demonstrate that we are not running or rushing away from the experience of prayer.

The Aleinu is more than a prayer, its main function being to help smooth the transition of a movement between worlds. As we take the final step back from the ethereal space of prayer and return to our worldly journeys, the Aleinu assists us in re-joining, re-membering and re-connecting to the world.

PRACTICE

1]

Praying as a Child:
With no Doubt or Worry,
Anytime and for Anything

FOR ALL THE BENEFITS OF PRAYING WITH THE
INTRICATE AND DEEPER INTENTIONS, SOME-
TIMES A PERSON IS JUST NOT UP TO ENGAGING
THE MIND IN SUCH AN EXAGGERATED MANNER.
Their heart simply desires to be open and communi-
cate freely with Hashem. At times, we might want to
put the mind aside for a few moments and just be in
a heart space.

The Baal Shem Tov says that even after Rabbi Nachunya ben Hakana, a first century sage, had mastered all the deeper intentions connected with prayer, he would still pray like a little child. This echoes an older teaching that speaks of many great scholars who would say that they too pray "with the intention of a child". In other words, they would pray with simple faith and openness.

Heart prayer, where the mind is not so actively involved, is often more intense and high on energy, but is not always sustainable. Mind prayer, where the emotions are bypassed for a more conceptual or philosophic approach, runs the risk of evolving into a state of pure transcendence that is completely detached from the here and now — the place of real life and responsibility.

We need both. We need the mind to create the context, and we need the heart to feel the connection. But sometimes, many times even, a person should just pray like a child, pure and simple.

Reb Chaim of Tzanz, a famous scholar and sage, was once praying in great fervor and ecstasy, running about and whispering something. One of his disciples, wishing to hear the deep mystical chants being recited over and over again by his illustrious teacher, went behind him and heard him repeating: "I mean nothing but You, nothing but You alone".

The simplicity of the prayer is the profundity. Simple and direct. To Hashem alone, as a simple child, I pray.

PRAY ANYTIME:

Children also do not have the sense of the restriction of time. You cannot tell a child: "We are on our way to your aunt's wedding, it is not a good time to cry." A child cries when they are hurt. We also do not have control over what they are going to say. They say what is on their minds and they say it whenever they want, until they reach some form of maturity.

When we pray like a child we pray when we want, whenever we feel the urge, and for whatever we want. Nothing is too big, nothing is too small, and no time is better than the next.

When Rabbi Chaninah ben Dosa went to study Torah from Rabban Yochonan ben Zakkai, the latter's son fell ill and the teacher turned to his disciple: "Chaninah, request divine mercy for my son that he may live." Reb Chaninah promptly laid his head between his knees, prayed and the boy was saved. Seeing this, Rabban Yochonan ben Zakkai said: "Had Ben Zakkai stuck his head between his knees for an entire day, the heavenly court would pay no heed to him!" Hearing this admission, his wife turned to him and said: "Is Chanina greater than you?" "No" he responded, "rather he is like a servant before the king, while I am like a minister before the king" *(Berachos, 34b).* A minister is a higher position than the butler, yet, the minister has set times to come discuss matters with the king, whereas the butler, the servant, is with the king at all times.

Most of the time we may be like ministers, but sometimes, to truly access the King in a spontaneous manner, in order to request, to express, to articulate a dream, a yearning, a desire, to cry from pain or rejoice in exaltation, to sense awe or sing in gratitude, to surrender or feel empowered, we need to reach out, connect, and try to make the connection from the place of a child, or as simple servant.

SPONTANEOUS PRAYER:

Spontaneity is the mark of a child. The Hebrew letters that make up the word *Tikkun* / perfecting, can be rearranged to spell the word *Tinok* / child. Part of our personal soul Tikkun is to reconnect with our inner child, to live with a childlike awareness, with wonder, amazement, excitement, and spontaneity.

Our prayers need to include a spontaneous element. We need to introduce throughout the day an openness to speak to Hashem, a spontaneity in our relationship with the Master of the universe.

Sometimes we pick up the phone to call our spouse or parents to find out how they are doing, what is happening at home, or maybe to ask them something. But sometimes, we just call because we have a moment to speak and connect. Prayer is the same way. Sometimes we just want to speak with Hashem and make a connection.

Our relationship with Hashem should also include a paradigm of best friends.

We need to learn to speak openly and truthfully to Hashem. Whether we are praising or complaining, speaking about our dreams or worries, something big or something very small, everything needs to be said. Hashem is always listening and not judging.

If one feels the need to sing, sing; if a need to cry comes up, cry. Whatever comes up is fine.

When we practice this form of spontaneous prayer we should do our best to 'speak' our prayers, and not merely to 'think' of them.

If you cannot find the words to say, say just one word, and say it over and over again. If you feel yourself mute or unable to open your mouth, make that the prayer; ask Hashem to open your mouth to be able to speak.

We should do all this in our own language.

Here is a simple guide to how one would practice this form of spontaneous prayer -assuming one needs a guide and it is not as spontaneous as one would desire:

• Step one would be to become aware of what you are about to do (pray) and in front of Whom you are about to do it (Hashem).

• Start speaking what is in your heart. Speak about everything as it comes up, and do so in your own voice and language.

• If nothing comes to mind, or you feel yourself unable to open up, make your predicament a prayer — ask Hashem to help you open up and speak your heart.

• If a sense of skepticism enters, and you begin thinking to yourself: "What am I doing? Who am I talking to?" Make that too part of the practice. Say:

"I have no idea what I am doing, I would like to feel close to You Hashem, but I do not even know what this means."

• If you keep on saying the same thing over and over again, that is ok too. You cannot bore G-d.

PRAY FOR ANYTHING:

When you pray "like a child" it is simple and pure, nothing is too big and nothing is too small.

We need to pray for clarity, wisdom, and health, but also, if we lost our keys we need to pray, connect, and trust in Hashem so that we find our keys.

Nothing is too big, and nothing is too small. If a person only prays when someone is sick, but does not pray when his toe hurts, or when he misplaces his keys, it shows that he does not truly believe in the power of prayer and that his prayers are mere knee jerk reactions or acts of desperation.

Once after the Amidah the students of Reb Pinchas of Karitz heard him say in Yiddish: "Master of the Universe, help us, that our house maid return to our home." His students thought for sure that this was some deep mystical prayer, maybe for the inner cleaner of his soul to return to his inner home. So they asked him what he means? "Simply", he said, "yesterday our maid left our home. She was upset and she left. I am asking Hashem that she have a change of heart and come back to work for us. Because who can I ask, if not from my Father in Heaven."

Just as we need to ask for our spiritual needs every single day, as every day brings new challenges, the same is true with our physical needs. According to Reb Bunim, if a person says to himself: "I have a good paying job, I do not really need to pray for my livelihood today", this is proof that his request for spiritual needs is not sincere. We need to have total trust in Hashem and be thankful for every single blessing in our lives, taking nothing for granted.

The Hebrew word for 'livelihood', *Parnasah*, and the Hebrew word for 'soul', *Neshamah*, have the same numerical value of 395. These two fundamental concepts are linked. If we only pray for Neshamah issues but not for Parnasah because we think that perhaps with regards to livelihood and financial stability we actually have some measure of control and we are our own masters, this demonstrates that we lack in our soul department, our spiritual development is not mature. We need to have total trust in Hashem with regards to all of life, including our spiritual, emotional and physical wellbeing.

There is a child-like quality when we pray with such simplicity. Then every situation of our life becomes an opportunity for us to connect with Hashem and reach out in prayer.

No Doubt:

What's more, the value of a child's prayer is that it is a prayer with little or no *Safek* / doubt. In this way, a child is like a Tzadik — unquestioningly confident in their faith that prayers are heard.

Before we begin to pray, we can and should take the time to explore and question: "What is prayer? Why should we pray? How does prayer work? Who am I praying to? Does not G-d already know?" But once a person is in the process of praying they are advised to let go of all their questions — all the 'whats', 'whys' and 'hows' of prayer.

It takes a level of distance, objectivity, and detachment to analyze the dynamics of prayer. But once we are subjectively involved in prayer, there is no longer any room for questions. To be sure, questions need to be asked. We need to understand what we are getting into. But once we begin, we need to let go of the questions. And on a deeper level, the questions actually disappear the more we get into it.

As in any relationship, before you enter into it you should ask the appropriate questions: "Am I ready to be in a relationship? Is this the right person? How is this relationship going to work?" But once you are deeply involved in the intimacy of the relationship there should no longer be any doubt — so long as the relationship is healthy and happy, of course. You need to be present with certainty and conviction in the root of the relationship in order to allow it to flower and flourish. You cannot continually analyze the love you are feeling, because when you do so you are robbing yourself from feeling that love.

Prayer works the same way. All the preliminary aspects of the practice, the questions and uncertainties, should be taken care of before the actual praying of the prayer. During this stage of doubt and wrestling, Hashem is still an object, an abstract idea to be contemplated, an external entity, an 'it'. But once the process of prayer ensues there is no more room for discussions, doubts or skepticism. Hashem becomes the subject, the intimate, the confidant, a Living Presence.

INTERNAL DIALOGUE
TO QUIET THE INNER SKEPTIC:

If, for some reason, doubt reenters your consciousness as you are praying, you may want to pause for a moment and have an internal conversation with yourself, which could go something like this: "Right now I am in the middle or praying. You, the voice of doubt and skepticism, have a place in my life, and a very important place to be sure, as you guard against naivety and gullibility, but please not now. Right now, I want to call forth my inner voice of clarity to be present and articulate. I want to speak openly and honestly with Hashem from my deepest self. I want to pray with confidence and conviction."

In the place of pushing away the doubt, you are able to acknowledge that it too has a time and place, just not right now. For as mentioned earlier, "prayer is a time of battle", and the time of battle is no time for philosophical doubt or existential uncertainty. It is a time for confidence and decisive action.

EXPERIENCING CERTAINTY WITHIN PRAYER:

In any long-term and loving relationship the rationalization of emotion can help you get to a certain point of commitment and identification. But ultimately, mere mental ratifications cannot provide the unwavering support and guiding light necessary for the mysterious journey through the labyrinth of love. Once you begin to rationalize feelings or passions they become statistical and stale.

Similarly, we need to enter passionately into prayer in order to enter the 'irrational', emotional, and intuitive side of the relationship. We need to be able to access the spontaneous, the potential, the poetic. Try to forget, for a moment, how the prayers are supposed to work and just pray. Express yourself, become a lover of the Infinite One. And as a lover deeply in love, move out of the incessant questioning of the skeptic-mind. Music, like prayer, cannot be fully explained from a purely mental or rational perspective, and in fact, it should not be — to do so takes away from the immediacy of the aesthetic experience. We need to enter into our prayers in a similar fashion.

Through the act of prayer we attempt to move from a place of question and doubt to a place of certainty and faith. There are times that we may feel the need to live within the place of questioning, and there is plenty of room for that. In prayer however, we need to live in the place of the answer. The answer is the certainty.

Before we say the Amidah prayer, which is the peak of the prayers, we declare loudly such an 'answer', and the answer is: *Hashem Echad* / G-d is One. According to our sages, the declaration of the Shema was originally said as a response, an answer, to a question. The story goes that while Yaakov was on his deathbed, he began to question his children's commitment to their spiritual way of life — he questioned their faith. They responded with the very words that have become the primary declaration of our faith, the Shema: *"Shema Yisrael, Hashem Elokeinu, Hashem Echad /* "Listen Yisrael (Yaakov), the Most High is our G-d, G-d is One!"

The Shema is the experiential answer to the most existential question. The Shema is the preeminent declaration of simple faith in perfect unity. And, being as it is a certainty, we need to make sure that when we say the word, Shema, we pronounce it precisely as Shma, and not as, She-ma. *Shma* is listen. *She-ma* means 'maybe', or perhaps. We need to imbue our declaration of the Shema with a degree of conviction and understanding.

And all the more so, during our prayers in general, we should attempt to pray from a place of deep certainty and faith. Be confident that Hashem hears your prayers.

For not only are we instructed to pray from a place of certainty and simple faith, as does a Tzadik, but the very act of prayer itself catapults us into such a state, the station of a Tzadik. *Tzedek L'fanav Yehalech*

/ "righteousness walks in front of him". This, says the Gemarah, "refers to prayer" *(Berachos, 14a)*. Rashi comments on this passage by saying that, *Matzdiko L'Bora* / "one becomes righteous in front of his Creator". This implies that through prayer, as we are standing in front of our Creator, we become wholly righteous. We become like a Tzadik in the presence of Hashem.

Through prayer, as explained earlier, we create a unity between the *Shechinah* / the Immanent aspect of Hashem, and *Kudsha B'rich Hu* / the Transcendent aspect of Hashem, between lack and perfection. The Zohar refers to the level of the Shechinah, which is currently in a state of exile, as a level of, *Ulai* / Maybe *(Tikunie Zohar, Tikun 69)*. When we enter into deep prayer, a place of Yichud, we move from a place of uncertainty and doubt, from the place of 'maybe', into a place of clarity, a place of certainty and faith.

In life there is ample room for doubt and questioning. There is even the concept of 'holy doubt' on the level of *Keser* / crown, which is a doubt wherein 'everything is possible'. This is a mind-state in which a person is open to the existential experience of miraculous surprise inherent in a place of infinite potential. Prayer is a place of certainty and clarity, wherein the 'doubt' which may be experienced is holy and opens one up to infinite possibility.

As we stand up to recite the final passages of Pesukei D'Zimrah before the blessings of the Shema, we say, *VaYevarech David Es Hashem* / "And Hashem blessed Dovid..." The first letters of each of these four words are: *Vav, Dalet, Aleph, Yud*. When combined in order, this spells the word, *Vadai* / Certain. As we move from the Second Rung of the Morning Prayers into the Third Rung, from the place of praise and emotive exuberance into the clarified mental-state of certainty as represented by the Shema, we move into a place of crystallized clarity and simple faith devoid of all negative, crippling doubt.

No Worries:

A healthy child in a healthy environment enjoys, for the most part, a worry free existence. To pray like a child is to rid oneself of worry, at least for the time one is praying. During the peak of prayer we are able to enter a Shabbos-like existence, a place of peace and serenity, a place of perfection.

The initial recitations said during the first rung of prayer, where we speak of the various offerings that were consumed on the Altar of the Holy Temple, are translated metaphorically and understood inwardly as representing the offering up and expiration of all of our worries, whether for *Parnasa* / making a living, *Refuah* / health or *Hatzlacha* / success in any other matter of our life *(Likutei Torah, Hazinu, 78d)*. This is not to imply that we stop doing, trying, or working hard — Heaven forbid — but rather that we continue our 'doing' with the elimination of any crippling worry or incessant anxiety.

In prayer we are able to access new perspectives of limitless abundance and thereby do away with our worries for a rejuvenating moment of peace and security. We do not need to sacrifice any longer, rather we are the sacrifice, offering up and surrendering our worries, insolence, and self-centeredness.

We may continue to pray for livelihood, for health, wisdom, or success but we do so without any of the worry or anxiety so characteristic of our day-to-day striving. There is a freedom in this type of prayer. We become responsible adults with a child-like quality. We are, in the moment of our prayer, like a child with no worries, free and open to new possibilities, not rigidly attached to a particular set narrative. And yet, just because we have less worry and more faith, does not mean that we are oblivious to the pressing needs of livelihood, health, or success. We pray for the concerns of the content of adulthood within the context of a worry-free childhood.

2]

Praying with
Joy, Love, Fear & Awe

OUR SAGES TEACH THAT IT IS ESSENTIAL THAT
WE PRAY WITH JOY. There is tremendous harm that
comes about when a person prays from a place of depression. Furthermore, says the AriZal, when someone prays from a place of *Etzev* / depression, they will
not be able to receive the Light and flow that becomes
revealed to them during prayer.

In the Torah, and throughout the liturgy, the Children of Israel are referred to as both the "servants of Hashem", as well as the "children of Hashem". Servants serve their master out of fear, while a child's relationship with his parents is founded on love. On the surface, either approach works. But on a deeper level, to serve Hashem in love without the external, surface level of fear is the higher and holier path. Fear is a condition of restriction and smallness. Love, by contrast, functions in a place of openness and full expression. Either way, we should always serve Hashem from a place of pure joy. Whether we are in the place of discharging an obligation or offering up a devotional gift of energy and awareness, we must always serve Hashem with joy.

The difference between praying with depression or praying with joy, says the Magid of Mezritch, can be appreciated in the analogy of one who comes before a king in tears, or one who comes before a king in song. The former approaches the king and pleads with bitter sobs for help and assistance. The king, who cannot bear to see this person suffer, may in fact grant this person's request out of a sense of pity. Imagine now one who approaches the king carrying a beautiful instrument playing soothing and uplifting music for the king. The king is then aroused with joy and grants whatever is requested of him with a sense of openness and pleasure. In this way, an abundance of kindness flows from the king.

Joy, desire and intimacy are some of the necessary ingredients in the creation of a new life. Similarly, for our prayers to produce fruit and manifest in a tangible way, our prayers must be evocative expressions of our joy, desire and feelings of closeness and vulnerability. A prayer is more readily accepted and speedily answered when said or sung in joy.

Of course, prayer is a serious and internal work. In fact, as mentioned earlier, it is called *Avodah* / labor. Prayer demands full disclosure and honesty, yet seriousness does not necessarily have to translate as being sad or depressed. On the contrary, it is "joy that breaks all barriers". When we enter prayer with joy and confidence we are reinforcing our intrinsic closeness with Hashem, as we are openly communicating with and cleaving to Hashem. Our manifest joy demonstrates our sense of being and feeling close.

CLOSENESS AND TREPIDATION:
SENSING THE MYSTERY
& FEELING FAMILIAR:

The Shulchan Aruch rules that prayers must be said "From a Place of Joy". They should also be said from a place of deep awe and humility.

Ahavah / love, and *Yirah* / fear - and on a higher-level - awe, are the two wings of prayer. Love and awe are the wings, says the Zohar, upon which our spirit takes flight. One without the other — love without awe or awe without love — no matter how profound or powerful, does not allow our souls and prayers to soar upwards.

If we only have the light of love with no vessel of fear/awe — meaning no reverence or sense of receiving and opening to the Above— then there is an abundance of inspiration and desire, but such ungrounded inspiration becomes like wasted seed, as there is no *Mekabel* / receiver or vessel, to collect and contain the blessings that the inspiration stimulated.

In prayer we seek to express our *Ahavah* / love, and the closeness we feel to Hashem, as well as our *Yirah*, / fear/awe, and trepidation in approaching the Infinite One. Ordinarily, the sense of closeness and the sense of trepidation arise in different moments during prayer. At the onset of prayer a person may feel overwhelmed in what they are about to undertake and experience — standing in the Presence of the Infinite One. Initially a person may feel his own lowliness, feeling far and distant. To counter these feelings a person may sing tunes of longing, of yearning, and of wanting to come close. But as one ascends the ladder of prayer, going deeper and higher, he begins to feel closer and closer. This generates, circulates and reciprocates more love and joy.

The movement of psycho-spiritual maturation generally travels along the trajectory from Yirah to Ahavah. But in a healthy spiritual process it will also return from Ahavah back to a higher form of Yirah, and then from Yirah back to Ahavah, ad infinitum. This is the spiral nature of spiritual development. The path is not purely linear, which would imply that we are moving ever-forward in a straight line of progression; nor is it only cyclical, which would mean that we keep coming back to the same place in the same way over and over again. But the nature of creation seems to organize itself in a series of spiral dynamics. We continue to come back to the same root of reality and identity, but on a different, deeper level and perspective.

To illustrate this process, we need go no further than the standard six-word blessing formula. The structure of a traditional blessing is that we begin with *Baruch Ata* / Blessed (or Source of blessing) are You, which is in the second person, very direct — "You!" And then we continue, "Hashem". We switch to the third person; this is more general, less intimate. We start by feeling close and intimate, as if being cradled by Hashem. When we say "You", we mean literally You, as if we are speaking to a close relative, a loved one, or a dear friend. Hashem, in our prayers, becomes a You — a subject — not an abstract object or idea, but a living presence in our life — a real You, who we feel close to and intimate with.

But then a deeper, higher awareness sets in and we begin to feel distant. A dreadful overwhelming sense of the Holy Transcendent Other sets in and we feel so far, so small, so alienated, so distant, and with the little strength we have left we say, "Hashem". And from this state of awe, suddenly a breakthrough occurs and once again we feel close, embraced, cradled and loved, and we say, "Elokeinu, our G-d". Then a deeper re-alization sets in and we once again feel distant. This vacillation continues throughout the process of pray-ing until we reach the Throne of Unity, where both feelings exist simultaneously as one.

This movement of feeling first close and then dis-tant, love and then reverence, vacillates continuously throughout the process of prayer. We are intermit-tently able to sense the immensity of the Holy Other, being overwhelmed by the mystery and majesty of the Creator and all of creation; and then we find ourselves feeling really close to and familiar with Hashem, as if we are being held in a Divine Embrace.

We are perpetually moving into and out of both of these feelings.

As a reflection of these oscillating feelings, between feeling embraced and overwhelmed, close and distant, our physical bodies respond in kind. At times during the prayers we sway from right to left, and at times, almost involuntarily, we sway from front to back. Moving from front to back is a movement of reverence — awe, bowing the head, submission. Moving from right to left, side to side, is similar to an act of showing affection and love as we feel ourselves cradled by Hashem.

The Union of Contrasting Emotions:

On a deeper level of unity within, these two feeling arise at the same time, at once feeling love and closeness with Hashem, while concurrently feeling awe, and perhaps even a fear and trepidation, while approaching the Mystery. In worldly matters, which exist in a place of duality, love is the antithesis of fear. When there is a full expression of Ahavah there is no Yirah, and when there is a strong sense of Yirah there is no Ahavah. When a person is, however, connected to Hashem, the Source, the Oneness, as the Sifri tells us, that person may, in the course of their Divine service, experience both love and awe simultaneously.

Yirah and Ahavah are each spelled with four letters. When one places the word Yirah above the word Ahavah, the word Yirah can be spelled with the first two letters of Yirah and final two letters of Ahavah, and Ahavah can be spelled with the final two letters of Yirah and the final two letters of Ahavah:
Yir-ah
Ahav-ah

On the deepest level, Yirah and Ahavah are One. This unity is paradoxical and non-rational, yet in the deepest mystical experience of Unity this anomaly is reality.

Ahavah is immanence, *Yirah* is transcendence. On the one hand we sense Hashem as beyond, and yet we also recognize that Hashem is also deep within. Hashem is both Infinite and Incomprehensible, and yet Hashem is also immediate and more real than observable reality. In fact, both immanence and transcendence are definitions and manifestations, and Hashem is expressed in all manifestations. Every-thing and no-thing are all within Hashem.

OPENING UP TO LOVE:

As mentioned, love and awe are the wings that carry us up. But how does one arouse love? True, there is an innate love we may feel towards our Creator, much like the natural love children have for their parents. But many times such a love is latent, dormant and obscured by all the other 'loves' of our lives — be they money, power, success, status or fame. So how do we reveal true love? How do we open up to love?

One way is through contemplation and meditation. Meditating on our lives and on all the gifts in our lives can arouse this love. As can a deep contemplation on the nature of *Hashem Echad* / the 'Unity of Hashem'. These two meditations can lead one to the state of *V'Ahavta* / "You shall (or will) love". In fact this is the progression that we follow in the liturgy. After saying the Shema, declaring the Unity of Hashem, we go directly into the V'Ahavta, the recitations that focus on our experience and expression of love for Hashem.

There is also another dimension of our experience that we can direct our contemplative awareness towards in order to reach a state of manifest love for Hashem, and that is through meditating on the dynamics of human love. We meditate on our finite love that has form, is exclusive and conditional, and from that place, through the art of analogy, we attain a pure, boundless love for the Creator and by extension all of creation — a love that is formless, infinite and all-inclusive.

The idea is that if we contemplate our love for others, we will arouse our love for and gratitude to the ultimate Other that is really One — Hashem. The smaller love allows for the greater love to blossom. It shows us the way, and even prepares us for a love encounter with the Infinite.

There is a Chassidic teaching that if you want to arouse your love for Hashem, think about the things in your life that you love, whether your spouse, parents, or children, and allow your love to expand from there.

When people open themselves up to a love that has form, that is finite and exclusive, the deeper they enter into the actual feelings that are generated by that love — not focusing on the actual object of the love, but the sensations and experience of it, stripping the sensation from the narrative— the more they can evolve from that particular expression of love to the pure emotion of love, a love that is formless, infinite and all inclusive. At first there is a directed love towards this or that person, and then there is just the sensation of love, unrelated to a narrative or subject, pure, boundless love.

A story is told by Rabbi Yitzchak of Acco about a princess who was once passing through a town. When a simple farm boy saw her, he cried out, "If only I could be with you". Hearing him, the princes responded harshly, "only in the graveyard could we possibly be together". Being a simple hearted boy he thought that she meant that he should go to the cemetery and wait for her to come to him. And so he went to the cemetery and waited. Nightfall came and she did not show up. But he trusted her, and he felt that he loved her, He waited and waited. Day by day his love and longing grew stronger and stronger, but his memory of the image of the princess slowly faded, and all he was left with was a pure love, unattached to any image or identity. By becoming open to this pure formless love, his love morphed into a love for the truly Formless Infinity, a love for the Creator and all of creation, and he became a great Tzadik.

LOVE FOR ANOTHER:

We all need to open ourselves up to loving others. This is true because our love for the Creator is expressed through our love for other human beings —

in that we are loving those whom our Lover loves —
and because our finite love for another opens us up to
the infinite love. On a deeper level, it is only by loving
and unifying ourselves with all of creation that we can
truly reveal our intrinsic connection with the deepest/
highest level of reality, *Achdus Hashem* / the unity of
Hashem.

The AriZal tells us that before praying we should verbally declare, "I hereby accept upon myself, the Mitzvah of the Torah, to love my fellow as myself". When
we can turn around in prayer and feel only love for the
person standing or sitting next to us, than we are in
essence, loving what Hashem loves.

The Iraqi scholar and Kabbalist, the Ben Ish Chai
brings down a custom that before praying the con-
gregants should turn around to the people standing
next to or behind them and gesture to them with their
hands, as if asking permission to begin praying, and
thus showing brotherhood, consideration and love towards each other.

In fact, one of the reasons peoples prayers are not answered is because they close their eyes and ears to the
cries of the needy. For as the verse says, "One who
shuts his ear to the cry of the poor, he too will call out
and not be answered" *(Mishlei, 21:13)*. So as we begin

praying, and throughout the prayers, it is extremely important to keep our hearts open to the compassion for and love of others.

Our sages tell us that if, "someone prays for the fulfillment of the needs of another and he also needs the exact same thing, he will be answered first" *(Baba Kamah, 92a)*. The simple meaning is straightforward: A person's prayers are answered when they can step aside and ask for the very thing that they need most, for the sake of another. But there is an even deeper interpretation: "If someone prays for another, and he needs the same thing" — i.e. he prays for the needs of others as if they were his own needs, or he feels another's pain or loss as if it were his own pain or loss — that person's prayers will surely be answered, both for the person whom they are praying on behalf of, as well as their own.

Parenthetically, this is something to keep in mind: If while in prayer, as you are trying to keep your heart open to the compassionate love for others and you find yourself being annoyed by the person sitting right next to you — maybe the person is speaking or they are making noise, their cell phone is ringing, they are sleeping, or they are just generally disturbing and distracting you from your focus in prayer — remember, everything in life is a messenger. The first thing to be aware of is that you do not become judgmental and self-righteous. The second step is to view that person as a messenger from Hashem sent to challenge your capacity to love unconditionally and concentrate completely. Though this person is generating a commotion from a place of their own free will, ultimately Hashem has paired this person with you in order to give you the opportunity to grow, to become more compassionate and deeply focused. The noise is only there to ensure that you are aroused to pray with even greater devotion and Kavanah until you will hear, but not be disturbed by, the other.

"In the Name of All of Israel":

As explained earlier, when we pray for our individual needs we should always enlarge our prayers to include all of those who are also in need. Our prayers should not only be about our individual selves. If we truly pray "in the name of all of Israel", then our prayers are answered more swiftly.

On a deeper level, the extension and expansion of our prayers is not simply so that our prayers will be "answered", but is rather so that our prayers are more intense and meaningful, with a greater measure of Deveikus. Reb Mich'ael of Zlotshov, would say before each prayer, "I hereby connect myself with All of Israel, whether greater than myself or lower. The benefit of binding myself with those who are greater is that through them my thoughts in prayer will be elevated. And the benefit of connecting myself with those of a lesser stature is that through my prayers they too will be elevated".

SENSE OF WONDER:

Besides love and fear there is also a dimension of prayer that allows us to be open to the possibility of wonder. Prayer can be a portal through which we pass on our way to the experience of radical amazement, standing in awe of the miraculous and intricate workings of creation and, by extension, of the Creator — the ultimate mystery that animates all of creation.

The recitations during prayers that continually direct our awareness to the renewal of creation each and every day seek to inspire a deep and detailed contemplation of the vastness of the cosmos and, in turn, generate the existential state of wonder. As creation is being continuously created anew each and every day, we also need to relive this truth in our own consciousness. In this way our sense of wonder shall never cease. In prayer, at least in the initial stages, there is a tremendous sense of being awestruck, feeling in a deep and tangible way the immanent presence of the Holy Other, and thus being overwhelmed by the mystery and majesty of the Creator and creation. One should feel blessed to bask in this state of radical amazement.

Isaiah the prophet implores, *Se'u Marom Aineichem /* Lift up your eyes on high and see who has created these" *(Yeshayahu, 40:26)*. Prayer is a practice through which we can lift up our eyes and be overwhelmed by the awesomeness of creation, and thus of the Creator. The Zohar *(Tikunei Zohar, Tikkun 50:86a)* takes these three Hebrew words, *Se'u Marom Aineichem /* "Lift up your eyes", and uses the first letters of each word to form an acronym for *Shachris /* the morning prayers, *Mincha /* the afternoon prayers, and *Arvis /* the evening Prayers. We are given the gift of prayer three times a day — morning, afternoon and evening — in order that we should take a few moments of every day and stand in contemplation, taking account of our lives and sensing the vast and mysterious wonder of creation and of the Creator.

LIVING WITH WONDER:

Life is fully lived when every moment is filled with excitement and wonder. When we are younger, life seems longer and fuller — a year of childhood seems much longer than a year in our adult life. This is because as children, we are living with a strong sense of wonder. We are experiencing so many more novel experiences. And as younger people we are so impressionable, every new experience is exciting and every newly discovered idea is stimulating. When we grow older, however, life seems more flat, stale, and habitual. Every day seems like the other and nothing is very memorable, and yet it does not have to be this way.

There are people who are considered dead even while they are still alive and walking about, says the Medrash. They are like the dead — showing no signs of movement, or more appropriately, of being moved — because, "they see the sun rising and they do not say the blessing "who creates light". They see the sun setting and do not bless "who causes the evening to become dark". They eat and drink and do not recite a blessing "that everything has come into existence through Your word". By contrast there are those who are fully alive, the Tzadikim, because for them, every moment they are alive is another opportunity for thanks and praise and they are continuously making blessings.

Making a blessing, taking a few moments to pause, to acknowledge and appreciate the experience, and to be thankful, allows us to continually live from a place of wonder and amazement. Without these moments of pause, reflection, appreciation and gratefulness we become indifferent, stoic to the mystery and wonders of life. Prayer and the continuous recitations of blessings throughout the entire day ensures that we remain alive and attuned to the miraculous unfolding of this vast and wonder-filled creation.

Tears & Pleasure:

There is a certain sense of *Ta'anug* / deep delight, and spiritual pleasure when a person is truly in awe. The Maggid of Mezritch teaches that when, for example, a person thinks about and meditates on how with each exhale he is returning his life force to the Source of Life, initially a person may experience a sense of trepidation and fear of losing their ego, of expiring, of being empty of that which sustains them — the breath. But then the fear brings the person to a sense of awe and a feeling of being overwhelmed by the awesome Presence of the Creator and the vastness of creation. Eventually the awe slips into a pure and heightened state of spiritual delight, the beatific dissolving of the small 'i' into the Ultimate I of *Anochi Hashem* / I am Hashem.

Often, the experience of being overwhelmed by a deep sense of Ta'anug manifests in the body in the form of tears. Not tears of sorrow or of longing, or even of joy, but rather tears of pure delight and spiritual ecstasy. If when in the midst of praying, whether formal or informal personal prayers, you involuntarily let out a cry with tears streaming down your face, but you are uncertain as to why — know that this is an indication, a sign, that your prayers have been accepted on High.

BEYOND FEELINGS, ENTERING THE TREE OF LIFE:

Love and awe are feelings. Feelings suggest separation, as a feeling either draws us closer — as in love — or repulses us, as in fear. Even awe and wonder, at least the way they are normally experienced, are still emotions. Unity is beyond emotions. Love and awe are the wings that allow us to rise upwards, but once a person attains a deeper measure of unity and Deveikus to Hashem there is no longer any movement. This manifests in a person when they have reached a point where they are entertaining love and awe simultaneously, or they have indeed transcended the sensations of feeling all together. Once you are One, in unity there is no longer any movement or feelings as we normally know them.

After Adam and Eve ate from the tree of knowledge and duality, they were banished from the Garden of Eden, which is the paradigm of unity. It says in the verse that, "Hashem stationed the *Keruvim* with their fiery spinning swords to the east of the garden of Eden, to guard the way to the tree of life" *(Bereishis 3:22-24)*. Accordingly, the function of the *Keruvim* / Cherubim, is to guard the tree of life. The Keruvim are representative of many ideas. One Kabbalistic interpretation is that they represent "love and awe". It is indeed love and awe that carry us to the gates of Eden, but to pass through those gates and attain a measure of unity, these too have to be surrendered and transcended.

Throughout prayer there may be moments where you feel overwhelmed with love, and then right afterwards move into a state of awe. And yet at other moments you may enter into a suspended and motionless experience of Deveikus. Even though you find it difficult to hold onto these emotions, or these states of motionlessness, do not despair. Prayer is called *Avodah* / labor, work. Prayer is a time of battle. To attain any measure of permanence is a struggle that demands a lot of time, effort and perseverance. Most people pray with peaks and valleys — moments of joy and love, and moments of distance and separation, as well as moments when there are no feelings what so ever.

These are the ups and downs of prayer and spiritual practice. But we need not despair. Breakthroughs occur, so long as we are making the effort and continuously moving forward.

3]

Yesh & Ayin:
Attachment and Non-attachment-demanding and surrendering

Two Perspectives:
Everything is Good -
Sometimes it does Not Appear Good:

Let us revisit a story mentioned earlier in the text:

> *Once the Baal Shem Tov told his students they should*
> *pray for a certain decree to be nullified. Whereupon his*
> *student, Reb Zeev Kitzes, said, "Hashem is certainly*
> *a merciful Father in heaven and certainly whatever*

Hashem does is done for our own good." The Baal Shem Tov responded, "It is fortunate that Reb Zeev was not around during the times of the Purim story, for certainly he would have said the same about the decree of Haman."

True, "everything the Merciful One does He does for our good", but it is also equally true that we are embodied in physical form and so, for the most part, we view this world through the prism of the five senses and when something seems wrong on the physical plane, it hurts. And because it hurts we pray for a shift and change of that reality. In truth, we pray not only because it hurts, but even deeper, we pray because that is what Hashem wants us to do when it appears to hurt. That is in fact the good concealed within the pain or misfortune — our prayers and spiritual realignment.

When we see an apparent injustice such as a person's or people's suffering and we pray for a change in the Divine will, we are fulfilling the Creator's desire that we protest injustice. So on the one hand there is a sense of *Bitul* / a total acceptance of Hashem's manifest will as is, and yet we also know that Hashem wants us to be co-creators and to consciously collaborate and influence the process of bringing a new Divine will into being.

Acceptance is not resignation as long as there is still hope that change is a possibility, even if not a probability. There is a delicate balance between these two perspectives. For example, a person who is sick should not just resign themselves to the fact that they are sick. Rather, the approach is that of acceptance, meaning that, "I accept this is the will of the Creator and I am aware of my situation, and yet I am not resigning myself to it, but am taking action by praying for healing, getting rest, eating right and going to visit a doctor." Resigning oneself to reality implies a sense of helplessness in the face a fixed outcome. Acceptance of reality implies an acknowledgment and even appreciation of the way things are, while still maintaining that a change of circumstance is always possible.

ALL PRAYERS ARE ANSWERED:

It is through prayer that we are able to enter into a more spiritually evolved existential state of *Ayin* / a no-thing-ness. On the Ayin level of prayer our prayers are always answered. The 'answer' is reflected in whatever the reality actually is, as there is a full acceptance of 'what is' as being the perfect will of Hashem.

From a place of Ayin the ultimate goal of prayer is the act of praying itself, not the success of our petitions being granted, though that too can occur. Perhaps this is one of the greatest obstacles in the path of prayer. We tend to be more desirous of or satisfied by end results than we are with the means that get us there. We judge and value people by what they have achieved, but not by how hard they worked at getting it. Success is measured by what one actually has, not on honest effort. If we surrender this mode of thinking and pray from a place of Ayin we will find our prayers more meaningful, and indeed more 'answered'. Even though at times on the level of Yesh there is no alteration of the facts on the physical plane and it seems as if nothing has really changed but our perception, it is our perception that really makes all the difference, certainly as far as our role in our relationship to the circumstances of life.

From this perspective, the goal of prayer is prayer itself. R. Yehudah Ha'Levi writes that for the *Chasid* / the pious, all hours of the day are pathways leading to the hour of prayer, and for this the Chasid longingly and lovingly awaits.

Through praying we leave the paradigm of *Yesh* / ego-oriented and physical existence, where perception is finite and limited, pixilated and fragmented — and enter into the Infinite perspective of *Ayin*, where everything is limitless, whole and complete. Normally we see fragmentation, we see the immediate; something looks good, because its good right now, or something looks bad, because it is bad right now. Through prayer we 'cut-away the weeds', the underbrush, and are able to sense the bigger picture, the Infinite Unity of it all. Again, perhaps nothing external actually changes, but we change, and in that place of Ayin and surrender creation is revealed to us as "perfect".

THE NEED TO BE HEARD:

Prayer is an essential, existential need of the human being. It is, in a way, the definition of what it means to be human. Human beings stand erect with the ability, and thus the innate desire, to look upwards and connect with the Creator of the universe. This is done primarily through prayer. Prayer comes naturally to the human, erupting spontaneously and developing systematically throughout all of history.

The human is called a speaking being — as opposed to the still beings, such as rocks and minerals, the sprouting beings, such as plants and all things that grow, and the living beings, such as the animals and all beings that roam and swim and fly and crawl. Prayer seems to be an instinctual inheritance of the human race, along the same survival oriented lines of genetic transmission as eating, bathing and clothing our-selves. We have the capacity to enter into relationship, to communicate, to look upwards and inwards, be-yond ourselves, and so we do.

The very fact that we have needs to be fulfilled, such as what and how we are going to eat and survive, is in itself a blessing, a gift from the Creator. Because the need forces us to fulfill an even deeper need — the need to pray, to seek, to ask, to communicate, to con-nect with that which is beyond and deep within us.

"Upon your belly you shall go and dust you shall eat all the days of your life" *(Bereishis, 3:14)*. This is the 'curse' of the primordial snake as depicted in the beginning of the Torah. The Kotzker Rebbe asks: Is this in fact a curse? If a person would have his food ready for him at all times it would seem to be a blessing. But the Kotzker flips this perspective on its head and states that this is the greatest curse possible: To have all your needs in front of you without desire or yearning to receive them. The longing awakens the dormant abil-ity, and thus the prayer, to look up to the Heavens in praise and petition in order to receive in humble service. This is one of the greatest blessings we have in life.

On one level, when we pray we are simply asking

Hashem to listen to us. Not to grant us health, wealth, or wisdom (of course these too) — but just listen to us. "G-d, we need to know that You are listening". We want to sense that You are aware of us and that You care.

What we really want, the deeper desire within all of our desires, is to be "heard"; as in, "to be heard as one good friend listens to the other "*(Yerushalmi Berachos, 9:1).*

Think of this in terms of a relationship. For example: Two people are in a relationship and one comes home late one night, turns to the other and says, "I had such a hard day at work, a co-worker was nasty to me". And the other person immediately responds, "You should stay away from that person". This is the wrong reaction. What their partner wanted was not a resolution to their problem, but just that they should listen.

Most times what we want in a relationship is for the other person to be a good listener and accept what we are saying and acknowledge how we feel. We are often not looking for resolutions, or ways to fix something, as much as we are seeking a sensitive and sympathetic ear.

This is what we are telling Hashem when we pray. Deep down, all we want is to know that You are listening to our hopes, dreams, sorrows and afflictions. We want to know that You are with us on our path, through all the peaks and valleys.

Think again in terms of a relationship. For instance, a relationship is not doing too well and in the course of a heated argument one spouse tells the other: "You know, you did not take out the garbage", or, "you did not clean up after yourself", or "you are always late". The other person then fixes the problems, takes out the garbage, cleans up, starts showing up on time, and yet, the relationship is still not repaired. Why? Because the root problem was not this issue or that issue, but that the other spouse is not truly listening to what is really bothering the other.

What we really want from You Hashem is to know that You are listening to our problems.

BREAD OF SHAME:

We begin our prayers from a place of *Yesh*, a strong sense of I. In the Yesh reality we want to feel that Hashem hears our sorrows and is with us in our pain. Slowly we move from Yesh into a more Ayin-like space. Ayin is not the place where we are being "heard", but is much deeper. From the perspective of

Ayin, we are, as much as possible, unified with Hashem — the speaker and listener are undifferentiated.

For the most part, we need to aspire to enter into and exist within both Yesh and Ayin. Going into and out of Ayin and Yesh means that we need to entertain both these notions concurrently. On the one hand we have humility and surrender. But on the other hand, we realize that it is our prerogative and right, a G-d given right no less, to pray and ask for alteration and change within our reality.

Part of the order of creation is that the creation below receives from Above through their own initiative and prayer. According to the arousal below is the arousal Above. Since the Creator desires our goodness at all times there is a Mitzvah for us to pray every day, and through our prayers to draw down an abundance of success and blessing into our lives. But this does not suggest a relinquishment of our responsibility to do in addition to pray for that which we need or desire in our lives.

The dynamics of creation is such that the Creator does not immediately give us everything we need. The reason for this is because the Creator wants us to be more than passive recipients of blessing, but rather active partners in a co-creative relationship. Hashem, the Ultimate Source of goodness, wants us to receive the greatest of all possible goodness. And what is the "greatest of all possible goodness"? When we are able to receive that which we have worked for, that which we have earned. When we are able to do this, we become, in a way, like the Creator. Instead of just 'receiving' sustenance and blessing from the Creator, we become active 'creators', and what we receive is dependent on what we create. Because of this, when we receive blessing or bounty that we did not work for, it is referred to as the "bread of shame". Receiving in such a way taints our appreciation for such bounty and blessing.

In life this means that when we pray for what we want, we are not seeking to eliminate the necessary hard work we must do on our part in the physical world. Rather, prayer is a compliment to all the work we do. And as we do, we pray for the clarity and strength to do more and better. In this way, we are not mere passive receivers, but rather active partners in Creation. We are then able to receive that which was prepared to be given to us in the first place, but now by way, in part, of our own efforts as co-creators.

By asking for and actively pursuing and participating in receiving blessings we are not only fulfilling our deepest truth, but because of that, Hashem loves us even more. According to the Medrash: The more we ask and pray, the more Hashem loves us *(Tehilim, 4:3)*. Unlike with human interaction, where the more a person asks another for a favor, the less likely the favor is to be granted, and slowly the person may even become annoyed with the other. Not so with regards to our relationship with Hashem. On the contrary, the more we ask, the more love is shown. The love increases the more we ask, as the act of prayer itself is an act of love on our part, which arouses a greater love from Above. And even deeper, the more we are creators of our own reality, the closer we are to the Creator.

HASHEM WANTS TO GIVE US:

"More than the calf desires to be nursed, the cow desires to give milk" *(Pesachim, 112a)*. In a manner of speaking, the Creator's delight in providing for our needs and fulfilling our prayers is greater than our delight in having our prayers answered. Hashem's desire to give is even greater than our desire to receive.

Rabbi Meir Ben Gabbai speaks of the mystical concept of *Avodah L'Tzorech Gavoha* / "Service for the Sake of Above", which plainly means that our actions have an effect in the realms Above. There are many ways how this can be interpreted. One way is that since the Creator is the Source of all goodness and "the nature of the good is to give goodness", when we pray and our prayers are granted the Creator's desire to give goodness is fulfilled.

PRAY WITH CHUTZPA & HUMILITY:

There are two pockets in our trousers. In one pocket, suggested Reb Simcha Bunim we should keep a scrap of paper with the words: "the entire world was created for me alone" *(Sanhedrin, 37a)*; while the second pocket should contain another piece of paper, this one in-scribed with the words: "even the mosquito preceded you in the order of creation" *(Medrash Rabbah, Vayikra, 14:1)*. These two notes represent the requisite balance of Yesh and Ayin consciousness that we must have at our disposal to navigate the perpetual motion of life and our relationship to Hashem.

From the perspective of Ayin, the Unmanifest Source, the world of Yesh, existence, is as no-thing. And so as we enter into Ayin consciousness through our posture of surrender in prayer, we feel that our ego, our Yesh, is to us like nothing, and thus we pray from a place of deep humility. Yet, from the perspective of Yesh, our story of life is very significant and of great importance, in fact it is Hashem who created our Yesh and thus it too has tremendous value. When we pray from a Yesh perspective we are praying with great confidence.

One of the archetypal narratives of the power of prayer in the Torah is the story of Chanah who was a barren woman and eventually had a child who grew up to become the master prophet Shmuel or Samuel. Our sages explore some of the prayers she uttered in her distress, prayers filled with holy Chutzpa *(Berachos, 31b)*. She said for instance, "Sovereign of the Universe, of all the hosts and legions that You have created in Your world, is it so hard in Your infinite capacity to give me one son?" She also said: "Sovereign of the Universe, if You see to it (that I have a child) — good. If not...I will force You". She turned to the Master of the universe and said: "Sovereign of the Universe, everything that You have created in the woman is there for a purpose — eyes to see, ears to hear...bosom to nourish a suckling..."

This type of prayer echoes the dialogue between Avraham and Hashem when Avraham learned that the city of Sedom was about to be destroyed. Avraham turns to the Creator of the Universe and thunders: "Will You sweep away the righteous with the wicked? Suppose there are fifty righteous within the city... Far be it from You to do such a thing...Shall not the Judge of all the earth deal justly?" These are very harsh and strong words on the part of Avraham. But then right away he says: "Now behold, I have ventured to speak to Hashem, although I am but dust and ashes" *(Bereishis, 18:23-27).*

Notice how Avraham is moving from a place of demand and questioning — "Shall not the Judge of all the earth deal justly" — to a place of total humility and acceptance, saying "though I am but dust and earth". They are both true — surrender and questioning — and true every at moment.

Rashi, the classic commentator on the Torah, tells us *(Ibid, 18:23)* that when Avraham entered into a dialogue with Hashem about Sedom he entered "to speak harsh words, to appease, and for prayer". These three approaches to relational interaction seem to be three divergent paths. The Maharal says that all three of these concepts are different modes within prayer itself. Prayer is sometimes harsh words, where we demand, and sometimes prayer is appeasement, acceptance and surrender.

Ultimately, prayer includes both requesting and surrendering. There are words that are known as contranyms, which is when a word means two opposite things simultaneously. One such word is a word related to prayer. The Hebrew word *Ana*, which means, 'please', as in *Ana Hashem* / please Hashem, can also be translated as 'thank You'. *Ana* can mean both 'please' and 'thank you'. And in fact, prayer is both. Yesh represents the 'please', in the form of a request; and Ayin represents the 'thank you', in the state of surrender. In prayer, both of these states — the please and thank you — are occurring concurrently.

BELIEVE IN THE POWER OF YOUR PRAYERS:

Within the place of Yesh itself, where we feel the need to question, plead and pray for change, there are two modalities. There is a *Tefilas Ani* / a prayer of the poor, which is said by one who has nothing physically and feels completely depleted, empty and lacking any merit. And then there is a person who prays from a place of confidence and demand. This is referred to as a *Tefilas Ashir* / prayer of the rich, which is expressed by the person who feels entitled, deserving, and demands change. What gives us the holy Chutzpa to pray this way? It is definitely not because one feels like he is praying with such Kavanah that his prayers should be answered. But rather this Chutzpa comes from the Torah itself, which gives us and empowers us with the Mitzvah to pray. Using the words of the Torah itself we turn to Hashem and say: "And You have said, I will surely do good with you" *(Bereishis, 32:13).*

There is a delicate balance between these two approaches that needs to be secured, a harmony between self-confidence, the feeling that you matter and are of importance, and a healthy dose of humility that ensures that confidence does not turn into arrogance.

Some people suffer from an inflated sense of self-confidence in their worth and abilities, while even more people suffer from a lack of belief in themselves and their potential.

In the time of the Great Flood, Noach was told in advance to build an Ark and that a flood would occur, and yet he did not pray for his generation to be saved. Unlike Avraham and Moshe, says the Zohar, who did pray for the people of their generation, Noach did not. Why not? Noach, we are told, was a "small believer." Not that he was a "small believer" in G-d and that a great flood will occur, rather he was a "small believer" in his own self. He had little faith in his potential and in the power of his prayers to make a difference, and as such, he did not pray. To pray we need to both believe in ourselves, and believe that our prayers can truly effect change.

Humility is integral to prayer, the feeling of "I am empty, Hashem please fill me". Yet, if you are too humble, our humility may keep us away from prayer.

You may reason: "How can little old 'me' make any difference? Can I really effect change in the world? Can I really stimulate the Divine presence to be more revealed in this world?"

At times we need to feel like a servant pleading with his master, and at times we need to feel like children asking from their parents. There is a time for everything. All and all, when we pray we need to believe in ourselves and believe that our prayers can have a dramatic effect for the good. "Blessings attach themselves to the blessed, but blessings do not attached themselves to the cursed". This speaks to the basic law of attraction. The mere act of feeling blessed and worthy, if not for our actions than for the purity of soul that resides within each and everyone, brings down blessings to our lives and to all those we are praying for.

BELIEVE IN A HEALED WORLD:

We need to believe in the power of our prayers and believe in the possibility that things can be different.

The Torah tells the story of Yoseph being sold into slavery and after many years of being reunited with his brothers and beloved father. At the end of Yaakov's life, Yoseph goes to his father to receive blessings for his children. Yaakov says: "I never Philalti that I would ever see your face again, and Hashem has granted me to even see the face of your children!" *(Bereishis, 48:11)*. What does *Philalti* mean? Rashi interprets Yaakov's statement to imply: "I was so devastated by your absence that I never would have filled my heart to think the thought that I would ever see your face again." As such, the word *L'Hispalel* — which means to pray — from the same root as Philalti, would mean to consciously and mindfully fill our hearts and minds to think thoughts or dream dreams of what we desire to see in this world, a world that is healed and perfected.

To pray means to fill our hearts with the 'impossible' dream. To fill our hearts with prophetic vision, when death will be banished from the face of the earth and Hashem will erase all tears, bringing all humanity back together in absolute peace.

To truly pray is to fill our hearts with a vision of, "A time where there will be no hunger or war, no jealousy or rivalry. For the good will be plentiful and all delicacies available as dust. The entire occupation of the world will be only to know Hashem...and the earth will be filled with the knowledge of the Creator, as the waters cover the sea."

APPENDIX I

Ten Sounds, One Source:
The Vowels and the Sefiros

During the course of the prayers there are various potential Kavanos one may utilize, which stem from a Kabbalistic understanding of the prayers. These intentions are related to the *Ten Sefiros* / the Ten Divine Attributes, through which Divine Unity is expressed and flows into apparent multiplicity.

There are also ten Hebrew Vowels (including silence), which correspond to the Ten Sefiros. When any of these vowels are placed under or next to a letter they create a particular sound/charge for that letter to carry into creation and consciousness. One can then combine these 3 symbolic systems (the Sefiros, the Vowels, and various Kavanos) to animate their prayers and irrigate their awareness during prayer.

There are nine "sounded" vowels, with the tenth being the "silent" vowel, which carries no sound. The four-letter name, Hashem, has no intrinsic vowels. As we are uncertain of how these four letters are pronounced, or even if they are pronounced at all, this name can thus be scanned and read with various vowel combinations depending on the specific Sefira/ Sound one intends to meditate on.

A LIST OF THE VOWELS
AND THEIR CORRELATING SEFIROS:

1. Kametz (aw) ‌ᴛ *Keser, deep desire & primordial will*
2. Patach (ah) — *Chochmah, wisdom and intuition*
3. Tzeirei (ei) •• *Binah, reason and cognition*
4. Segol (eh) •‌• *Chesed, kindness and love*
5. Sh'va (uh) • *Gevurah, strength and boundaries*
6. Cholam (oy) ‌ᴵ *Tiferes, beauty and compassion*
7. Chirik (ee) • *Netzach, victory and perseverance*

8. Kubutz •‌• (U- vowel under the letter)
   Hod, splendor and humility
9. Shuruk ‌ᴵ (U—vowel on top of the letter)
   Yesod, foundation and relationship
10. No vowels (silence)
    Malchus, kingship and receptiveness

THE VOWELS SOUNDS AND THEIR RELATIONSHIP WITH THE SEFIROS:

As mentioned, it is taught that the particular sounds of the vowels arouse and stimulate specific responses within us and within the order of creation.

1] *Kametz is Keser.*

Kametz is *Keser*. *Keser* is the Crown of the Tree of Life. *Kametz* is the 'aw' sound; this is the sound of holding, concealment and self-containment, it is a closed sound. The word *Kametz* actually means 'closed' *(Vayikra, 2:2)*. It is a tight fisted sound, so to speak, a sound that is difficult to come out. The reason for this is because sound is a product of movement and movement suggests a separation from Unity. The *Ein Sof* is One, Unified whole. There is no interior and exterior, higher or lower, there is only One. The Sefiros are the 'finite' screens through which the One is projected into and perceived by the many. This implies separation. Keser is the bridge between the Ein Sof and the lower Sefiros, so it holds the tension of One versus multiplicity, unity versus separation, stillness versus movement. Being in this intermediary position it contains both sound and the anxiety of expressing sound, like a seed about to burst forth and bloom.

2] *Patach is Chochmah.*

Patach is *Chochmah*. *Chochmah* is wisdom and intuition. Within Chochmah there is the beginning of an opening. *Patach* is an 'ah' sound, as in something opening up, a new understanding, an "ahhh" moment. The word *Patach* actually means 'opening'.

3] *Tzeirei is Binah.*

Tzeirei is *Binah*. *Binah* is Understanding. *Tzeirei* is an 'ei' sound. When something begins to make sense. After the initial "ahhh" sound, there is a corresponding 'ei' sound. This shift in vibrational frequency represents the movement from an initial intuitive grasp of an idea on the big picture level, to a more thorough understanding of its constituent parts. This takes patience and a certain degree of the critical faculty represented by the 'ei' sound. In addition *Tzeirei* is comprised of two dots. The two dots suggest a process of understanding via the drawing of parallels, analogy, association and analysis.

4] *Segol is Chesed.*

Segol is *Chesed*. *Chesed* is Loving-kindness. *Segol* is the 'eh' sound. The 'eh' sound is an expressive sound, a sound of release. In addition to its sound, the shape of the vowel is also significant. The *Segol* is in the shape of a triangle made up of three dots, with two on top and one on the bottom. This formation is a depiction of the process of synthesis. It shows that it wants to give, to lower and offer itself to the other.

5] Sh'va is Gevurah.

Sh'va is *Gevurah*. *Gevurah* is strength and boundary. *Sh'va* is the sound of 'uh', an inward moving sound. The *Sh'va* indicates that you are taking a pause, a stop, a restriction, in order to reflect. It is the pause before the letting go. The root of the word *Sh'va* means to sit or to settle (i.e. to stop).

6] Cholam is Tiferes.

Cholam is *Tiferes*. *Tiferes* is Beauty. *Cholam* is the 'Oh' or 'Oy' sound. This is the sound of feeling compassionate, empathetic and merciful.

7] Chirik is Netzach.

Chirik is *Netzach*. *Netzach* is Victory. *Chirik* is the 'Ee' sound. It is an enduring and penetrating sound. It is a sound of perseverance.

8] *Kubutz is Hod.*

Kubutz is *Hod*. *Hod* is Thankfulness and Humility. *Kubutz* is the 'OO' sound. It is a sound of wonderment and spender. This is the essence of *Hod*.

9] *Shuruk is Yesod.*

Shuruk is *Yesod*. *Yesod* is the Foundation. *Shuruk* is also an "OO" sound. But this vowel is placed in front of the letter, unlike the *Kubutz*, which is under the letter. This suggests a movement outward. This is the idea of *Yesod*, connecting to others and forming relationships.

10] *No vowels — Malchus.*

No vowels — *Malchus*. *Malchus* is the Kingdom, the world, tangible reality. It is not about "you", but about the other. Malchus is the "other", the receiver. It has no sound of its own. It only receives sound as it is acted upon.

A MAP OF THE BODY:

R. Chaim Vital, the primary disciple of the AriZal, writes in *Shar Ruach Ha'kodesh (p. 57b)* that a person should meditate on the fact that he is a throne/seat for the inner world of *Atzilus*, the world of perfect unity where the 'light' and the 'vessels' are one. A person's body was created to reflect the ten Sefiros and their relationship with the vowels and the name of Hashem. To internalize this, he records a kabbalistic meditation designed to include the 4-letter name of G-d, the human body, the Sefiros, and the Vowels. This meditation, he writes, is especially pertinent before the prayers as well as during the internal breaks within the structure of the liturgy. Each Sefira vocalizes the Four-Letter Name with a different vowel, based on the correspondences developed above.

> *The head* is a seat for the Name *Havayah* (Hashem) with the vowel *Kametz*
>
> *The right part of the brain* is a seat for the Name *Havayah* with the vowel *Patach*
>
> *The left side of brain* is a seat for the Name *Havayah* with the vowel *Tzeirei*
>
> *The right arm* is a seat for the Name *Havayah* with the vowel *Segol*
>
> *The left arm* is a seat for the Name *Havayah* with the vowel *Sh'va*
>
> *The body (torso)* is a seat for the Name *Havayah* with the vowel *Cholam*
>
> *The right leg* is a seat for the Name *Havayah* with the vowel *Chirik*
>
> *The left leg* is a seat for the Name *Havayah* with the

vowel *Kubutz*

The procreative organ is a seat for the Name *Havayah* with the vowel *Shuruk*

The crown of the Bris/Covenant is a seat for the Name *Havayah* with no vowel

TO HASHEM ALONE WE PRAY:

It is important at this time, as we are exploring these Kabbalistic approaches to prayer, to emphasize the core Jewish belief in radical unity. One must never confuse the Sefiros with independent entities that have any existence outside of Hashem.

On one hand the Medrash *(Tehilim, 91:8)* says: "why are the prayers of the people of Israel not answered? Because they do not know the Name." This suggests that in order for our prayers to be answered on any level we need to know the particular Name and evoke the proper expression of Hashem. In other words, prayer needs a direct focus and a specific address to access the aspect of The Infinite One that we seek to awaken.

And yet, on the other hand, when we pray we need to direct our focus, "To Hashem and not to Hashem's attributes" *(Medrash Sifri)*. This seems like a contradiction. Should we think about and meditate on specific "attributes" of Divine expression or on Hashem alone? Do we focus on the Sefiros and the names or do we think only about Hashem Alone? Do we focus our attention on the Source or direct it to the Vessels that channel the forces of the Source?

Of course it is unanimously understood that we must pray to Hashem alone. But if we are praying to the Source, why think about the Sefiros at all? Not only does it seem inappropriate, but, if anything, these contemplative meditations upon the Sefiros would appear to distract us from thinking about Hashem at all. This quandary deserves our attention.

During the fourteenth century, the *Rivash* (Rabbi Yitzchak Ben Sheishes) asked the illustrious sage R. Don Yoseph Ibn Shushan of Saragossa this question: "Who is it that we pray to? Should we simply pray to the essence of Hashem or should we direct our intention towards the Sefiros?" *(Teshuvahs Rivash, Teshuvah 157)*.

The gist of his reply was as follows: When we pray, we pray only to Hashem. And yet, just as it is in the earthly realm, so too is it in the Heavenly realm. If one were involved in litigation seeking justice, he would request the king to order the magistrate to judge him. He would certainly not ask that the treasurer be ordered to hold court. Similarly, if he wanted a gift he would ask the king to order the treasurer, not one of the royal guards. If he wanted bread, he would ask the baker, and wine — the wine-maker, and so on. As the world below mirrors the worlds Above, when we ask for mercy from Hashem we keep in mind the emanation of mercy, and when we seek justice — the emanation of strength; though all the while our focus and request is directed to Hashem alone.

Though an analogy has been drawn, a clear distinction must be made as the Tzemach Tzedek explains *(Shoresh Mitzvas Ha'Tefilah, Chap 8)*. Whereas the king and the ministers are two separate beings and it is the minister who carries out the decrees of the king, with regards to Hashem there is no separation, only unity. Hashem, the Infinite One alone, is the judge and the dispenser of all decrees. The relationship between the formless Infinite One and the Multiple Sefiros is simply that the Infinite, as it were, uses the Sefiros as tools and lenses to reflect and reveal Oneself within the world below. The 'vessel' of Chesed is used to manifest the light/energy of kindness, and the Sefira of Gevurah is accessed to channel stringency and discipline. But there are no independent existences. There is only Hashem, period. And it is only Hashem who listens to, answers and accepts our prayers.

Part of the problem of focusing your Kavanah on the Sefiros while trying to pray to Hashem alone is, as the Ramak says *(Pardes Rimonim, Shar 32:2)*, that when a person is thinking about the Sefiros he may *Megashem the Sefiros* / conceptualize them as physical and independent entities, as if they are separate objects, which they most certainly are not. In this way the person is confusing the Vessel for the Light and thereby causing a blemish in his perception of the interwoven fabric of creation.

The Ramak also says that if a person is meditating on one particular Sefira during the course of his prayers, then it would in fact seem that he is *Mafrid* / separating, the Sefiros from the core of Ultimate Unity. Whereas the whole purpose of prayer, and for that matter life itself, is to realize and reflect the *Yichud* / unity, of everything.

These are serious contradictions and complications that deserve our deepest consideration. The answer the Ramak gives is that our attention must always be directed towards the Light, the *Ein Sof*, the limitless, the Infinite, the Unity. And yet the formless Infinite One becomes vested in the Sefiros in order to be able to be perceived and related to within the finite world. Our focus is always on the Light, the *Ein Sof*, which is revealed and unified within the structure of the Sefiros. When we sense how the Light is unified with the vessel then the Sefiros themselves are called "holy names."

ONE LIGHT, AND (SEEMINGLY) MANY VESSELS:

It cannot be restated enough: While there is the revealing of the Light through the vessels, still the essence of the Ein Sof itself, even while vested within the vessels, remains unified and undivided. The essence of the Light does not change by descending and diversifying into multiple vessels. True, the Divine will manifests itself differently in different situations and circumstances. For example, to one person it will come through the vessel of loving-kindness (chesed), while to another it will come through the vessel of restraint (gevurah). Still, we must know that the light does not change, only its reflection and revelation changes. The same Light is seen in different variations through the filters and lenses of the different Sefiros.

The change that occurs through prayer is not a change in the Ein Sof, as Hashem is changeless and cannot be influenced. But rather, Hashem's will reveals itself in another "form", so to speak. Whereas before prayer the Light may have appeared "red" as Gevurah (harsh judgment or illness), perhaps now after one's prayers, the Light appears in the "color" of Chesed, as kind-ness.

The Ramak draws a parallel of a single ray of clear sunlight being filtered through many colored funnels. In reality the light never changes. In the eyes of the observer, the red funnel looks like it contains red light and the blue funnel like it contains blue light. But this is only the perception of the observer. The light itself is forever the same and does not change. The perception of the observer is what is different, not the Light itself.

PRAYING TO HASHEM:

It is important to reiterate that although the Divine flow is manifest to us through the various vessels, nevertheless, when we pray we pray to Hashem alone. The vessels are merely the vehicles that carry the Divine Light to and through us. They possess no independence or separate existence of their own. The only force is Hashem and in fact, there is only Hashem. And yet it is from this world — the world of duality, relationship, paradox and separation — that we humbly reach out in love and awe as we pray to Hashem alone.

APPENDIX II

Yichud Zah V'Malchus –
Unification between Zah and Malchus

MALCHUS ELEVATED INTO ZAH VS. ZAH DRAWN DOWN INTO MALCHUS:

The act of prayer is to elevate *Malchus*, which is, before the prayers, in a condition of 'lack', into *Zah* /Completion. When prayers are answered, meaning when Malchus is elevated into *Zah* / life, which is Malchus, is then fully realized and fulfilled. The blessings of the *Shemonei Esrei* are materialized as Malchus is filled. This is what occurs in the *Amidah*, the elevation of *Malchus* into *Zah*.

Keep in mind that if Zah would be drawn down into Malchus nothing would actually be 'answered' or changed, and yet everything would appear to be fulfilled. Malchus represents something that is missing.

Zah, relative to Malchus, represents fulfillment and completion. If Zah would be drawn down into Malchus, Malchus would take on the properties of Zah and thus be instantly fulfilled. Nothing on the ground would actually need to change for it to be perfect. But when Malchus elevates through our prayers into Zah it retains its own properties, which is that something is 'missing', yet it is unified with Zah and everything that was missing before is now fulfilled.

IN THE SEQUENCE OF THE PRAYERS:

But before there can be this Yichud between Zah and Malchus we need to draw down 'mind' into Zah. The reading of the Shema is about bringing *Mochin* / mind, into the Emotions, into Zah. We experience our emotions in the world of Yetzirah, the second stage in the prayers, and then we bring them into Beriah during the third stage of prayer, the Shema, so they can be filled with 'mind.'

Once Zah is filled with Mochin, Zah can have a Yichud with Malchus and produce 'children', i.e. the prayers are answered. The actual Yichud of Zah and Malchus occurs during the Amidah, the main body of the Tefilah.

Just as on a physical level, unity between two people

that does not have any Mochin or intention cannot produce children, the same is true spiritually. Hence the teaching that, *Ein Kishu Ela L'Daas* / "there is no physical arousal without intention". For the male (Zah) and the female (Malchus) to unify in a way that produces results and brings down blessings, Zah has to be filled with Mochin. In the reading of the Shema we are bringing Mochin down into Zah. In layman's terms, we are bringing understanding into our emotional conditioning. Only then can Zah unify with Malchus in the act of Tefilah.

Essentially, the Kavanos, intentions of the AriZal in prayer is to bring a Tikkun, correcting to Zah and Malchus, the masculine and feminine, by drawing down and adding Mochin, mind to Zah. When Mochin is added to Zah it creates an active, as opposed to a passive, Zah, which when Zah is active, pulsating and alive it unifies with Malchus, and Malchus is then filled and elevated.

ZAH AND MALCHUS IN TIME:

Zah, which is Redemption, is also reflected in the idea of Day. Day represents revelation and clarity. While Malchus, which is Prayer, is the notion of Night. Night has no light of its own, like Malchus or the moon. It represents that which is in a state of lack.

Tefilah represents an expression from within the existential condition where something is "not complete" and is in the process of being filled.

The time of exile is Malchus and the time of redemption is Zah. For now, so long as there is still a condition of exile, Malchus is quiet and it is in a process of *Balah* / absorbing, and not *Palit* / giving. Therefore, the Amidah is said quietly. There is no place for Malchus to express itself.

In a time of Galus the feminine (Malchus) aspect of the Divine remains as a recipient and does not influence. It is quiet, still, low. And even when it is being filled, it is merely in a condition of absorbing. However in the time of redemption, when Malchus will finally be 'filled' completely, the feminine aspect will become influential and the 'voice' of the female will be heard, and heard loudly. We will hear in the streets, *Kol Chason, V'Kol Kalah* / "the voice of the groom and the voice of the bride" *(Yirmiyahu, 7:34)*. As a reflection of this meta-historical dynamic, today the Amidah is said quietly, while in the time of Ultimate Redemption and Unity the Amidah will be said loudly. We will reveal a space that is beyond and includes both sound and silence.

ZAH AND MALCHUS-
VOICE AND SPEECH:

Zah and Malchus also correspond to the names *Havaya*, *Hashem* (Zah-Tiferes) and *Ado-noi* (Malchus). They in turn correspond to the two dimensions of speech in prayer.

Whenever we utter words we have the pure undifferentiated sound, as well as the particular sounds formed by the potentials of the month, lips, teeth, palate, which become words. So there is *Kol* / Sound, and *Dibbur* / Speech. *Kol*, which is transcendent of particularities, corresponds to Havaya. *Dibbur*, which creates distinctions and separations in the sound, is related to Ado-noi.

In prayer we need to have intention to create a Yichud between Zah and Malchus. But a question is asked: "Since we need to direct our intention in prayer to 'Hashem and not to the attributes', how can we direct our Kavanah in prayer to the Yichud of Zah and Malchus?" More perplexing is that if we direct our Kavanah entirely and solely to the Ein Sof, which is Limitless and Infinite and thus inaccessible and un-influencable, to what or whom are we praying to?

Of course we pray to Hashem alone. Our focus is always to the 'Light' that becomes enclosed and vested within the 'vessels', which are the Sefiros, in particular in the Amidah Zah and Malchus. And yet it is precisely in the place of 'vessels' that there is the possibility of relationship and variant viewpoints.

The Kavanah is towards the Ein Sof and beyond, to the Essence.

There are three dynamics in prayer:

1] *Dibbur*, which is Ado-noi.

2] *Kol*, which corresponds to Havaya.

3] *Kavanah*, which corresponds to the Ein Sof.

These three words together equal 298 (Ado-noi-65, Havaya-26, Ein Sof-207 = 298). Two hundred and ninety eight in numerical value can spell the word *Rachamim* / Mercy, or compassion. The unity between the three, as the Ein Sof is manifest to us in the details and Dibbur of our lives, is a revealing of Divine compassion and is therefore the answer to our prayers.

SPEECH CREATES THE VESSEL TO RECEIVE BLESSING:

Not only do we pray with words, our own Malchus, but sit is through words that we create and make the vessel to absorb and receive blessings. Hashem will bless you, the Torah tells us, *Ka'asher Diber Lachem*

/ "as He has spoken to you" *(Devarim, 1:11)*. But it can also mean: Hashem will bless you "as your speech is", i.e. according to your prayer.

Hashem's blessings are always there, but when we speak and pray we create the proper vessel to absorb and channel these blessings.

SPEECH CREATES REALITY:

The Baal Shem Tov teaches that the words of our prayer create reality. Prayer is often viewed as a paradigm in which the prayer beseeches the Creator to grant all of the heart's desires, requesting that all of needs may be fulfilled in the most immediate and gentle way. Once submitted, the prayer no longer has control as to whether or not these requests will be granted.

The Baal Shem Tov revealed that the answer to the prayer arrives in the manner in which the prayer is formulated. When we say heal us, we are creating healing; when we say bless us, we are creating blessings.

Divine speech creates reality; G-d said, "Let there be light", and there was light. Basic human speech, on the other hand, is a reflection of Divine speech, shaping and contextualizing our reality as opposed to actually creating it. However, sometimes our words become the embodiment of Divine speech, and are imbued with the power to now create reality.

When we pray with *Deveikus/* cleaving, and when we pray with awe and love, we become one with the Creator and prayerful speech shares great resemblance to Divine speech with its power of creation.

This is the deeper reason why we need to be very specific with what we pray for, because we will get it! The Medrash speaks of a person who is trudging along in the desert. When his legs begin to tire, he prays, "Please G-d, if only I had a donkey." A moment later, he noticed a Roman officer standing nearby. The officer had stopped traveling as his she-donkey had gone into labor. The Roman noticed the man and ordered him to carry the colt on his shoulders. The man sighed, "I asked for a donkey, but did not ask correctly." *(Ester, 7;24. Orach Chayim, Devarim, 3;23).* The man prayed for a donkey in the hopes that it would carry him, but he did not specify that and therefore, received a donkey whom he had to carry!

It behooves us to be mindful of our words, especially while in deep prayer. The yearnings which we give voice to will be the realities which we live.

APPENDIX III

The Names of Hashem:
In greater detail

YUD-HEI-VAV-HEI
Hashem –The Name

The Four-Letter name is the *Shem Ha'mefurash* /the explicit name, otherwise known as the *Shem Ha'etzem* / the essential name. In English this name is called the Tetragrammaton. In the times of the Holy Temple the High Priest would guard the sanctity and secret pronunciation of this name and utter it only once a year on Yom Kippur in the Holy of Holies. But today, in the absence of The Holy Temple, this Name is not pronounced. The precise pronunciation and articulation of these four letters, Yud-Hei-Vav-Hei, has been lost over time through bitter exile. Since it is not verbalized or pronounced, it is simply called *Hashem* / The Name.

Perhaps this name may never have had a vocalized linguistic pronunciation, as one would vocalize a word, representing instead the perpetual inhale and exhale, expansion and contraction, or running and returning of all of creation. This very name can be understood as the constant motion and sound of breath, or in fact, of Hashem breathing creation into being in each and every moment anew.

This is the highest and deepest name. In the image of the early Kabbalists, it is both the "seed and the actual tree in its totality" — the whole that is greater than the sum of its parts. In relation to this name, all the other names are mere branches, or isolated parts of the tree. One way to refer to this name is *Ha'va'ya*, which is a permutation or rearranging of the four letters that comprise this name. *Ha'va'ya* means literally *Haviya* / bringing being into being. This is understood as referring to the Ultimate Being, which is the source and stuff of all beingness. The Ultimate Being that does not depend on anything else to exist; Primordial being, which gives rise to all past, present and future manifestation, thereby bringing all "things" into existence ex nihilo - i.e. some-thing from no-thing.

The last three letters of this Name, *hei–vav–hei* creates the word *Hoveh*. The root of this verb means, 'to bring into being'. The first letter *yud* serves as a prefix to the word Hoveh, modifying the verb to represent that this is a perpetual action. The creation of all created being is ever present and continuous.

The four letters, *yud–hei–vav–hei*, when rearranged, can spell out the words for past — *Hayah* (hei-yud-hei), present — *Hoveh* (hei-vav-hei), and, when you exchange the *Vav* for another *Yud* (the Vav is understood as an elongated Yud) you can also get the word future — *Yi'hiye* (yud-hei-yud-hei). This name then represents the simultaneous totality of all past, present and future — infinite transcendence, beyond any conception of time, extending from before the past, into the present moment and on into the future and beyond.

These four letters from among the entire 22 letters of the Aleph Beis, when spelled out, have the least numerical value of any other letter. The *Yud* is 20, as in *Yud*-10, *Vav*-6, *Dalet*-4 (20). The *Hei* is 12, as in *Hei*-5, *Aleph*-1 (6). *Vav* is 12, as in *Vav*-6, *Vav*-6 (12). All other letters have much larger numerical values. For example: *Beis* is 412, as in *Beis*-2, *Yud*-10 and *Tof*-400 (412). *Gimel* is 83, as in *Gimel*-3, *Yud*-10, *Mem*-

40, *Lamed*-30 (83). Infinity takes up, as it were, the least possible space. This is similar to the analogy of a black hole, which is an entire Universe's worth of matter contained in a single infinitesimally small dot.

Understood as the source of all being, these four letters reflect the entire inner structure of creation: the four inner worlds, four winds, four directions and four rivers that all lead back to the Infinite One. This name, as well as the Kabbalistic four-world model of reality, also contains within it the 10 *Sefiros* of the Kabbalistic Tree of Life. The 10 Sefiros are the 10 Spheres or Lenses through which the One Formless and Timeless Light of Infinity is refracted and reflected into finite being as it comes into the world of form and process.

Viewing the inner image of the "four worlds", or stages, of creation in a descending order, the highest level is known as *Atzilus*. This world is understood as nearness to and emanation from pure spirit. It is the world/reality/perspective where the "vessel" is completely unified with the "light"; where all that is seen/ felt/experienced is the Divine Primordial Infinite One Light of Creation, the initial "point" of all being. All form, whether linear or circular, begins with a single point. This corresponds to the smallest, most fundamental letter — the Yud. The form of the Yud can be found in all the other Hebrew letters. In fact each letter begins with a Yud, a point, and from there the form of the individual letter takes shape.

In the Creative Process outlined in the beginning of *Beresheis* / Genesis, this corresponds to the first sentence in which all of creation was conceived on a macro-cosmic level. This is referred to as the creation of "the Heavens and the Earth". This is the Big Picture, as yet undefined or understood as a step-by-step gradual process of unfolding. This is the initial lightning flash of inspiration in which "the end is wedged in the beginning" *(Sefer Yetzirah)*. This is the tiny infinitesimal dot of a black hole, wherein an entire universe is contained. This world, Atzilus and the Yud in the Tetragrammaton, corresponds to the *Sefira* of *Chochmah* / wisdom.

From this un-self-conscious state of near "no-thingness", pure desire, and uninhibited inspiration, comes the beginning of the creative process of some-thing emerging from nothing, order out of chaos. This is the world of *Beriah* / Creation, represented by the Upper Hei of the Tetragrammaton. It is in this world that the vessel begins to separate ever so subtly from the light. Ideal form begins to emerge in potential. But it is still not yet a full "thing". It is still a thought or word.

The Hebrew word for 'thing' is the same as the word for word / *D'var*. This is illustrative of the Torah's developmental creative process. What begins as a 'word' manifests as a 'thing'. This is the journey from the *D'var* of the Creator to the *d'var* of Creation — from the Upper Hei to the Lower Hei. But at this stage, the stage of the Upper Hei, we are still in the realm of Divine Thought.

The Hei is the crucible, the womb, the place of transformation and gestation. The Yud or seed of creation enters into the Hei and begins to take shape in order to manifest its limitless potential as a unique entity. This all corresponds to the *Sefira* of *Binah* / understanding.

This phase of creation is similar to the 'list making stage' of organization and prioritization, where the jumbled mass of raw energy and undefined substance, with no particular formation or function, begins to coalesce into some kind of crystallized abstraction which will allow it's organic emergence into reality or being.

This step in the process of becoming corresponds to the second sentence in *Bereishis* where "the earth was without form and empty…but then the Divine Spirit/Wind was hovering and began to move over the surface of the waters". The initial desire to create was present and the Idea was beginning to take shape as to how Creation would come about, but there were still no tangible individuated manifestation.

Next emerges the world/reality/perspective of *Yet-zirah* / formation. This is where "things" begin to take shape in particular configurations. The vessels are becoming more pronounced and less identified with the Light. The subtle vibrations are becoming more dense and compact on their way to becoming real 'things'. Consequently, the Vessels begin to take on enough substance to give birth to the beginnings of some sort of self-consciousness, or sense of aloneness and uniqueness. This movement downward, as it were, is reflected in the letter Vav, which is in the shape of a line.

The Vav is understood as a ladder connecting the Heavens to the Earth, or inspiration to manifestation. Vav is the sixth letter in the Aleph Beis, and therefore it corresponds to the six days of creation, as well as all of the "let there be…" statements in Bereishis. All of these creative intonations or generative vibrations that give birth to the world, beginning with Light and concluding with Humanity, occur during the Six Days of Creation. The Vav can thus be understood as the channel or conduit of the creative process as it evolves from pure formless inspiration into its ultimate actual form and manifestation.

The Yud is the initial intuitive inspiration / *Chochmah*. The Upper Hei is the drawing up of the Divine Blueprint, the visioning in detail, *Binah*. And the Vav is the gathering together and orchestration of the resources and energies necessary to bring the ultimate vision into actual reality. For as detailed as a blueprint may be, without the actual tools, supplies and personnel the house will never be built. The Vav and the world of *Yetzirah* correspond to the six emotional Sefiros: *Chesed* / loving-kindness, *Gevurah* / strength, alternately translated as *Din*, judgment, *Tiferes* / harmony, *Netzach* / victory, *Hod* / submission, and *Yesod* / foundation.

The final stage of this creative process manifests in the Lower Hei of the Tetragrammaton and the World of *Asiyah* / action. Asiyah is the world/reality/ perspective of physicality, materiality, individuation, freewill, responsibility and consequence. Asiyah is the world of apparent illusion, where the Light is most obscured or obstructed. But from a more transformative perspective, it is only in Asiyah, where both form/ vessel and substance/light are able to come back together in mutual relationship. This occurs through an existential commitment between Creator and creation known as covenant.

Covenant is a highly evolved sense of relationship, which transcends the confines of contractual obligation. This kind of integral relationship is dependent on the depth and degree of respect for and receptivity of each partner. This is ultimately the meaning and purpose of the spiritual life: to train us to respond to the Divine Other — which is really only One — with sensitivity, respect, awe and love.

The world of Asiyah corresponds to the Lower Hei and the Sefira of *Malchus* / kingdom. Malchus is the bottom of the spiritual food chain, the archetypal receiver, the ultimate empty vessel, the moon, the mirror, the absorber of all energy flowing downward into the world.

Above this entire developmental structure of Creation is *Keser* / the crown, which is represented by the *Kot-Zo Shel Yud* / the spike atop the letter Yud, the point where infinity and the earliest emergence of finite being merge. This point is above and beyond even the world of Atzilus, and thus nothing about it can be defined or described. This non-world corresponds to the White Fire upon which the Black Fire of the Text emerges from and appears upon. This is the silence before the sound, the stillness beneath the surface, the soil before the seed, the ground of all being.

While the Tetragrammaton is inherently connected with the totality of all reality, it is also specifically related to the aspect of divine mercy and compassion.

The sages teach that initially the world was created with the attribute of *Din* / strict judgment, through the Divine Name *Elokim*, as will be explored further on. This is what is referred to as 'Natural Law', in which there is no room for error. You touch fire and you get burned, end of story. Only angels could survive in such a world, for they have no freewill and therefore no capacity to 'miss the mark', so to speak. And so, that first world was shattered, because it could not sustain itself, it was too rigid. There was no leeway within the universal and objective laws of pure nature.

Our world, the world in which we currently exist, was then created through the attribute of *Chesed* / loving-kindness', mercy and compassion, with the giving of the Torah at Mt. Sinai through the Divine Name of the Tetragrammaton. Essentially this opened up the space for forgiveness and 'second chances', i.e. *Teshuvah*, to exist. Meaning that in this world, it is not so much about not falling, as it is about getting up again after you do fall. This leaves us room to make mistakes, to learn and grow, to expand, embrace and be embraced.

As the Tetragrammaton represents Transcendence and Infinity, it is also the name most associated with miracles or acts that seem to defy the more or less fixed laws of nature.

Today, when this name is written, as it is throughout the Siddur, it is pronounced as *Ado-noi*. When pronouncing the name Yud-Hei-Vav-Hei as Ado-noi, meditate on the meaning of both names.

ADO-NOI

Today the Tetragrammaton is pronounced as Ado-noi. So in a way Ado-noi is the garment, or the vessel, through which the Tetragrammaton vests itself within creation. Ado-noi represents the immanence of the Divine, which allows for the utterly Transcendent Infinite One to be experienced and expressed within creation.

Besides being the proverbial bulb for the Light of the Tetragrammaton, the name Ado-noi is also a name of its own. It represents the *Adon haKol* / the Master of all. This is the simple definition as recorded in the *Shulchan Aruch* / the code of Jewish Law. On the most basic level, Ado-noi represents G-d as Master, Lord and Ruler. It is a name with overtones of hierarchy and monarchy, two things that are generally distasteful to modern sensibilities. Nevertheless, there is much to be learned from this name and the element of submission to a higher power, which it quietly requires.

The essence of Ado-noi can be accessed and experienced in the quality of Divine Majesty and Exalted awe-inspiring beauty within the universe. If the created world is the kingdom of G-d, then the name Ado-noi represents the Master of that kingdom, the one who we ask for and answer to. This is why the name Ado-noi is used in place of the Transcendent name, the Tetragrammaton. The unpronounceable name is so high, so other-worldly that we need a more accessible name like Ado-noi to feel close and familiar enough to call on and be called on by G-d in order to live in accordance with G-d's will.

Ado-noi is connected with the Sefira of *Malchus* / the Divine kingdom. But contrary to contemporary negative feelings concerning the idea of lords and rulers, the conception of a true and righteous leader or king was one of humble servitude and radical responsibility to the needs of the people. It is this kind of compassionate and caring Ruler that we call upon when we approach the Infinite One through the name Ado-noi, for this is the name we most often use when petitioning G-d in prayer.

The letters in the name Ado-noi can spell: *Aleph*/One and *Din*/strict judgment. This implies the existence of the One within the Judgment. When we sense the Creator's presence, even within our trials and tribulations, we are able to connect with The One within our Judgment. Thus, we are able to feel that we are not abandoned or rejected, but rather that there is a Divine purpose for the hardships or concealments that we are going through. This awareness sweetens and transforms *Din* into *Rachamim* / judgment into compassion.

When the name Ado-noi appears on its own in the Siddur, fully spelled out as its own name, meditate on the meaning of Ado-noi as being the Master of all reality. But when Ado-noi is used as the 'stand-in' vocalization of the Ultimately Transcendent Four Letter Name, Yud-Hei-Vav-Hei, then meditate on the meaning of both names together. Hashem and Ado-noi, transcendence and immanence, bound together as one seemingly paradoxical but utterly integrated Unity.

YUD-HEI-VAV-HEI & ADO-NOI = AMEN:

The Yud-Hei-Vav-Hei and the name Ado-noi are also related to the word Amein, also pronouced as Amen. The word Amen is one of the most widely known and recognizable religious utterances. It is used as a type of choral response to punctuate the end of a prayer or blessing said in a group. Functionally, Amen serves the purpose of a collectively articulated affirmation to the truth and sincerity of the prayer or blessing that was just said.

The Gematria or numerical value of the name Ado-noi is 65. Ado-noi: Aleph—1, Dalet—4, Nun—50, Yud—10 = 65

The Gematria or numerical value of the Tetragram-maton is 26. Yud-Hei-Vav-Hei: Yud—10, Hei—5 Vav—6 Hei—5 = 26

The numerical volume of the word Amen is 91. AMeN: Aleph—1. Mem—40. Nun—50 = 91 91= 65+26. AMeN= Ado-Noi + Yud-Hei-Vav-Hei

Amen represents the unification of these two primary names of G-d: the Tetragrammaton and Ado-noi.

Therefore, Amen represents the unity between infinite transcendence and immediate immanence, between the concealed inner secret/Sod and the revealed outer surface/Peshat, between reality in a static state of perfected being and reality in a dynamic process of perpetual becoming. The exclamation of "Amen!" bridges this ontological abyss. It is, in essence, an exclamatory statement declaring that All is One!

Every time in prayer when we say Amen, which is an acknowledgement and affirmation, we are confirming and establishing that the Transcendent Source of all blessing is tangibly felt and present in our own life, in real time, and that, in truth, there is no separation or dichotomy, but only the ultimate reality of absolute unity between Hashem and Ado-noi.

Amen is an acronym that stands for *E-l Melech Ne'eman* / G-d is a faithful King *(Shabbos, 119a)*.

Amen also comes from the Hebrew word *Uman* / worker, and *Umnas* / trade. This alerts us to the understanding that it is not just simply a magical chant that will forge unification in all realms, rather that our spiritual life demands hard work and constant striving for unitive awareness. This is the great work of unification and integration within ourselves, our families, our communities, and within the whole world — may it be speedily in our days, *Amen*.

ELOKIM

The code of Jewish law defines the name *Elokim* as the mighty ruler and sovereign of the heavens and the earth. If Yud-Hei-Vav-Hei is the Source, then Elokim is the Force. Elokim is the orchestrator and director of all natural forces, the force of forces.

Elokim represents G-d of creation, in contrast to Yud-Hei-Vav-Hei which represents G-d of revelation and redemption. Elokim creates the world. Yud-Hei-Vav-Hei redeems the world, taking us out of our Egypt, so to speak.

We get a glimpse of this powerful name as we meditate on the physical laws of nature and the deep symmetrical order, pattern and rhythm of creation. It appears to us as the script and story line of created reality.

Elokim is connected with the notion of *Din* / strict judgment, as well as the Sefira of *Gevurah*, which sets limitations, boundaries and apparent constrictions. This can be seen in the Laws of Nature themselves, where there are fixed laws and limits to the ways things work. Fire is hot. If you touch it, you get burned. Water is wet. The sun comes out in the day. If you throw something up in the air it will eventually come down. This is the level of the universe governed by strict judgment. If you step over the line or cross the natural boundary there is a predetermined consequence. Yud-Hei-Vav-Hei represents *Tiferes* / compassion, and forgiveness. Elokim represents Din and Gevurah, 'judgment', 'strength', boundaries, and discipline. The natural world is governed by Elokim via the Laws of Nature. The deeper reality is governed by Hashem, which is why there is room for Teshuvah or returning and realignment, miracles, revelation and freewill.

The creation of the physical, the dimensional and quantifiable, emerges from Elokim. The first words of the Torah are that, "In the beginning Elokim created the heavens and the earth." Heaven and earth, up and down, all plurality and polarity are created through Elokim. That is why the name Elokim is spelled in the plural, as the suffix implies many. It is not *Eloki* (singular), but rather *Elokim* (plural).

This linguistic plurality refers to the multitude of creative forces put into motion by the One Mover of many forces. The name Elokim and its relationship to the transcendent oneness of the Tetragrammaton speaks directly to the dynamic tension of maintaining a belief in One G-d in a world seemingly dominated by multiplicity.

The creation of duality occurs through a radical *Tzimtzum* / concealment, and withdrawal of the Infinite Light, in order to create a vacated space or fertile void, within which the finite world of individuated beings has the freedom to emerge as soon as Elokim creates it and puts it into motion. Physical reality, time, space and essentially all of nature are reflections of this Divine force. So much so, that the word for 'nature' in Hebrew, *Ha'Teva* — has the same numerical value as the word Elokim. Both Elokim and Ha'teva equal 86.

"For the sun and (its) shield are Hashem (and) Elokim" *(Tehilim, 84:12)*. Sun and shield represent light and vessel, or soul and body. Elokim is the finite vessel that contains, albeit in a concealed manner, the Infinite light of Hashem, the Tetragrammaton. That is to say that nature contains, conceals, and communicates the Infinite Light of G-d. This teaches us that G-d is not 'out there', but is truly 'right here', in this world. The Creator is hidden with creation, waiting to be discovered and acknowledged.

Thus Elokim, which as mentioned equals 86, is comprised of the combination of the Tetragrammaton (26) and the word for vessel, Kli (60).

26 + 60 = 86
Yud- Hei- Vav- Hei + Kli = Elokim

Being that Elokim is the vessel of Yud-Hei-Vav-Hei, the letters of Elokim can be scrambled and divided and it will still represent this idea. Therefore, we can split the name Elokim into two words: *Eilam* / muted, and *Yud–Hei* / the seed of the Tetragrammaton. Elokim is thus the shield that mutes and muffles the Yud-Hei, the infinite Divine energy. But being as it is a shield, the name Elokim also protects the Infinite Light, allowing it to manifest itself, albeit in a hidden way, in this world of multiplicity and materiality.

Deeper still, the name Elokim itself embodies both its finite revealed self and its infinite concealed self. Hence, the name Elokim can also be divided into the words: *Mi* / Who, and Eile / These — "Whose (G-d's) are These (Creations)?". This is a rhetorical question that alludes to the Hidden Holy One, Hashem. All aspects of creation are thus posing the ultimate question to us: "Whose are These?" The answer is: Creation belongs to the Creator.

SHECHINAH

Shechinah is not a Divine name per se, rather it represents the "a glory of creation", indicating to the observer that the Creator is present. *(Emunos V'Deios. 2:10. Kuzari, 4:3. Moreh Nevuchim, 1:19, 1: 25).*

On a deeper level, the Shechinah is the "glory of the Creator" *(Ramban. Bereishis, 46:1)*, and it represents the feminine and indwelling presence of Hashem. We get a glimpse of this name when we sense the poetry of creation and the resonant archetypes interwoven within the details of all reality.

Before the daily prayer *Baruch She'amor* (and many people say this passage before any important Mitzvah) we vocalize the intention that our actions be "For the sake of the unification of *Kudsha B'rich Hu*, 'The Holy One Blessed be He' and the *Shechinah*, the feminine indwelling presence".

When we recite this prayer we facilitate an awareness of our actions and that which is transcendent becomes immanent and readily accessible.

Berich Hu / Blessed be He, represents the masculine, detached, transcendent aspect of divine energy. An all-encompassing life force that remains unaffected by our finite actions or inaction. The feminine Shechinah represents that which is *Shochen* / dwelling within, a presence permeating the finite and immediate realm of our daily lives.

Appropriately, the word Shechinah numerically equals 385, as does the word Asiyah or doing — the fourth world of action and physicality.

Shechinah: Shin—300, Chof—20, Yud—10, Nun—50, Hei—5 = 385
Asiyah: Ayin—70, Shin—300, Yud—10, Hei—5= 385

Being as we are physical creations of this world, whatever we do influences the Creator, as it were, on the level of the Shechinah. For with all of our positive and life-affirming actions and intentions, we are "elevating the Shechinah". And for all of our negative and narrow-minded actions and intentions, we are causing the Shechinah to "fall", or go into exile. We are, essentially, the "limbs of the Shechinah". Every one of our harmful actions not only affects us negatively, but also has cosmic influence, as we in effect blemish the Indwelling Divine Light apportioned to earthly existence. In turn, we end up distorting, as well as reducing, the Divine energy immanent within creation. Thus any time we are in exile, the Shechinah is in exile as well. Conversely, when we are redeemed there is also redemption for the Shechinah.

The cosmic "fall" of the Shechinah is representative of the disunity between the immanent and transcendent aspects of The One, the mutual estrangement of the male and the female, the separation of the upper and lower waters, the exile of the Shechinah from Kudsha B'rich Hu. To redeem and uplift the Shechinah we must seek out and acknowledge the infinite divine energy that is contained within, as well as encompasses, all of creation. Doing a *Mitzvah* — a transcendent, compassionate and noble act — allows each one of us to reach for the infinite, in order to create an opening for the transcendent to enter into the realm of the immanent and to inspire the desire for re-unification between Kudsha B'rich Hu and the Shechinah.

On a personal level we are able to perform a *Yichud* when we bring together the way we feel and the way we act, aligning them in a perfect and seamless harmony.

E - L

The name *E-l* represents the attribute of supernal and boundless kindness. It is thus related to the Sefira of

Chesed / loving kindness. The verse in Psalms says, "the Chesed of E-l is present all throughout the day" *(52:3.)* We sense this aspect and expression of the Divine in the kindness we experience and actualize within our own life, and within all the goodness, nurturing and benevolence of creation as a whole.

In the course of our prayers, the name E-l often comes with an epithet attached to it, as in, *E-l Elyon* / the Most High E-l, or *E-l Gadol* / the Great E-l.

There are two methods of counting the "Thirteen Attributes of Mercy" expressed in the Torah *(Shemos, 34:6)*. These attributes were revealed to Moshe by Hashem and are understood as the Divine qualities that we most want to activate within the true and compassionate Judge as we seek forgiveness and counsel. In addition, these are the attributes that we as humans are most encouraged to actualize in our own lives as we seek to emulate "the ways of G-d" in our dealings with creation.

One way to count these Thirteen Attributes, which is based on the literal interpretation of *Rashi* and the mystical understanding of the *AriZal*, is that the first of the thirteen attributes of mercy is the name E-l, rather than the Tetragrammaton (which is the other way of counting the 13 attributes).

Before there is any movement from within a point of Oneness to the creation of or interaction with (apparent) duality in the form or substance of an "Other", there needs to be a desire to express and to offer the bounty and gifts of One to an "Other." This initial desire to create and share the universe is rooted in the aspect of E-l, Divine goodness and kindness. And as the sages teach that "the nature of the good is to do good", we are able to ascertain that since creation came from a "good" place, a Divine Desire to share and to give, then the true purpose of all creation is "for the good" of that creation. In turn, we can also surmise that the purpose of such a creation is to also "do good" in order to continue the cycle of nurturing and sharing such goodness with an "other" apparently separate existence. For, as the Torah teaches, "it is not good for a human to be alone" *(Bereishis 2:18)*.

To review: first there arises a desire to connect, to relate, to give, and then because of this desire, the Infinite (Hashem) contracts and conceals OneSelf into the level of Elokim, which facilitates the creation and maintenance of the physical and the multiple.

As it says in the Book of Psalms *(50:1)*, *E-l Elokim Hashem (Yud-Hei-Vav-Hei) Diber Va'yikra Eretz /* "E-l, Elokim, Hashem spoke and he called forth earth". The primordial desire to create an 'other' comes from the attribute of E-l, the aspect of Divine kindness, *Chesed*, a kindness that desires to contract (*Tzimtzum*) in order to create the space necessary for the appearance and existence of an "Other" upon whom One can then bestow loving kindness and blessing. Once there is this desire, only then can there begin the actual process of creation, which occurs through Divine speech — i.e. communication, which necessitates an "other" in order for there to be a significant and satisfying dialogue — i.e. for One to actually feel heard.

ELOKA
Elokei, Elokeinu

Eloka represents another aspect of divine kindness. Whereas E-l is that initial flash of the desire to share with and to care for an 'other' that leads to the contraction and creation of a space for such an 'other' to exist, Eloka represents the actual extension of that kindness, which in turn infuses all dimensions of creation. E-l can thus be seen to represent the intention and desire to do good, and Eloka can be understood to represent the actual doing of that good.

The name Eloka is comprised of four letters. The first two are Aleph and Lamed, which make up the name E-l. The next two letters are Vav-Hei, the final two letters in the Tetragrammaton (Yud-Hei-Vav-Hei).

If E-1 is Chesed alone, then the final two letters in the Four Letter Name represent the six emotional attributes in totality (the Vav), as well as the final Sefira of Malchus (the Hei) — the receiver, the mirror, the other upon whom the good is bestowed. The lower dynamic of the Vav-Hei is connected with the actual world of creation, and thus these seven Sefiros are embodied and embedded within the seven days of the weekly cycle. Eloka is thus Divine kindness that permeates all spaces and times of created existence.

Other names connected with E-1 are *Elokei* or 'my Eloka', and *Elokienu*, 'our Eloka'. In both of these permutations, the name becomes more personal — my G-d who does good, or our G-d who bestows goodness.

Elokei is also comprised of four letters: Aleph and Lamed for E-1, and Hei-Yud (the first two letters in the Tetragrammaton). The higher dynamic of the Yud-Hei is transcendent and beyond this world. Thus Elokei and Elokeinu represent a Chesed that is rooted in the initial inspiration and intention to do good that is not channeled to all of creation, as in Eloka, but is instead experienced very personally as being routed directly to me or us. This is a more intimate and unique encounter with the supernal loving kindness that resides within the attribute of E-l.

YA-H

The name *Y-ah* (Yud-Hei) is created from the first two letters of the Tetragrammaton, the Four Letter Name of Hashem. *Yud*, as explained represents *Chochmah* / 'Divine Wisdom' and intuition, while the Upper Hei reflects *Binah* / 'Divine Reason' and understanding. The reality of this name is sensed in the inner divine wisdom and intelligence that permeates all of creation.

More precisely, Ya-h is connected with the Sefira of *Chochmah* / wisdom.

This name represents the innate ability within us all to form a conscious and co-creative perspective of our life's purpose and meaning, the wisdom of life, as well as a coherent narrative of our soul's story and trajectory.

Suffering and anxiety occur when a person's life seems meaningless. When all that is observed is the 'vessel' or tunnel, one cannot see any 'light'. In other words, mental and emotional suffering occurs precisely when one is unable to find any purpose or direction to their own experience. Ya-H is revealed when one is able to understand the wisdom within all creation, even within apparent suffering. One is then able to realize that there is always some form of wisdom to be gained and learned from every encounter and experience. It is then understood that nothing is empty of meaning or devoid of wisdom.

Yud and Hei are the deeper hidden aspects of the name of Hashem. As the lower dynamic, the Vav and Hei are more revealed. Our world is primarily governed by emotions and instincts, as represented by the Vav and lower Hei. For instance, most people function from an emotional and unconscious place, with the conscious mind being less of a controlling factor or influence on their actions or reactions. *Gan Eden* / the Garden of Eden, is the world of Binah and beyond, where Torah and Divine Mind are revealed.

The transformative perception of suffering, which is able to grasp how the essence of any experience is always for the purpose and potential of eventual good, comes from Y-aH — i.e. from wisdom and understanding.

During the prayers, and in particular during the morning Shachris prayers in the section of *Pesukei*

D'Zimrah / the verses of praise, we continually offer praise to Y-ah. For example, the word *Halleluy-ah* is comprised of two Hebrew words: *Hallelu* / praise, and *Y-ah*. At the end of the verses of praise we conclude with *Kol Ha'neshamah Tehallel Y-ah* / "let all living beings, with every breath, praise Y-ah!" *(Tehilim, 150)*.

Praise is a revealing agent. Through praise we reveal and draw down into the world, as well as our own lives, the power of Y-ah — the divine wisdom, goodness, purpose and meaning within all aspects of our life, even into the places and experiences that seem meaningless, trivial or devoid of purpose.

SHAD-DAI

The name *Shad-dai* conjures up various images and interpretations, which though seemingly unrelated, all express one fundamental idea — the notion of divine protection and nurturing; that which shields, borders and secures boundaries.

Shad-dai is exemplified by the Sefira of *Yesod* or foundation and the position of the back.

Yesod is connection, relationship and foundation. Proper boundaries allow for greater possibilities in relationship, preparing and paving the path of ultimate unification.

The Sefira of Yesod realigns, re-focuses, re-adjusts and re-members disparate elements within the construct of a greater unity, and is thus connected with the aspects of nurturing and healing, which are ultimately about wholeness and integration.

The word *Shad-dai* can be translated as ' enough'. The Medrash tells us that, "as the *Olam* / world was being created and expanding endlessly, Hashem said to the world *Shad-dai*, 'Enough!'" Shad-dai sets limits to define margins and boundaries within which growth and nurturance can take place.

We are commanded in the Torah to place a Mezuza upon the gates, boundaries and doorposts of our homes, buildings, and rooms. Inscribed on the outside of a Mezuza is the letters *Shin-Dalet-Yud*. These letters comprise the Divine name Shad-dai. This is spiritually appropriate, as Shad-dai is a name that sets limitations, securing what is inside, literally and metaphorically, making sure that no outside negative influence enters the defined space and protecting the home and the ones who live within its boundaries. When Mezuza is spelled in the plural, as Mezuzos, we can find and form the words *Zaz Maves/* move aside death, alluding to the protective nature of the Mezuza. Furthermore, the letters Shin, Dalet, and Yud making up the Divine name Shad-dai, can also be viewed as an acronym for *Shomer Dalsos Yisrael* / 'Guardian who protects the doors of Israel'.

The Divine light of Shad-dai is related to the measured amount of energy regulated within the universe. This is referred to in the teaching: *S'Dai B'elokus B'ol-ama* / "for there is a sufficient amount of divinity in His world". Shad-dai is that nurturing aspect that provides nourishment in such a way that even a little suckling gets the perfect amount to be satisfied — just "enough".

For this reason, the name *E-l Shad-ai* in the Torah is always associated with blessings for children. Indeed, when people pray for children they should meditate on this name *(Rokeach, Sodei Razia)*. The 'filling letters' of the name Shad-ai, meaning the 'children' of the Shin, Dalet, and Yud are (for Shin) Yud/10 and Nun/50, (for Dalet) Lamed/30 and Tof/400, and (for Yud) Vav/6 and Dalet/4 = 500. 500 is the numeric value of the words of the command to Adam to, *Peru V'revu* / "be fruitful and multiply". The minimum fulfillment of this Divine command is to have a son and daughter. This is reflected in the name Shad-ai when one considers that according to tradition the male has 248 main body parts and the female body has an additional 4, totaling 252. 248+252=500.

Paradoxically the word Shad-dai, directly related to the Hebrew word *Shadayim* / that which nourishes the young suckling *(Shir Hashirim, 8;1)*, can also denote the concept of a destroyer, as in the word *Shoded* / meaning to break and destroy. The name Shad-dai is thus reflected in the ebb and flow of creation. Nature is continually being created as well as decomposing, building itself up while at the same time being pulled down in one continuous rhythmic dance of life and death. There is a perpetual movement that fluctuates back and forth. But within all this motion and transition there is always the guiding hand and nurturing element of Shad-dai to both nature and nurture all of creation toward its next stage of development, whether that is towards apparent growth or decay, for truly all is one.

The name Shad-dai is also related to what are referred to as concealed miracles. These are 'miracles' that appear vested within nature such as meaningful synchronicities or a series of unlikely but 'miraculous' events. This is as opposed to a miracle that defies the laws of nature, such as the splitting of the Reed Sea as the Israelites escaped Egyptian bondage. This is the experience of the miraculous in a way that does not fly in the face of natural law, but rather works within the confines of nature, and in effect nurtures nature towards a higher point of its inevitable evolution.

When the name Shad-dai appears in the Siddur with the prefix E-l, which is Chesed, these two Divine Names are joined, thus representing the divine flow of blessing into creation to the extent that the receiver of the blessing is able to say: "Enough! I am filled."

TZEVAKOS

The literal translation of *Tzevakos* is, "Lord of the Heavenly Hosts" or "Master of Legions". Though this name does not appear in the Torah as one of the names of Hashem, it is recorded often in the book of Prophets and is a Divine name that is found frequently throughout the prayers.

This name is connected with the celestial orchestrating element of the Creator, the aspect of the Divine that organizes, cares about and is intimately connected to all the intricate details of the innumerable legions, whether they are stars in the sky, people on earth, or fish in the sea — "to all of them He assigns names" *(Tehilim, 147)*. This gives us the sense that we are all on a "first name basis" with Hashem, that G-d truly knows every miniscule speck of creation by name. This is especially miraculous and inspiring in that it melds together the philosophical idea of an exalted and abstract universal G-d with a concerned, familiar and personal G-d. This is what it means when we call G-d "the Lord of Hosts". We are able to sense this name in that place where the Infinite collapses upon the interface of the finite.

The name Tzevakos is related to the Sefiros of *Netzach* — 'victory', endurance, and eternity — and *Hod* — 'humility', submission, devotion and gratitude. When the name is written with a prefix of Hashem, as in "Hashem Tzevakos", it is connected with the right column and expansive Sefira of Netzach. And when it is written as "Elokim Tzevakos", it is related to the left column and restrictive Sefira of Hod. Netzach is situated above, while Hod is below.

Being that these two Sefiros are from the outer implementary emotions, *Ne'hi* (Netzach and Hod), this name is "outside" the body of Torah as it were, and is only first recorded in the book of Samuel when Chanah, the mother of the prophet Samuel, uses it in prayer *(Samuel 1:11)*. And indeed these two Sefiros, Netzach and Hod, are identified most closely with prophecy, being as they are represented by Moshe/ Netzach and Aaron/Hod. Thus we can see that this name was acknowledged and articulated in the experiential encounter with the Divine via prayer and/or prophecy.

Numerically speaking, the name Tzevakos equals 499, and with 1 added for the word itself it comes to a total of 500. Symbolically, the number 50, and by extension 500, is a number that relates to fully realized quantities of time, and for that matter, space.

500 is understood as the time and space of the world. Our sages teach that, "From earth to heaven is a journey of five hundred years. The width of heaven is a journey of five hundred years. Between the first heavenly realm and the next heavenly realm is a journey of five hundred years, and similarly between each successive heavenly realm" *(Chagigah, 13a).*

This is highly symbolic and poetic language that is meant to convey, through a series of analogous juxtapositions, the awe-inspiring scale and proportion of all creation. It also may be meant to infuse us with an awareness of humility and our own insignificance by communicating the breadth and depth of creation, while at the same time revealing the concealed miracle that Hashem, even within such an expansive multiverse, still knows every aspect of creation by name.

The name Tzevakos suggests the aspect of the Divine that orchestrates so thoroughly because it cares so lovingly for all the multiplicity and diversity of creation. Hashem is the One Creator of all the myriad legions and hosts of creation and is thus a Creator that is intimately involved in all the "five hundred" details of creation.

Although from one perspective G-d is infinite and utterly transcendent, Hashem also chooses to care, listen and heed every individual's particular request and is able to respond to and call us all by name. There is the *Tzava*, "the Legions" — the many — but these many embody the *Os*, "the sign" or signet of the One.

A Talmudic tale:

> *Rabbi Eliezer said, "from the day the world was created, there was no man who called the Holy One, blessed be He, Tzevakos until Chanah. Said Chanah as a barren woman praying for a child before the Holy One, "Sovereign of the Universe, of all the hosts and legions that You have created in Your world, is it so hard in Your eyes to give me one son?" A parable: To what is this matter like? To a king who made a feast for his servants and a poor man came and stood by the door and said to them, "Give me a bite", and no one took any notice of him. So he forced his way into the presence of the king and said to him, "Your Majesty, out of all the*

feasts which you have made, is it so hard in your eyes to give me one bite?" (Berachos, 31b).

By evoking the name Tzevakos, Chanah was addressing the One who interacts intimately with the many. By saluting and stressing the vast intricacy of the celestial realms all the way down to the tiniest grain of sand, she was seeking to activate that particular element of the Divine in order to draw down blessing from the Infinite One to her place of finite constriction and pain. Chanah's prayers initiated and allowed for a collapse of the Infinitely Expansive Unity of G-d to exist within a constricted space of apparent finitude, suffering and sorrow. When there is this kind of merging of the One and the apparent many, the latter melds into the former and life is filled to capacity with abundant blessing and divine influx.

APPENDIX IV

ANA B'KOACH:
Understanding the Power of the
Ana B'koach Prayer

The Ana B'Koach prayer as a whole represents a movement from one state to another; it is a transitional prayer.

It is comprised of seven verses corresponding to the seven days of the week, which in turn are a reflection of the seven emotional Sefiros through which the Divine energy sustains and nourishes our manifest universe. Sunday corresponds to the first attribute of

Chesed, loving-kindness, Monday is Gevurah, severi-
ty, constriction, and so forth.

Being that *Ana B'Koach* represents the seven sefiros it
is recited in the liturgical process whenever there is a
symbolic ascent of Divine energy from a lower plane
to a higher one, or whenever there is any movement
from one reality into the next.

THE 42-LETTER NAME CONNECTED WITH CREATION:

Ana B'Koach is also known as the 42-letter name of
Hashem. As there are 42 words in this prayer, the
initial letters of each word, when combined, create
the 42-letter name of Hashem. This Divine name
is connected with creation and the first verses in
the Torah that speak of creation. The authors of the
Tosefos write in *Chagiga (11b)* that this name is connected with the first two verses in the Torah *(See also
R. Abulafiah, Chaye Ha'Olam Habba, p. 57)*. Years later, the
Ramak *(Pardes Rimonim, P'ratai Sheimos)* explained that
the 42-letter name corresponds to the first 42 letters
of the Torah. He comes to this conclusion through
various methods in *Gematria* such as *At-Bash*, (where
the Aleph is exchanged with the final letter Tof, and
the second letter Beis is exchanged with the second
to the last letter, Shin), A'Y'K (where the letters are

divided into the single, double and triple digits; as in
1 through 9 (Aleph through Tet), from 10 through 90
(Yud to Tzadik) and 100 through 900 (Kuf through
final Tzadik), and others.

The beginning of the Torah is a journey through the
creation of time and space and Ana B'Koach is deeply
related to this unfolding process.

SIX LETTERS SUBDIVIDED:

Another way to approach the Divine Name within
Ana B'Koach is line by line. Instead of combining all
42 letters together in one long Divine name that is
particularly related to the creation of the world and
beginning of the Torah, one can also approach Hashem one line at a time. This results in 7 6-letter names
of Hashem. There are six words in each of the seven
lines of Ana B'Koach that correspond to the six sur-
faces of a cube: up, down, right, left, front, back. These
six directions are connected with the verse from the
vision of Yechezkel that says, "With two [wings] they
covered their faces, with two [wings] they covered
their feet and with two [wings] they flew."

Seven six-letter names are thus found in each line using the first letter of each of the six words in that line.

These names are meant to be scanned and visualized but never pronounced. As each line corresponds to a specific day of the week, each six-letter acronym gives us a meditation for that day. The first line/name is about Sunday; the second, Monday; the third, Tuesday; and so forth.

THE 42-LETTER NAME:

The 42-letter name is related to Moshe and the Burning Bush, the first direct encounter that Moshe has with the Divine. When Hashem first appeared to Moshe in the mystery of the Burning Bush, Moshe asked Hashem: "By what name should I call the Infinite One?" Hashem responded, *"E'heye Asher E'heye,"* which has been translated to, "I will be as I will be".

The numerical value of the name *E'heye* is 21:
- Aleph = 1
- Hei = 5
- Yud = 10
- Hei = 5

The name E'heye, when repeated twice as it is in this Divine Name, yields a total gematria of 42.

The Name *Mab* also has this numerical value

(Mem/40, Beis/ 2=42). This name expresses the Divine as timeless and eternal, forever with His people in their sorrows and tribulations. When recited from the heart, Ana B'Koach evokes this same kind of revelation from on high.

Forty-two is also connected with the 42 letters contained within the four-letter name of Hashem, Yud-Hei-Vav-Hei. This name has four letters which, when spelled out, become ten letters. When these ten letters are spelled out, there are 28 letters. When these three levels of the Name are added up together, they equal 42.

Yud – Hei – Vav – Hei = 4

Spelled out:
Yud: Yud – Vav – Dalet + Hei: Hei – Yud + Vav: Vav – Yud – Vav + Hei: Hei – Yud = 10

Spelling the spelled out:
Yud: Yud – Vav – Dalet | Vav: Vav – Yud – Vav | Dalet: Dalet – Lamed – Tof | Hei: Hei – Yud | Yud: Yud – Vav – Dalet | Vav: Vav – Yud – Vav
Yud: Yud – Vav – Dalet | Vav: Vav – Yud – Vav | Hei: Hei – Yud | Yud: Yud – Vav – Dalet = 28
4 + 10 + 28 = 42

The Name *Mab* (Mem + Beis = 42) is additionally connected with the sefira of *Gevurah* / restraint and restriction. Restriction is necessary, as a builder of desire and momentum, for an elevation from a current state to a higher level; therefore, this prayer is recited whenever we reach a place of elevation.

THE 42-LETTER NAME CONNECTED WITH MOVEMENT FROM SLAVERY TO FREEDOM:

There can be no elevation without this name as it embodies the ultimate elevation, the progression from slavery and constriction to freedom and expansion. This journey of 42 is reflected in the story of our exodus from Egypt, a place of constriction and limitation. The etymological root of the Hebrew word for Egypt / *Mitzrayim*, is *Metzar* / constriction. In Mitzrayim, the Israelites were literally slaves who were then given freedom. Internally, they were enslaved to their lower selves. Leaving Egypt represents a movement into genuine freedom. Before they were able to reach their full freedom, to enter the Promised Land, they were engaged in 42 journeys (elaborated in the Torah portion of *Maasei*). These are known as the 42 journeys, which according to the Baal Shem Tov, represent the 42 stages a person goes through in life.

As the 42-letter name represents a movement bridging one reality to the next, this idea is reflected in the Mourner's Kaddish, which is the bridge that connects to healing after the separation of death. In Kaddish, there are seven words beginning with the letter *Vav*, from *V'yishtabach* to *V'yis-halal*. Similarly, there are seven general names in Ana B'Koach. Vav is the sixth number (7 x 6 = 42). Here, we also see that each of these words has six letters just as there are six letters in each acrostic name of Ana B'Koach.

NOT TO BE PRONOUNCED:

At all times, the full 42-letter name is present, but one line and one acronymic name of the seven is most felt each day (as mentioned above).

These names are very sacred indeed and certainly should not be pronounced. In tractate *Avodah Zara (17b-18a)*, our sages speak very harshly regarding those who pronounce the 42-letter name in full. In tractate *Kidushin* the Gemarah reveals the following:

"Rav Yehudah said in the name of the Rav: The 42-letter name is entrusted only to him who is unassuming, humble, middle-aged, free from anger, never gets drunk and is not insistent on his rights. And he who knows it is heedful

thereof and observes it in purity, is beloved Above and popular below, feared by man, and inherits two worlds: this world and the future world."

As there is an inherent meaning to these Divine Names, they are only to be scanned and visualized. The *Rishonim* / early commentators, have different views on how these names should be read. One view sees each line as one whole name, another holds that there are three letters per name and thus two names per line. Thus the names should be said as two words together, as in the first line, *"Ana b'koach - gedulas yemincha - tatir tzrurah"*, so as not to say the Names.

THE NAMES & THE DAYS OF THE WEEK:

As mentioned above, the 42-letter name is connected with creation and is linked to the first verses of the Torah, which speak of creation. This is a name very closely associated with the weekly unfolding of time, the six days of the week and Shabbos.
Rav Hai Gaon (939-1038), one of the last sages of the Gaonic period, deciphers the names and how they relate to the days of the week.

Sunday: Avag Yatazt
• Av – father, implying

> our Father in Heaven
> • Yud and Gimel -
> Thirteen Attributes of Mercy
> (numerically, Yud is 10, Gimel is 3 = 13)
> • TaZT -
> breaks, as in breaks all levels of kelipa,
> concealment and constriction

On this Sunday level, there are little or no conceal-ments. In the Torah, Sunday is called *Yom Echad* / Day One, and not *Yom Rishon* / the First Day. Day One is only unity and oneness with the One, The *Av* / Father, and His Thirteen Attributes of Mercy emanating from the crown, the sphere of *Keser, Arich Anpin.* This is a time of perfect and complete unity coming from the holiness of Shabbos, before plurali-ty, before work mentality. Just to draw a further con-nection between this concept of Oneness and these Divine Names, the Hebrew word for One / *Echad*, equals thirteen.

The meditation for Sunday is to bring the conscious-ness and unity of Shabbos into the weekdays. Instead of being pulled down by the ensuing week to come, we should meditate and have kavanah to feel lifted up by the Shabbos that has just completed and that irrigates the coming week.

Kavanah
• Chesed – Kindness – Openness – Giving
• Consciousness: Tree of Life, Unity
• Energy: Love

Monday: Kara Satan
    • Kara – to rip asunder, to break apart
    • Satan – consciousness of duality,
      otherness and separation

The Torah discusses the second day as the creation of separateness and division. On this day, there is the division between higher and lower waters. The Medrash adds that it is the creation of *Gehenom* / hell.

The second day is so much related to division that the words, "It is good", which appear in all other days of creation, are omitted on this day. Hell is the opposite of unity. Inwardly, it is a state that arises from living in a state of separation from the complete reality of unification with our Source. Consequently, this is a name for breaking the Kelipa of separation and ripping it open to reveal that even the Satan is a Divine force.

Sam-El, another name for Satan, is spelled with the closed letters *Samech* and *Mem*, indicating that in this closed and cut-off state Divine Energy cannot reveal itself. When these closed letters are open, their Divine root is exposed and we understand that *Sam-El* is actually *E-l*, G-d, and the attribute of Chesed.

Monday is the beginning of many peoples' workweek. Even when people work on Sunday, that day is still very much connected with the modality of Shabbos. Come Monday, we must once again interact with a world of duality, concealment and a satanic consciousness of me, not you, this, not that — where time and space seem separate and our lives are compartmentalized by palm pilots and appointments.

Due to the powerful forces of separation on Monday we need to meditate on opening our blockages. Instead of feeling stuck, closed, or shut out, we can break the strength of the kelipa of duality and remain connected.

Kavanah
• Monday - Gevurah
  – Strength – Concealment – Separation
• Consciousness: Break and destroy all sense of disconnection and separation, remain connected
• Energy: Strength

Tuesday: Negdi Kash
  - Negdi – in front of me
  - Kuf – stands for kavod,
    indicating glory
  - Shin – stands for *Shamayim* / Heaven,
    indicating the *Shechinah*, the immanent
    presence of Hashem within the world.
    The glory of Hashem is before me.

The third day, Tuesday, corresponds to the Shechinah, residing in the *Malchus* of the third pillar, the middle column of balance and harmony. If the middle column is the trunk of the Tree of Life, Malchus is its life giving fruit. On the third day of creation, the Torah tells us that the earth gives over her fruit, just as Malchus is the manifestation and result of all the higher branches of sefiros that flow into and animate it. This is the idea of Malchus, the Shechinah, the mother earth giving birth to new life.

Tuesday represents routine, the same as Monday, just another day. It is a double day, thus in the Torah the word *tov* / good, repeats itself twice on this day. Our Tuesday's meditation is to realize the majesty and glory in our actions, in nature, in the routine of life, and how the entire world is filled with Hashem's glory, even that which seems trivial.

Instead of being bored or jaded by the routine and re-dundancy of the week, realize that within everything is Hashem's glory.

Kavanah

• Tuesday - Tiferes –
  Middle Column – Harmony – Beauty
• Consciousness: Balance, beauty
• Energy: Compassion

Wednesday: Ba'tar Tzatag

> • Tar — *Atara* / crown
> • Beis and Tzadik – numerically equal-ing 92, indicating 92 angels on high.
> • Tag – crown

On the fourth day, there is an allusion to two crowns, which rule over and guide the earth and angels (angels being the *Mazal* / guiding forces, of creation). This idea of the *Mazalos* interacting with the Creation is referred to in the Medrashic teaching that, "There is no blade of grass that does not have a Mazal (angel) over it that gently taps it and (continually) says 'grow'" *(Bereishis Rabba, 10:6).*

The double set of crowns refers to the two great lumi-naries of the earth, the sun and moon, both of which were fully created and began functioning appropriately on the fourth day.

Wednesday embodies circular motion, orbit, sun and moon and the *Mazalos* / stars and planets. On a personal level, if Tuesday is the beginning of routine, Wednesday represents deep routine, like the stars in their circuit, the third day in a row of repetition. It is circular motion, which also allows us to have a sense of predictability and perseverance.

Wednesday's meditation is on all of the crowns above our head. We should meditate on returning the 'crown' to its rightful place. We often misplace our sense of servitude during the busy workweek, confusing our real priorities with those which the world seeks to impress upon us. In truth, we need to be the crowned ones, along with Hashem, and not get stuck in routine, allowing ourselves to be mastered by the work that we do throughout the week. Instead, we must be our own masters with the power of the Master of the Universe to direct our own lives.

Kavanah
• Wednesday – Netzach – Victory – Perseverance
• Consciousness: Perseverance and Mastery
• Energy: Endurance

Thursday: Chakav Tana

These six letters form an acronym: *Chosem ketz, bo tamun (v)nistar ayin* / the seal of the end in which is hidden the seventy (two-letter sacred name of Hashem).

There are two types of seals: *Chosem Shoke'a* / receding seal, and *Chosem Bolet* / protruding seal. For example, if one were to seal with wax and the letters of the seal are hollow, the letters on the wax will protrude. If the letters of the seal protrude, the impression on the wax will be hollow. Inwardly speaking, when there is arousal from below, we are a protruding seal bringing ourselves to outward creativity and a sense of self and there is an impression Above, the Light which is reflected is dimmed. However, when we enter into a state of a receding seal, *Hod*, humility, and *Bitul*, nullification, of separate ego, we allow the deepest hidden Lights to be unclothed and revealed.

Thursday is the last full weekday and a seal of the week as Friday is already Erev Shabbos. There can now begin to be a shift in perspective from an outward and assertive modality to a more inward and reflective state of being, a mood of thanksgiving.

The idea of hiddenness is also reflected in the creation of the fifth day: Fish. By their very nature, fish are hidden away in the depths of water.

Hiding is generally a gesture of humility, the attribute of hod, which is related to gratitude. Angels were created on Thursday (according to one opinion in Medrash), and their archetypal image is one of singing praise and thanksgiving.

The Gemarah *(Rosh Hashanah, 31a)* tells us that the Song of the Day that was sung in the Holy Temple on Thursdays was a chapter from Psalms that begins with, "Let us sing praise to Hashem since birds and fish were created to offer praise to His name." Rashi explains that when a person sees all the various types of birds, he offers praise to the One Who created them.

Thursday is deeply connected with being grateful and offering up praise. Inwardly, the feeling connected with the week winding down is that of gratitude and for some, a sense of relief. Thus Thursday is the colloquial night of celebration.

The natural tendency when a successful week comes to a close is to offer praise. Sometimes that praise can be directed towards oneself, thinking it was one's own skill and genius that brought about the success. Instead of feeling smug and arrogant, like protruding seals, we need to meditate on how everything we have in our lives is truly a gift — even our skills and genius are gifts from Above.

Kavanah

- Thursday - Hod – Humility – Thanksgiving – Praise
- Consciousness: Introspection, deeper insight and gratitude
- Energy: Inner Insight

Friday: Yagal Pazak
- *Yagal* – to reveal
- *Pei* - stands for pisron, the "interpretation", revealing
- *Zayin* - stands for z'man, "time"
- *Kuf* - stands for ketz, "the end"

Hashem will reveal the Ultimate purpose of creation during the end of time. This is the sixth day of creation in which the human being was created. The purpose of creation is potentially realized through our actions, as co-creators of our creation. On Shabbos we connect with our spiritual selves, the inner purpose; while during the week we connect with our outer physical selves, the external actions. One completes and compliments the other.

We move from weekday outward activity to Shabbos inward restfulness on Friday. We can realize our work's purpose on this day of rest and enjoyment. Friday serves to connect (*Yesod*) work with rest and rest with work.

The workweek is now complete. If a person finds him or herself to be preoccupied by the work load, now is the right time once again to further connect with one's family, friends and community.

Friday's meditation is to bring everything we have done during the workweek to its realized purpose and to become attuned and aligned with Shabbos. Instead of remaining connected with work and dragging it into the home, thus bringing the weekday into Shabbos, we need to channel our *Yesod* / sense of connection and intimacy, towards our inner selves, family and friends.

Kavanah
- Friday - Yesod – Foundation– Intimacy – Purpose
- Consciousness: inward focus, inner peace
  and tranquility with oneself and with one's family
  and friends
- Energy: Connecting

Shabbos/ Saturday: Shaku Tzis
> - Shin - stands for sheish, the
>   number six
> - Yud - the letter looks like
>   a point and stands for the

Center of All Existence,
Hashem, the infinitesimal
Point of Infinity
• The remaining four letters
spell the word - *k'tzovos* /
directions. Hashem is the
center of all reality.

Within the six directions — up-down, right-left,
back-front — is the midpoint, which is *Malchus*.
Shabbos is malchus, the middle point of the cube,
pointing to all of the outer directions. The midpoint
is not a direction as it has no movement or any kind
of doing at all. It is a state of pure being, a space to
come from.

The meditation for Shabbos is that everything revolves around Shabbos, the Yud within the center of
the cube of time and the six directions of space. Not
only is Shabbos the culmination of the week just past,
it is the harbinger of the week to come. We should
aspire for all of our doings to come from a place of
deep being, and our weekday should flow naturally
from and into our Shabbos.

Kavanah
• Shabbos - Malchus – Non-Doing and Being
• Consciousness: Now, the eternal moment,
immortality

• Energy: Receiving

BLESSING AFTER THE NAME:

After we have completed this name, pronouncing the words and the visual scanning of the letters, we say *Baruch Sheim…*, "May His name be blessed…," much like we say after pronouncing the Shema. In the Temple, every time the high priest was heard saying the Holy Name, the people responded with Baruch Sheim. Today, if one of the Divine names is pronounced in vain, we say *Baruch Sheim*.

The Divine names in Ana B'Koach are connected with elevated Temple consciousness, as our sages explain. We therefore conclude the prayer with Baruch Sheim, the response given in the Temple when the name of Hashem was heard.

GLOSSARY

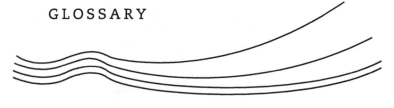

of hebrew words

Aleph Beis: The Hebrew Alphabet

Alter Rebbe: Literally, the "old Rebbe". Rabbi Schneur Zalman of Lidai. (1745 – 1812). Profound Chassidic Master and Teacher. Beloved student of the Maggid of Mezritch. Founder of the Chabad school of Chassidim.

Amidah: The "standing" prayer. The most essential prayer of the daily prayers.

AriZal: Acronym for "The Lion, Rabbi Yitzchak (Isaac) (Luria) of blessed memory" (1534-1572). The father of contemporary Kabbalah. His teachings are referred to as Lurianic Kabbalah.

Asiyah: Actualization. The world of action, of manifestation, of doing. The physical world as we know it.

Atzilus: Emanation. Nearness. A world that is close enough to its Source, that it feels itself a mere extension of its Source.

Avraham: Abraham.

Avodah: Service and work. More specifically spiritual work, as in prayer.

Ayin: Emptiness, no-thing-ness. The Unmanifest

Baal Shem: Master of the good name. A Baal Shem was a mystical healer, mostly using amulets. The most known Baal Shem was Rabbi Yisrael (Israel) Baal Shem Tov.

Baal Shem Tov: The mystic and profound teacher, Rabbi Yisrael (Israel) son of Eliezer (1698-1760). The legendary founder of the Chassidic movement.

Bereishis: The first book of the Torah (the five books of Moses), otherwise known as Genesis.

Beriah: Creation. The world of intelligence. Where reality is just beginning to emerge as a separate existence.

Binah: The attribute of comprehension and understanding.

Bitul: Self-nullification, a total acceptance of the Divine's manifest will. The transparency of the ego.

Chochmah: Wisdom, intuition. The spark of intelligence.

Chassidim: Followers of the spiritual path of the

Baal Shem Tov.

Chassidic Master: A leader and teacher of Chassidim.

Chesed: The act of loving kindness. Expansiveness and giving.

Chovas HaLevavos: Duties of the Heart. The moral, philosophical text by Rabbi Bachya Ibn Pakudah. (1050 - 1120)

Chozeh of Lublin: The Seer of Lublin. Rabbi Yaakov Yitzchak Horowitz. Chassidic master, teacher and leader. Known as the "seer" due to his intuitive powers.

Da'as: Knowledge, awareness. The ability to take information and apply it to life.

Deveikus: Cleaving, being unified. The spiritual sensation of being one with G-d.

Din: The attribute of judgment and setting of boundaries

Eliyahu Ha'navi: Elijah the master Prophet

Gemarah: See Talmud

Geulah: Redemption

Gevurah: The act of holding back, withdrawing. Inwardness and restriction.

Halachah: Jewish law.

Hashem: Literally "The Name", what is said instead of the Tetragrammaton, the predominate name of G-d in the Torah. This name of G-d is written with four Hebrew letters, the Yud-Hei-Vav-He. Being that this name is not pronounced it is called "The Name".

Hisbodedus: The spiritual practice of being alone. Also, known as the practice of speaking to the Creator openly, as one would converse with a best friend.

Hislahavus: Open and displayed emotions, excitement.

Kavanah: (Plural; **Kavanos**) Intention. Focused mindfulness. Specifically focus on the words of the prayers, or the general focus of what one is doing when praying.

Kelipa: (Plural: **Kelipos**) Literally, husk or husks.

That which conceals and covers over the truth of reality.

Magen Avraham: Rabbi Avraham Gumbiner. (c. 1635 – 1682). Polish Rabbi, Talmudist and leading Halachic ruler, often his rulings are aligned with the Kabbalistic understandings.

Ma'ariv: The evening prayers.

Machshavas Zaros: Foreign thoughts. Intruding thoughts that enters the mind involuntarily.

Maggid of Mezritch: Rabbi DovBer (? - 1772) the primary student and accepted successor of the Baal Shem Tov. Great scholar and the disseminator of Chassidic teachings and practice.

Maggid of Koznitz: Rabbi Yisrael (1773 - 1814). Chassidic master, teacher and author. Known as a miracle worker and great scholar.

Malchus: royalty; receptiveness. The reality as is. The state of lack. The feminine attribute

Medrash: Rabbinic writings of allegory and narrative, often containing the 'behind the scenes' stories that fill out the Biblical narrative; part of the oral tradition of Torah.

Mincha: The afternoon prayers.

Mitzvah: The commandments of the Torah, also understood as good deeds. Ritual obligations, or actions, that connect the doer with his deepest self and with his Creator.

Mitzvos: The plural for Mitzvah.

Moshe: Moses

Moshe Rabbeinu: Moses our Teacher

Musar: A ethical, educational and cultural movement that developed in the 19th century in Eastern Europe, particularly among Lithuanian Jews. Founded by Rabbi Yisrael of Salant.

Ohr Ein Sof: The Infinite Light of the Creator, although light is but a metaphor for a creative and sustaining force.

Rabban: Rabbi in Aramaic, the language of the Gemerah.

Rabbi Akiva: The great and wise sage of the Talmud,

who lived in the latter part of the 1st century.

Rabbi Meir Ben Gabbai: Spanish mystic, author. (1480 - 1547). A great synthesizer of Kabbalistic teachings.

Rabbi Yitzchak Ben Sheishes: Also known as the Rivash, which is an acronym for his name. Spanish Talmudist and Halachic ruler. (1326 – 1408).

Rabbi Yaakov Emdin: A leading German Rabbi, prolific author and thinker. Known as a zealot, for his fierce battles against any forms of heresy. (1697-1776).

Rabbi Yehudah HaChasid: Preeminent German mystic, author and moralist. (1150- 1217).

Rabbi Yitzchak of Acco: Early 14th Century Mystic and Author. Student of the Ramban, when the Ramban lived in Israel.

Rambam: Acronym for Rabbi Moshe Ben Maimon. Also known as Maimonides (1135- 1204) the great Jewish Spanish rational philosopher and codifier of Halachah.

Ramban: Acronym for Rabbi Moshe Ben Nachman. Also known as Nachmanides. (1194 - 1270) Prominent commentator, philosopher and physician.

Ramah: Acronym for Rabbi Moshe Isserles (1530 – 1572). Preeminent Polish Halachic ruler, mystic, author and thinker.

Ramak: Acronym for Rabbi Moshe Cordevero. (1522–1570) Mystic and author. Leader of a mystical school in 16th-century Safed, Israel, before the AriZal. A great synthesizer of Kabbalistic teachings.

Ran: Rabbi Nisan. 14th Century. Spanish commentator and Halachic ruler.

Rashi: Rabbi Shlomo Yitzchaki. (1040 – 1105). The preeminent commentator on the Torah and Talmud.

Rebbe: Chassidic master and teacher.

Reb: Affectionate term for Rabbi.

Reb Eliezer Ezcari: 16th century, rabbi, poet, mystic and moralist. Lived in Safed, Israel.

Reb Elimelech of Lizhensk: Chassidic master and teacher. Student of the Maggid of Mezritch. The Rebbe of many Rebbe's and Chassidic dynasties. (1717- 1787).

Reb Chaim of Tzanz: Rabbi Chaim from the town of Tzanz. A Chassidic master and teacher. Known as a great scholar and mystic.

Reb Chaim Volozioner: Rabbi, author, Talmudist and ethicist (1749 –1821). Student of the Gra of Vilnah, and founder of the first modern Yeshivah.

Reb Chaim Vital: Rabbi Chaim Vital. Master Kabbalist and author. Prime disciple of the AriZal. (1543 -1620) See AriZal.

Reb Levi Yitzchak of Berditchov: Rabbi Levi Yitzchak the Rabbi of Berditchov. A Chassidic Rebbe and profound teacher, a disciple of the Maggid of Mezritch. Known for his love of Israel. (1740 - 1809).

Reb Mendel of Kotzk: The Kotzker. Chassidic master and teacher. Known for his sharp intellect and relentless pursuit of truth.

Reb Mich'ael of Zlotshov: Profound mystic and ecstatic teacher. (1731 - 1786). Student of the Baal Shem Tov.

Reb Nachman of Breslov: Rabbi Nachman who lived in the town of Breslov. A Chassidic Rebbe and profound teacher, grandson of the Baal Shem Tov.

Founder of the Breslov branch of Chassidim. (1772-1810).

Reb Pinchas of Koritz: Rabbi Pinchas from the town of Koritz. Early Chassidic Rebbe. (1726 – 1791)
Reb Tzodok HaKohen of Lublin: Chassidic master and teacher. Profound scholar and prolific author. (1823 – 1900)

Reb Simcha Bunim of Pshischah: Chassidic master and teacher. Known as a wise and truthful person. (1765 - 1827).

Reb Zusha of Anipoli: Chassidic teacher and beloved figure. Student of the Maggid of Mezritch. (1718-1800).

Reb Yaakov Yoseph of Polonnye: One of the early students of the Baal Shem Tov. Teacher and author. His book was the first Chassidic text published. (1710 – 1784).

Sefirah or Sefiros: The 'vessels' or 'lenses' that refract and reflect the Infinite Light in order that it can manifest in the finite, created reality; a series of cosmic/consciousness transducers that help to transform Infinite Light into finite form.

Shabbos: Shabbat. The seventh day of the week, a sacred day of rest.

Shachris: The morning prayers.

Shaloh Ha'Kadosh: The name of the books by Rabbi Yeshayah Halevi Horowitz. (1570–1630). Profound mystic and author. Shaloh is an acronym for Shenei Luchos Habris. Ha'Kadosh means the holy.

Shechinah: The Divine presence within creation. The feminine, the indwelling presence.

Siddur: Prayer book. The order of the prayers.

Shulchan Aruch: The Code of Jewish Law. Written by Rabbi Yoseph Caro.

Targum: The original translation of the Torah –the Five Books into Aramaic.

Tehilim: The Book of Psalms

Tzimtzum: The (apparent) cosmic Divine withdrawal. The contraction of the Infinite Light to make room for finitude.

Tzadik (plural; Tzadikim): A righteous person. Also,

refers to a spiritual master or miracle worker.

Talmud: Literally the learning. The Rabbinic writing that contain Halacha, law, and Agadah, lore. Part of the oral tradition of the Torah. Also known as the Gemarah.

Tefilah: The Hebrew word for prayer

The Ben Ish Chai: The name of the books by Rabbi Yosef Chayim, the great Iraqi scholar, Halachic ruler and Kabbalist. (1832 – 1909).

The Chidah: Rabbi Chayim Yoseph David Azulay. (1729- 1806). Sefardic Rabbi, prolific author and world-traveler.

The Chayit: Rabbi Yehudah Chayit (1462–1529). Spanish Rabbi, Kabbalist and author.

The Maharal: Rabbi Yehudah Loew. (1512 -1609). Profound thinker, mystic and philosopher.

The Mabit: The book by Rabbi Moshe of Trani. 16th-century Rabbi, thinker and author.
Torah: Generally refers to the Bible, the Five Books of Moses. In broader definition, this terms includes the entire canon of Jewish thought.

Yaakov: Jacob. One of the patriarchs of the Bible.

Yesh: A something. Individual, separate existence.

Yesod: Foundation; relationship. The masculine attribute. World as perfection.

Yetzirah: Formation. The world of pure emotion. Reality in process, in flux, in a state of emergence. A world in the process of becoming.

Yichud: (Plural, Yichudim). Unity. Unification. Unifying a physical action with a spiritual intention. In prayer Yichud is a spiritual intention (Kavanah) when saying the words of the prayers.

Yoseph: Joseph

Zohar: The Primary, multi-volume work of Kabbalah. Teachings date back to the 1st century sage Rabbi Shimon Bar Yochai. Published and made public in 1290's.

END NOTES:

CHAP. I.
Prayer: A Quest for Unity:

*The Rambam posits that there is a Mitzvah to pray at least once a day. *Safer Ha'Mitzvos, Mitzvah 5. Hilchos Tefilah, 1:1. Safer Ha'Mitzvos Rasag. Esei 2.* The Medrash Sifri *(Parshas Ekev, 41)* and the Gemarah *(Taanis, 2a)* write that prayer is the "service of the heart". See also *Baba Metzia, 107b. Medrash Tehilim Chap 66. Medrash Mishlei, Chap 1. Zohar 3, p. 257a. R. Yoseph Albo's Safer Haikkarim, Maamor 4:20. Akeidas Yitzchak, Parshas Tzav, Shar 58, p. 13b. R. Moshe Metrani, The Mabit, Beis Elokim, Shar HaTefilah, Chap. 15, p.63.*

How does the Rambam know that prayer is a Mitzvah each day? From the verse, "you shall serve Hashem with all your heart". And as mentioned earlier, we know that the service of the heart is prayer. But how do we know that there is a Mitzvah each day to pray? The Mabit answers in Kiryas Safer (beginning of Hilchos Tefilah) that since the verse says, "You shall serve Hashem your G-d, and He shall bless your bread and waters" *(Shemos, 23:25)*, the Torah is implying that just as water and bread is needed each day, the same is true for prayer. *See also Lechem Mishna, ad loc.* The Pri Chadash adds *(Orach Chayim, 89:1)* that the idea of, "to bless your bread and waters", refers to a slice of bread and cup of water in the morning and evening, the same being true for prayer. Based on this, it would seem that the Mitzvah is to pray twice daily. This is as the Mahari Perlo suggests in *Safer HaMitzvos Rasag Esei Bies (Jerusalem 1973), p.56*. Indeed according to some opinions it is a Mitzvah to pray twice daily *(Ibid. 70b)*. Interestingly, Rabbeinu Bachya comments on *(Devarim, 13:5)* and brings another verse as the source for praying each day.

The Ramban on the other hand is of the opinion that there is no Mitzvah from the Torah to pray daily, and that one should only pray when in need, see Ramban commentary on *Safer HaMitzvos, 5. See also Safer HaChinuch, Mitzvah 433. Safer HaMitzvos Katan, Chap. 11*. This is also the opinion of the Behag *(Baal Halachos Gedolos)*, who omits prayer as one of the positive Mitzvos. See also the *Tzemach Tzedek. Derech Mitzvosecho. Shoresh Mitzvas Ha'Tefilah, Chap. 1*.

It appears that the Ramban would agree that on Yom Tov prayer is a Torah law. *Ramban. Vayikra. 23:2*, as explained by the *Beis Yoseph. Orach Chayim. Siman 487. Pri Megadim. Siman 490*. Though see *Minchas Asher. Vayetze, Siman 35*. Perhaps, to answer the Minchas Ahser's question and to confirm the opinion of the Beis Yoseph, the Way how to pray; in public, with nice cloths is perhaps Rabbinic, but the actual idea to pray on Yom Tov is in fact a Torah law.

The Ramban does not count Tefillah as a Torah Mitzvah, being that prayer is the backbone of all Mitzvos. See also *R. Schneur Zalman of Liadi. Likutei Torah, Parshas Balak, p. 70b*.

Much like all general principles that are also not counted. See *Rambam, Safer HaMitzvos, Shoresh 4*. Note: This is the same reasoning offered by some commentators as to why the Rambam does not count Teshuvah (only the actual confession) as a Mitzvah. *Minchas Chinuch, Mitzvah 364*.

The *Aruch HaShulchan (Orach Chayim, 89:4)* explains that Tefilah is not counted as a Torah Mitzvah (according to some opinions) since it considered even higher and more integral, much like the spine of the body. R. Eliyahu of Vilna, the Vilna Gaon, writes that through doing a Mitzvah one does a Tikun to one body part. With Tefilah however there is a Tikun to the entire body. *Gra, Berachos, 28b*.

* Prayer needs intention. *Eiruvin, 65a*. Thus argues the *Toldas* that even according to the *Rambam*, when we pray today, while we are in exile and we do not have full intention, it is only a Rabbinic mitzvah. In fact, the Rambam and Ramban are not really arguing. The Rambam is speaking of prayer in Temple times, whereas the Ramban is speaking of prayer today. *Toldas Yaakov Yoseph, Parshas Yisro*.

* Four steps on the ladder of prayer. *Zohar 1, p. 266b — and Part 3, p. 306b. Tikunei Zohar, Tikkun 45. Shaloh Ha'Kadosh, Shar HaShamaim, p. 127. Likutei Torah, Parshas Beshalach, p 2b*.

* Prayer being similar to an offering which needs fire. See *R. Yitzchak Aramah. Akeidas Yitzchak, Parshas Tzav, Shar 58, p. 13b*.

* Prayer without intention is like a body without a soul. *Chovas Ha'Levavos, Shar Chesbon HaNefesh, 3:9. Safer Hayashar, Shar 13, p. 124. R. Yaakov Emdin. Sidur Beis Yaakov. Hakdamas Ha'Mechaber, p. 6.* The Ramak writes that prayer without intention does not rise to Heaven. *Pardes Rimonim, Shar 31;5.* Without Kavanah Kelalis, General Intention, there is no object of prayer. See *R. Chaim Brisker. Chidushei Reb Chaim, Rambam, Hilchos Tefilah, Chap 4:1.* Without intention, not only has the person not fulfilled his obligation to pray, but the actual 'entity' of prayer does not even exist. The *Lubavithcer Rebbe, Likutei Sichos, Vol. 22, p. 117–118.* See also *Shulchan Aruch Harav, Orach Chayim, Siman 101, the end. Magen Avraham, Chap. 101:5.* See also, *Safer Chassidim, Os. 585, and Os. 785. Rambam, Moreh Nevuchim, 3;51.* The first blessing of the Amidah (Smak. Bach, ad loc) needs *Kavanah Peratis /* Individual Intention, and without this intention the person praying has not fulfilled the obligation. *Tur, Orach Chayim, Siman 101.* Today, the consensus is that most people have trouble with proper intention and therefore even without *Kavana Peratis these parts of prayer should not be repeated. Ramah. Ad loc.*

* Prayer without intention and heart is similar to a king who requests a meal of roasted meat and the servants bring to the king the coal, a fork and knife, but not the meat itself. *R. Chaim Yoseph David Azulay. Chomas Anecha. Yeshayahu, Chap 29.*

* Without Kavanah the words of prayer are likened to a mindless bird chirping. *Chovas Ha'Levavos, Ibid.* The Rambam

writes that if a person prays without intention he might as well be digging holes in the ground or chopping wood. *Moreh Nevuchim, 3:51.*

* Prayers create Yechudim Above. *Pri Eitz Chayim, Shar HaTe-filah, Chap 7.*

* For the parable of the king, see also; *Keser Shem Tov, 97. Baal Shem Tov, Torah, Noach, 125. Degel Machana Ephrayim, Parshas Ki Tetze. Likutei Sichos 9, p. 271.*

CHAP. 2.

Prayer-book:
A Guided Tour through the Portable Homeland Prayer

* In prayer we need both *Keva* / routine, and Kavanah. "When you pray, do not make your prayer a routine (mechanical) act, but rather an entreaty of mercy and supplication before G-d." *Avos, 2:13.*

* *Ta'am Tefilah. Ohr Yechezkel, Emuna, p. 196.*

* The main idea of prayer is the inner intention to become close

to Hashem. "And his "banner", *Digulo*, over me is *Ahavah*, love. *Shir Hashirim, 2:4.* The Medrash says, "If an ignorant person reads "hate" instead of "love" as in, *Ve'ayavta* instead of *Ve'ahavta*, Hashem says, "His 'mistake' (*Dilugei*) is beloved to me." *Medrash Rabba, 2:13.*

* Need to know the inner Kavanah and the outer literal meaning of the words. *R. Yechezkel Londa, Node B'yehudah, 1.* See also *Yoreh De'ah 93.*

* Connecting to the letters themselves. *Keser Shem Tov, 2, p. 17b. Baal Shem Tov, Torah. Noach, Amud HaTefilah.*

* Sometimes it would even be appropriate and beneficial to say the entire blessing in one powerful extended exhale, especially, if one is struggling with extraneous thoughts intruding your focus. *R. Meir Poprosh. Ohr Tzadikim, 5;15. R. Aaron of Zelichov. Ohr HaGanuz, Bechukosai. Chidah. Teshuvos, Yoseph Ometz. 70;1.*

* The Chasam Sofer writes that a person who cannot himself meditate on all the Kavanos, should better cleave his thoughts to his ancestors, who were able to pray with the Kavanos, and thus, it is as if he prayed with all the Kavanos. *Chasam Sofar, Shemos, 14.*

* At times, a person can say the prayers very quickly because his heart is on fire with the love for Hashem and the words flow

through his month as if on their own. *Tziva'as HaRivash, p. 4d.* The opposite would be to hold onto each word and not wanting to part from it. See *R. Tzvi Elimelech of Dinov, Igra D'Pirka, p. 62.* Each letter is a rose and one collects them with tender care. *See Likutei Ma'haran 1:65.*

CHAP. I.

General Preparations: Time/Space/Consciousness

* The Shulchan Aruch rules that one should pray in an enclosed area since it brings about humility. *Orach Chayim, Chap 90:5.* Rav Kahana says: "A person who prays in a valley is brazen" *Berachos, 34b.* The *Tosefos (Chatzif, ad loc)* explains that this applies only to one who prays in an open place that is populated and thus distracting. Thus, throughout history there has been a practice to pray formal or informal prayers in the fields, as we find by *Yitzchak Bereishis, 24:63.* And also in the later practices of the AriZal and Reb Nachman for example.

* Even a blind person should pray in a space with windows. *Kaf Ha'Chayim, Orach Chayim, 90:20.* Also the windows should face Jerusalem. *Rambam, Hilchos Tefilah, Chap. 5:6.* See also *Shulchan Aruch, Orach Chayim, Chap. 90:4.* See also *Zohar 2, p. 251.*

* *Makom Kavuah* / Designated Place. The Gemara teaches, "One who sets a place for prayer, the G-d of Abraham will help him" *Berachos, 6b.* A Makom Kavuah should be selected even at home. *Yerushalmi, Berachos 4: 4.* In the Shulchan Aruch it seems implied *(Orach Chayim, 90:19)*, and the Mishna Berura confirms *(Ibid: 59)*, that even when praying at home one should designate a place for prayer. One of the reasons for this is because a person concentrates better in a familiar place. See also *R. Yitzchak Abuhav, Menoras Ha'Maor, Ner 3, Klal 3, Chap. 10, p. 303.* "And his family members will not distract him" *Shulchan Aruch Ha'Rav, 90:18.* Hashem's presence is found throughout the entire world, yet a place where one prays continually becomes that much more holy and thus their prayers are more susceptible to be answered. *R. Moshe Metrani, Beis Elokim, Shar HaTefilah, 5.*

* Regarding a Gartel. Already in the times of Rashi, when men began wearing pants in Europe, the custom of wearing a belt at mid body as a preparation for prayer because of *Heichin Likras Elokecha*, and also to separate the upper and lower parts of the body, became less practiced. *Machzor Vitry.* Yet, most opinions agree that even if we do not need to wear a belt in prayer, assuming we don't normally wear a belt, still as a *Midas Chassidus* we should wear a belt. The Shulchan Aruch rules we should wear a belt because of *Heichan. Orach Chayim, 91:1-2.* Today if one does not normally wear a belt it is Midas Chassidus to wear one. *Mishnah Berurah, 91:4.* It appears that according to the *Shulchan Aruch Harav* a Gartel has to be worn, and not just because of Midas Chassidus. *Orach Chayim. Siman 91:2.*

* One is not allowed to eat or drink before praying. *Berachos, 10b.* For the purpose of health one may eat and drink *Shulchan Aruch HaRav, 89:5.*

* We need to purify our heart before we enter prayer. *Midrash Rabbah, Shemos, 22:3.* See also *Menoras HaMaor, Ner 3, Klal 3, Chap. 11, p. 305. R. Yaakov Emdin, Sidur Beis Yaakov, Hakdamas Ha'Mechaber, p. 11.*

* Without Teshuvah our prayers are not answered. *R. Yehudah Ha'chasid, Safer Chassidim, 612-* in the name of the Rasag. Teshuvah before praying. *Psikta D'Rav Kahana, Chap. 30:191.*

CHAP. 2

Settling the Mind for Prayer

* Learn Torah or say Tehilim before prayer. *Keser Shem Tov, p. 27.*

* The Gemara *(Berachos 5b)* speaks of the sage Abba Binyamin who always tried to pray as close as to the time he woke up as possible. Rashi writes *(ad loc.)* that this means he did not learn before praying, as he may get too involved and forget to pray. If

the person appoints someone else to remind him to pray there is no problem. Many contemporary codifiers of law suggest an alarm clock as an agent to remind one to pray. Also, the Gemarah says that a person should not begin praying while in the midst of an unanswered Torah issue. *Berachos, 31a.*

* A person should not pray when angry. *Eiruvin, 65a. See; Tur Orach Chayim, 98.* See *Tosefos (ad loc.)* for the Torah source of this ruling. Today, the ruling is to pray either way. *Teshuvas Ha'gaonim, Sharei Teshuvah, 89 — and Mechaber, Siman, 98:2.*

* Emptying themselves of ego. *R. Mendel of Vitepsk. Pri Ha'aretz. Vayakhel-Pekudie.* See also *The Magid of Koznitz. Avodas Yisroel, p. 164.* See *R. Yisrael DovBer of Vilednick. Shearis Yisrael, p. 3.*

* Hispashtus Ha'Gashmiyus serves as a good introduction to prayer. *Tur. Orach Chayim, 98.* See also: *Shaloh Ha'Kadosh, Asarah Hilulim, p.319. Nefesh Hachayim. Shar 2;14.*

* There are many details regarding the law of not offering a formal greeting before praying. Overall, there are two prohibitions: One is not to go visit a friend to say even good morning before praying. The other is not to extend a formal greeting, as in the word Shalom, even to a person you happen to meet on the street. Although, saying good morning is never an issue. *Shulchan Aruch Harav, Orach Chayim, 89:3.*

CHAP. 3.

Dealing with Foreign & Negative Thoughts Before and During Prayer

* Prayer is similar to, and is offered in the place of, the offerings in the Temple. Just as with an offering, we need to make sure that we do not entertain distracting thoughts while praying. *Shulchan Aruch, Orach Chayim, Siman 98:4*. We should at least secure a basic understanding of what the words mean. *Ibid, 98:1*.

* For this reason the AriZal offers little advice about what to do with foreign thoughts. On the other hand, from the school of the Baal Shem Tov and his students there are elaborate solutions as to what one should do when foreign thoughts enter the mind. According to the method of the AriZal the mind is "filled" with divine thoughts and Kavanos, there is no room for other thoughts. This is similar to when a person is truly preoccupied with a thought or an experience, for example in a moment of crisis, then no other thoughts enter their mind in a distracting manner. A person becomes very clear minded and focused when the issue at hand is very personal and pertinent. The Baal Shem on the other hand suggest a much more simplified and embodied approach to prayer. He does not emphasize the use of complex Kavanos, and instead suggests that a person should truly try to enter into the simple sound and vibration of each word and letter. Thus, Prayer becomes

a much more vibrational experience, rather than intellectual. Due to this shift in awareness, the mind is not as 'occupied' as in the Arizal's method of intense intentions. Therefore, 'foreign thoughts' are much likelier to creep into one's consciousness. They must be dealt with. This is the explanation for why the Arizal's teachings do not focus on strategies to deal with foreign thoughts, and the Baal Shem Tov's do.

* The Baal Shem Tov teaches not to dismiss a prayer without intention. *Ben Peros Yoseph, Toldos, 277.* The *Kamarner (Shulchan Ha'tohar)* derives many laws based on this principle of the Baal Shem Tov. Yet, sometimes the Shulchan Aruch rules that we need to pray over specific prayers if said with no intention. The *Bnei Yisachar* suggests, that a person should not think, I need to pray over because I did not have good intention, rather, I need to pray over to have more intention, to add more sanctity.

* With regards to the verse *Lev Tahor* see also: *Machtzis Hashekel. Shulchan Aruch. 98:1. Mishnah Berurah 98: 2.* R. Pinchas of Koritz teaches that a person should continuously recite the verses Shema Yisrael and Baruch Sheim. *Medrash Pinchas. Os 8.* This helps with quieting intruding thoughts in prayer. *R. Aaron Roth. Shomer Emunim. Maamar Hashgacha Peratis. Chap 3.* Reb Aaron also speaks a lot in his books about the value of affirmations, one that he suggests for intruding disturbing thoughts is "I hereby nullify all negative, despicable, damaging thoughts, that enter into my heart/mind when I pray or study Torah at all times, that they are all nullified and I have no desire of them, at all." *Ibid.*

* The practice of reciting or meditavely thinking the verse in Vayikra is quoted in *Kaf Hachayim, Orach Chayim. 98: 9.* See also *Sidur Ha'AriZal –R. Shabsi Rashkaver- p. 16.*

* The Magid of the Mishnah revealed to R. Yoseph Caro, the Beis Yoseph, that to purify thoughts he should say seven times, the passage, (which is also the beginning of a hymn sung Friday evening) *"Mah Yafis, U'ma Ne'amt, Ahava B'tanugim* - how beautiful and how pleasant is this love of pleasure", and the words *Kera Satan* – break open Satan. Many Sefardic sources, such as R. Yoseph Chaim Azulai and the Kaf Ha'chayim, write, that if a person is looking to break negative patterns of thoughts, he should than meditate on the words "Kera Satan-break open Satan", Satan represents all forms of constriction and limitations, including all constricted, limiting, ego-centric thoughts.

* The word *Pi* stands for *Palti* and *Yoseph.* These are two biblical figures who overcame temptation in the face of temptation. *Sanhedrin. 19b. The Magen Avraham (Orach Chayim. 98)* writes that it is not a proven method and thus should not be done during the prayers, during the Amidah itself. The three times Pi is also related to the word Pi which literally means a Mouth. The three Pi's refer to the three "mouths" that "opened" miraculously in the desert, the "mouth of the earth" the "mouth of the donkey" and the mouth of the well." *R. Tzvi Elimelech of Dinav. Devarim Nechmadim. Avos.* The numerical value of Pi is 90, three times 90= 270, as the word *Rah*, negative, so the three times spitting and saying Pi erases and lets go of the negative.

* Thinking of business to break negative thoughts. R. *Klunimus Kalmish of Peasetzna. Hachsharas Ha'Avreichim, Chap. 9. p. 125.*

* We are to place the letters of the Name of Hashem before us at all times. *R. Yitzchak of Acco. Meiras Einayim. Parshas Ekev. 11 - 22. R. Yoseph Caro. Maggid Mesharim. Parshas Vayikra. R. Chaim Vital. Shar Ruach Hakodesh. Derush 1. Sharrei Kedusha. 3:4.* This idea is brought down in Halacha. *R. Yehudah Ashkanazi. Be'er Heitiv. Shulchan Aruch. Orach Chayim. 1:3.* Visualization of the name of Hashem can assist to eradicate unwanted thoughts. *R. Elimelech of Lizhensk Tzetal Katan.*

* Kera Satan. *R. Chaim Yoseph David Azulai. The Chida. Devash L'phi. Erech Mem.* See also: *Kaf HaChayim. Orach Chayim. 98: 9.*

* Visualize being in Gan Eden to break negative thoughts. *R. Yaakov Yoseph of Polonnye. Toldas Yaakov Yoseph. Parshas Tetzave. p. 139.* See also: *Reishis Chachmah, Shar HaKedusha, Chap. 4*

* Visualize the words on the page in your thoughts to break negative thoughts. This is a proven practice. *R. Chayim of Viloshin. Nefesh Hachayim, Shar 2. Chap 13.* See also: *Rabbi Eliyahu Mani (associate and student of the Ben Ish Chai) Kise Eliyahu, Shar 3.* There is a teaching repeated in the name of the Gra,

Reb Chayim's teacher "He came in front of the king, he said, with the book, it was returned his negative thought" *(Megilah, 9;25)*. Homiletically, could mean, with the book (looking in the Siddur) all the negative thoughts are returned - nullified.

* Bodily movement shifts consciousness. *R. Pinchas of Kartiz. Imrei Pinchas, p. 136.*

* Clapping the hands to purify the air. *R. Nachman of Breslov. Likutei Aytzos, Tefilah, p. 157.* See also *Likutei Moharan, 1:46.* Clapping ones hands in prayer is an old Chassidic custom. *Noem Elimelech. Parshas Shemini. Degel Machane Ephrayim. Parshas Noach.*

*"A Nigun has the power to eradicate..." *R. Yoseph Yitzchak of Chabad. Sicha Yud Tes Kislev, 5708.*

* *Zimra – Zamer. Yeshayahu, 25:5.* See *R. Yoseph Gikatalia. Shaarie Orah, Shar 1, p. 7.*

* The Baal Shem Tov teaches that the reason a person has these thoughts is because the spark desires elevation. *Ben Peros Yoseph, p. 50b-c. Divrei Moshe, Parshas Lech Lecha.* Deeper still, the Baal Shem teaches that when a person is in deep deveikus and a thought arises it can be assumed that this thought is a minor form of Ruach Hakodesh. *Keser Shem Tov, chap. 195, p 25b.* See also, *Likutei Yekarim, chap. 12, and chap. 48.* The body's hunger is a physical manifestation of the soul's hunger. *Keser*

Shem Tov, p. 50.

* *Ha'alas HaMidos*, elevating the attributes. *Keser Shem Tov, chap. 171. Tzavoas Harivash, chap. 87.* See also *The Magid of Mezritch. Magid Devarav Leyokav, Likutei Amorim, Ohr Torah, chap. 37. Likutei Yekarim, chap. 194. Ohr Haemes, p. 2. R. Moshe Chaim Ephraim of Sudylkov. Degel Machanah Ephraim, Parshas Behaalotecha, p. 177. R. Nachum of Chernobyl. Meor Einayim, Parshas Shemos, p. 62. R. Yaakov Yitzchak Horowitz of Lublin. Zikhron Zos, p. 141.*

* From human/finite /formed/exclusive love can come Divine/ Infinite/ Formless/ Inclusive love. *R. Eliyahu ben Moshe Di Vidas. Reishis Chochmah, Shar Ha'Ahavah in the name of R. Yitzchak of Acco.* Experiencing pleasure of this world is but a small fraction of the Infinite pleasure of being close to Hashem. *Degel Machane Ephrayim, Vayigash, p. 66.*

* "How can you elevate the thought when you yourself are below?" *R. Schneur Zalman of Liadi. Tanya, chap. 28.* See also *R. Tzvi Elimelech of Dinav. Derech Pikudecha, Hakdamah 7, p. 26. R. Klunimus Kalman Maor Vashemesh, Parshas Re'eh, p. 581. R. Tzadok HaKohen of Lublin. Komtez HaMincha, chap. 16, p. 26.*

* There are points in person's life in which there are fewer struggles and in those areas perhaps a person can practice the elevation of Midos. See *R. Avraham Yitzchak Kaan. Likutie Yekarim, Ha'gaah, p. 58-59.*

*A person can be Tzadik with regards to certain issues in life. *R. Tzadok Ha'kohen. Tzidkas HaTzadik 58*

* The AriZal writes that there are no prayers from the time of creation until the time of redemption that are alike. *Pri Eitz Chayim, Shar HaTefilah 7, p. 17. Olas Tamid, Shar HaTefilah, p. 11. Shulchan Aruch AriZal, Orach Chayim, 89:1.* See also *Ramak. Shiur Koma, Hakdamah, chap. 13. Ohr Yaakar, Parshas Kedoshim, 4.* Everyday necessitates a new level of prayer. See *R. Chaim of Volozhin. Nefesh HaChayim, Shar 2:13, p. 129.* The Baal Shem Tov adds that the same is true with "foreign thoughts." The thoughts today are different than the thoughts of a day ago. *R. Yaakov Yoseph of Polonnye. Toldos Yaakov Yoseph, Parshas Va-yakhel, p. 75c.*

* If a person finds himself being disturbed by another person during prayer he should think to himself that surely this person is a Divinely sent messenger, teaching them to have more Kavanah in prayer. *Keser Shem Tov, p. 66. Tzavoas Horivash, chap. 120.* See at length *Tanya, Iggeres Ha'Kodesh, chap. 25.*

* Parable of the Baal Shem Tov. *Baal Shem Tov al Ha'Torah, Amud Tefilah 105.*

CHAP. 4.

Visualizations to Enter Prayer

* Through *Tziyur* what we know in our minds becomes knowledge of the heart, and the information is integrated. *R. Simcha Zisal of Kelm. Kisvei Ha'Saba M'Kelm, Part 1, p. 143-144.*

* The primary *Avodah*, Divine service, today is through prayer. *Eitz Chayim, Shar HaTefilah, chap. 7, 39:1-2. Tanya, Kutras Acharon. Maor Vashemesh, Parshas Vaeschanan.* Note: See also *Midrash Shochar Tov, Tehilim, 102.*

* When saying the Az Yashir we need to imagine that we ourselves are now crossing the Sea of Reeds. *R. Chaim Yoseph David Azulay, the Chidah, Avodas HaKodesh, Tziporen Shamir, chap. 24. Siddur, Tefilah Yesharah, Keser Nehurah.*

* It is preferable to pray somewhere further from one's home, to move away from ones mundane reality. *R. Yehuda Lowe, the Maharal, Nesivos Olam, Avodah 5.* See also *Sefas Emes, Parshas Vayerah*, with regards to entering the "two doors".

* Imagine oneself above the *Kipas Ha'Shamayim*, the "Cap of the Sky". *Tzava'as HaRivash, p. 17b.* See also *Rambam, Hilchos Tefilah, 5:4.*

* Imagining oneself moving higher and higher in the vastness of space. *Likutei Yekarim, p. 3.(Baal Shem Tov Torah, Parshas Ekev, 46.*

* *R. Chaim Vital* writes, "Therefore if you are praying, or desire to have proper intention, imagine that you are light...the light is a throne of life..." *Kesavim Chadashim, Sharei Kedusha 4, Shar 2:12.* In fact, we, our souls are "light". *Mishlei 20:27. Shabbos 32a.* We come from Hashem's light and return to the "light." On the one hand, the Mishnah says we come from a "putrid drop" and we are going to a place of "dust, maggots and worms." *Avos. 3:1.* Or "we come from a place of darkness... and go to a place of darkness." *Avos D'Rebbe Nason. Chap 19.* Or, "we come from a place of impurity...and go to a place to impure others." *Derech Eretz Zutah. Chap 3.* Yet, this is all with regards to the "body" the soul, however, is part of the Light of Hashem. See; *Shefa Tal Hakdamah,* and the soul returns to the "Throne of Glory". *Shabbos 152a.* "The spirit returns to G-d." *Koheles. 12:7.* Note there is another version in *Avos D'Rebbe Nason* "From where did he come from? From a place of fire, and he returns to a place of fire."

* Regarding visualization of being in the Holy of Holies. See also; *R. Yoseph Yitzchak, The sixth Chabad Rebbe. Igros Kodesh, vol. 8, p. 200. R. Klunimus Kalmish of Peasetzna. Hachsharas Ha'Avreichim, p. 32.*

When we pray the Amidah we should imagine that we are standing in the Beis HaMikdash *(Shulchan Aruch, 95:2)*, in the place of the Holy of Holies. *Mishna Berura, 94:2.*

* Picture yourself praying with Tzadikim that you have seen.

Yosher Divrei Emes, Os 33, and *Likutei Yekarim, 129a.* Imagine standing next to your Rebbe and praying. See the *Steipler Gaon. Kreina D'Igrata, Part 3.*

* The teaching of the Maggid is recorded in *Maggid Devarav L'Yaakov, p. 325.*

* The Baal Shem Tov teaches that when we pray we should have Kavanah that we are connecting with the Tzadikim. See: *Me'or Einayim, Parshas Beshalach.* This, says the Baal Shem is part of the L'Sheim Yichud declaration. R. Nachman of Breslov teaches that the words, "I hereby bind myself to all the Tzadikim of the generations", should be said as a verbal declaration before prayer. *Likutei Moharan I, 2:6, 9:4.* Note some other early sources: *Yosher Divrei Emes, 2:33. Be'er Mayim Chayim, Parshas Vayetzei.*

* R. Yoseph Caro writes that when we pray the Amidah we should "empty ourselves from all thoughts of body and imagine as if we are angels". *Beis Yoseph, Orach Chayim, 95:1. Mishna Berurah, ibid.*

* The Zohar speaks of the light of the Shechinah that rests above the head of the Wise. *Zohar vol. 3, p. 187a.* R. Eliezer Ezcari speaks about how this light is revealed on the heads of Tzadikim. *Sefer Chareidim, chap. 3, p. 32-33.*

* The quote about the light is from R. Eliezer Ezcari. *Safer Chareidim, chap. 65.*

* Reb Yitzchak of Homel writes that the Early Pious Ones would visualize how the Shechinah is surrounding them. *Ma'amor Ha'Shiflus V'Ha'simcha, 8.*

* At all times we should imagine ourselves in the midst of Hashem's presence. *Likutei Yekarim, p. 3.* Hidden within the Divine Light. *Baal Shem Tov, Torah, Ekev, 31.*

* The *Rambam Hilchos Teshuvah, 3; 7,* writes that a heretic is one who believes Hashem possesses a body. The *Ra'aved (ad loc.)* disagrees. For educational purposes, to train the mind to more subtle understandings, one can begin by conceptualizing Hashem in form. *Bnei Machshava Tova, 7*

CHAP 5.

Nigun –Song Before & During Prayers

* R. Yehudah Ha'Chassid suggests that we pray with songs to inspire us. *Sefer Chassidim, 158.* The brilliant sage Rabbi Meir would sing various melodies during his prayer. *Zohar, Rayah Mehemnah, Parshas Mishpatim, p. 114. Shaarei Teshuvah 2 (Chabad), p. 15.* Either a person can use song to induce contemplative consciousness or a more passionate form of prayer. It is preferable that the song organically flows from the person who is deeply praying. Alternatively, a person can use song to pray, or the prayer may evoke the song. *Baal Shem Tov al Ha'Torah, Aumud Ha'tefilah 21, Note 15.*

* R. Eliezer Ezcari. *Safer Cheraidim, chap. 66:30.*

* The four reasons for music in the Temple. *A) Rambam. Morah Nevhuchim, 3:45. B) Sefer Ha'Chinuch, Mitzvah 384. C) R. Shem Tov Ibn Falaquera. Safer HaMevakesh, p. 86.* See also *R. Moshe Yechiel Levertov Sefer Shemiras Hada'as, Maamor Nigun, p. 8-9. D) R. DovBer of Chabad. Kuntras Hispalous, p. 66.*

CHAP. I.

Feet Together at the Peak of Prayer

* We pray in the various positions to mimic the prayer positions that Moshe prayed in: sitting, standing, and prostrating himself. *Devarim 9:9, 9:18, 10:10.* See; *Tur, Orach Chayim, chap. 131.*

* The Medrash says that Israel will be redeemed in the merit of prostrating in prayer. *Yalkut Shimoni, Samuel 1, chap. 1:28.* When Rabbi Akiva would pray alone he would prostrate and kneel so often that if one were to see him in one corner of the room and would leave, upon returning one would find him at another corner. *Berachos 31a.* See also *Medrash Tanchuma, Parshas Chayei Sarah, chap. 5.* Today however, we do not actually prostrate. *Shulchan Aruch, Orach Chayim, Siman 131.* See *Rambam Hilchos Tefilah, 5:14.* See also; *Shulchan Aruch Arizal, p. 33.*

Chap. 2.

Swaying or Being Still

* *R. Chaim of Volozhin Nefesh HaChayim, Eitz Ha'Chayim, p. 432.*

* We sway to awaken our soul. *R. Yaakov Emdin. Sidur BeisYak-kov, Hakdamas Ha'Mechber, p. 12.*

* Swaying in prayer and thus all my bones are involved in prayer. *Zohar 3, p. 218b. R. David Avudaraham.* This is brought down in the *Shulchan Aruch, Orach Chayim, Rama 48:2.*

* *R. Pinchas of Koritz. Imrei Pinchas, p. 1.*

* When a person sways in prayer it appears they should try to sway from front to back. *Yesod Shoresh Ha'Avodah, Shar Ha'karbon, Tefilas 18. p. 83.*

* Sources for not swaying during the Amidah. *Shulchan Aruch, Orach Chayim, 48. Magen Avraham 4. R. Menachem Azaryah De Fano. Asarah Maamoros, Maamor Aim Kal Chai, 1:33. Rabbi Chayim Yoseph David Azulay. Avodas Hakodesh, Kesher Gudal, 12:1.* In fact there are Kabbalistic sources that write that one should not sway at all in prayer. *Teshuvhas Mahara Me'Panu, Teshuvah 113.* Perhaps this is assuming that the person at any point in prayer is in such deep Deveikus that there is no room for expression or movement.

* At the peak of prayer, during the Amidah there is no room for self –expression. See *R. Yehudah Lowe. Nesivos Olam, Nesiv Ha'Avadah, chap. 6.*

CHAP. 3.

Hands & Body Position

*"Rav Ashi said, "I saw with Rav Kahana that when there was trouble in the world, he would remove his cloak and clasp his hands saying, 'like a servant before his master'. At times of peace he would dress himself and cover himself and enwrap…" *Shabbos 10a.* According to the Rambam, Rav Kahana would always clasp his hands, both in troubled times and in a time of peace, and he most probably had his right hand over his left, upon his heart. *Hilchos Tefilah, 5:4.* The difference in various times was with regards to his dress. *Kesef Mishnah, 5:4.* The Rama rules that "in times of trouble one should clasp his hands like a servant before his master." *Orach Chayim, 91:6.* The AriZal would always pray the Amidah with his right hand covering his left. *Pri Etz Chayim, Shar Kerias Shema, chap. 29.*

* The custom to place the thumb of the right hand within the grasp of the left hand. *R. Menachem Azaryah De Fano. Asarah Maamoros, Maamor Eim Kall Chai, Part 1:33. Shulchan Aruch Harav, 95:4.*

* Lifting the hands above the head. *Melachim 1, 8:22. Divrei Ha-*

Yamim 2, 6:13. Ezra, 6:5. See also Shemos 17:11. See also, *Pirkei D'Rebbe Eliezer, chap. 44.*

* A person should not lift his hands above their head in prayer. *Zohar 2, Yisro, 67a.* This is only when a person lifts (both) his hands (with an open hand) for "no reason".

* Even with the proper intention there are limitations to how long a person should stretch his hands over his head. *Sefer Ha-Bahir, 138.* See also *Ramban and R. Bachya, Shemos, 17:11-12. Meiras Einayim, Beshalach. 17:16. Pardes Rimmonim, Shar 15:3. Asarah Maamoros, Maamor Chikur Din, 1:22.* See also; *Shaloh Ha'Kadosh, Meseches Tamid, 62.*

* Rabbi Akiva Eiger writes with regards to lifting the hands above the head in prayer that the Jews no longer have this practice as it has become adopted by gentiles. *Ha'gaas, Shulchan Aruch, Orach Chayim, 89:1.* When a person is drowning he wildly gestures with his hands and body to lift himself out of the water. Similarly, says the Baal Shem Tov, when a person is praying and is shaking his body he may be doing so to save himself from the "negative waters"; i.e. the intruding thoughts that wish to distract him from his prayers. *Lekutei Yekarim, p. 15a,* also *Ohr Ha'emes, p. 83b.*

* If the hands involuntarily fly upwards in a position of 'receiving from on High', "know, that this is a sign that your prayers have been answered and that in fact you are receiving from on High". *R. Pinchas of Koritz. Imrei Pinchas, p. 84.*

* The palm of the hand facing downward. *R. Levi Yitzchak of Berditchov. Kedushas Levi, Parshas Naso.*

* Outstretched hands represent the letter Shin. Left hand outstretched, right hand resting creates the letter Dalet. *R. Moshe Ibn Shem Tov. Nefesh Ha'Chochmah, Amudei Ha'kabalah 2, 2005.* See; *Sodos V'Taamei HaMitzvos, p. 43. Shaloh Ha'Kadosh, Meseches Chulin, Torah Ohr, chap. 18, p. 31 regarding Milah.*

CHAP. 4.

Eyes Open or Closed

* The Zohar speaks of praying with eyes closed. *Zohar 3, p. 260b. Shaloh Ha'Kadosh, Meseches Tamid 59, and Yesod Shoresh Ha'avoda, Shar 5, chap 2.* The AriZal would pray the Amidah with his eyes closed. *Pri Eitz Chayim, Shar Kerias Shema, chap. 29.* The AriZal would keep his eyes closed during the Amidah (both the private and the repetition). He did so also to imitate and embody the aspect of Rachel within the Shechinah, which is beautiful but "without eyes".

* It is a miracle that a person remains alive after prayers. *Sifsei Tzadikim, Parshas Beshalach.* See also; *Tziva'as HaRivash, p. 4b.* Reb Uri of Sterlisk would say his final goodbyes before prayers. *Imrei Kodesh, p 35.*

* Overall, when praying one should look into the Siddur. *Siddur Shalah. Kavanas V'Han'hagas Ha'tefilah.* The act of looking into the Siddur, the Gra of Vilna teaches, gazing upon the letters assist to negate intruding foreign thoughts. See *Shulchan Aruch, Orach Chayim, Siman 98, Biur HaGra.*

* The Aruch Hashulchan writes that, "a person should close his eyes during the Amidah, and if he does so he will merit to see the face of the Shechina at the moment of death." *Orach Chayim, chap. 95:4.*

* Eyes open, looking into the Siddur, when a person feels themselves on a lower level and lacking focus. Eyes closed when a person feels connected and fully engaged. *Tziva'as HaRivash, p. 4d.*

CHAP. I.

The Four Ascending Steps in the Morning Prayers

*"The hour of prayer is an hour of battle". ˆ See also; *R. Schneur Zalman of Liadi. Siddur Im Dach, p. 23b. Likutei Torah, Parshas Balak, p. 72a,* and *Ki Tetze p. 34c.* See also: *Zohar 3, p. 243a.* Sword is a reference to prayer. *Baba Basra, 123a.* The Targum translates the word sword to mean prayer. *Targum Unkolus, Bereishis, 48:22.*

* The Four worlds and the Four Sections of the morning prayers. See: *Pri Eitz Chayim. Shar HaTefilah, Shar HaKavanos, D'rushei Tefilas HaShachar, Derush 1. Olas Tamid, Shar HaTefilah, p.7a. Toldas Yaakov Yoseph, Vayikra. Ramchal, Derech Hashem, 4;6;14. Derech Pikudecha, p. 174. Nefesh Hachayim, Shar 2;18. Rashab, Kuntras Ha'avodah, chap 1. p. 233.* There are other ways to divide the morning prayers into four. See: *Rayatz, Sefer Ha'maamrom –Kuntreisim 1. p. 638. Maor Vashemesh, Beshalach, p. 196.*

* There is also the way to divide Shachris into seven chambers. These Seven Chambers correspond to the Ten Sefiros. 1) Heichal Livinas Hasapir- corresponds to Yesod and Malchus. 2) Heichal Etzem HaShamayim – corresponds to Hod. 3) Heichal Nogah- corresponds to Netzach. 4) Heichal HaZechus – corresponds to Gevurah. 5) Heichal Ha'Ahavah –corresponds to Chesed. 6) Heichal HaRatzon –corresponds to Tifferes (that is above Chesed). 7) Heichal Kodesh HaKadashim –corresponds to Keser/Kodesh, and Kadashim (plural) to Chochmah and Binah.

* Whereas generally the Yud corresponds to Atzilus, the Hei to Beriah, the Vav to Yetzirah and the final Hei with Asiyah, each inner world contains the entire Name. In Atzilus it is the Name as it manifests in 72, the Name Av, Beriah 63, the Name Sag, Yetzirah 45, Mah, and Asiyah 52, Ban.

The Name Yud/10 Hei/5 Vav/6 Hei/5 = 26. Yet, each letter,

as in the Yud, and the Hei, the Vav and the Hei

In the world of Atzilus the Name Hashem shines with the Yud's as the 72 Numeric value;

Yud/10, Vav/6, Dalet/4=20.
Hei/5, Yud/10= 15
Vav/6, Yud/10, Vav/6= 22
Hei/5, Yud/10=15
20+15+22+15= 72.

In the world of Beriah the Name of Hashem shines with Aleph/Yud, as the 63 numeric value;

Yud/10, Vav/6, Dalet/4=20.
Hei/5, Yud/10= 15
Vav/6, Aleph/1, Vav/6= 13
Hei/5, Yud/10=15
20+15+13+15= 63.

In the world of Yetzirah the Name of Hashem shines with Aleph as the 45 numeric value;
Yud/10, Vav/6, Dalet/4=20.
Hei/5, Aleph/1= 6
Vav/6, Aleph/1, Vav/6= 13
Hei/5, Aleph/1=6
20+6+13+6= 45.

In the world of Asiyah the Name of Hashem shines with Hei's as the 52 numeric value;

Yud/10, Vav/6, Dalet/4=20.
Hei/5, Hei/5= 10
Vav/6, Vav/6= 12
Hei/5, Hei/5=10
20+10+12+10= 52.

In ascending order; 1) Ban -52. 2) Mah-45. 3) Sag-63. 4) Av-72

* With regards to saying the Karbanos, the Sacrifices, sitting down see, *Mahadura Basra. Shulchan Aruch Harav, Orach Chayim, Siman 1;9.*

* Zimrah from the word Zamer. *Yeshayahu, 25;5. R. Yoseph Gikatalia. Shaarei Orah, Shar 1.* See also; *Likutei Torah, Parshas Nitzavim, p. 51d.*

* It is preferable to sit during the Shema. *Tur, Orach Chayim, 63.* See also; *Medrash Rabbah, Bereishis, 48:7.*

* The Amidah corresponds to the letter Yud, the upper masculine. Yet Tefilah, as will be shortly explained is also Malchus, the "feminine". Therefore one would think that we should sit while we pray, as sitting represents the "feminine". But just as the law with regards to blessing the new moon (feminine/Mal-

chus) is that it should be done standing *(Sanhedrin, 42a)*, the Amidah should also be said standing even though Tefilah is viewed as "feminine". We do this because when Malchus is in a state of receiving from Zair Anpin (the "masculine"), we need to stand. The blessing of the new moon is a Tikun for the moon. *Moar Anayim, Parshas Bereishis. Tola'as Yaakov, Birchas Ha'Levanah.* The same could be said about Tefilah, since the idea of the Amidah is that Malchus is "filled" by Zair Anpin and thus needs to be said standing.

CHAP. 2.

The Redemption of Prayer

* During the Amidah we do not say, Hashem Melech Ha'olam, "Hashem king of the Universe", even though any blessing that does not contain Malchus, "Kingship", is not a blessing, since the Amidah is connected with the blessings of the Shema, and therefore the Amidah does not need Malchus. *Tosefos Berachos 49.* This is a deeper connection between the two. Bringing redemption close to prayer is also the reason why Tefilah Va'sikin, "praying at the moment when night turns into day", has tremendous value — perhaps even more important (according to some authorities) than praying with a Minyan — since night represents that which is lacking, and day represents that which is revealed. When a person prays in these moments they are also unifying "night" with "day", Tefilah and Geulah, Malchus and Zah (Zeir Anpin).

* Rashi, in the name of the Yerushalmi, offers another reason why we need to juxtapose Geulah to Tefilah *Berachos 4b.* The simple reason is so that we begin Tefilah from a place of joy *Shulchan Aruch, Orach Chayim, 93:2.*

* On Shabbos there is a debate whether we need to connect Geula to Tefilah. *Haga'as Ashri. Berachos 1;10. Ramah, Orach Chayim, Siman 111.* See also; *Sh'ut, Shagas Aryeh, Teshuvah.* The inner reason why we would think that there is no reason to draw a direct connection from Geulah to Tefilah on Shabbos (or Yom Tov) is because on Shabbos (and Yom Tov) the Tefilah itself is Geulah, it is redemptive prayer, since we are not asking for any personal requests and there is no judgment.

* Redemption represents a reality where one is no longer bound and limited by all the things lacking. *Beis Yaakov (Ishbitz) Emor, p. 106b-107a.*

CHAP. 3.

The Essence of Prayer

* Rabbi Shalom Sharabi, the Rashash writes about the Kavanos during Tefilah and writes V'yichavein, have Kavanah, not V'yichashev, think. According to his son, this means that a person when meditating on these Divine Names he should not merely have in mind, intellectually, rather have in mind as if

his soul, experientially is ascending with the intension, Above.

* Rabbi Pinchas of Karitz writes that the path of the Baal Shem Tov is that when you have Kavanah you need to become like the Kavanah, become similar to the Kavanah. *Imrei Pinchas, Tefilah, 174.*

* Prayer on a deep level, is simply a mechanism to bring down the Infinite Light into the finite creation that is our reality. *The Alter Rebbe. Likutei Torah, Balak.*

CHAP. 4.

Silence & Sound in Prayer

*We need to speak the prayers. *Berachos 20b.* We need to pronounce the words. *Shulchan Aruch, Orach Chayim, Chap. 101:2. Magen Avraham ad loc.* Yet, "One who rises his voice in prayer shows a lacks of faith" *Berachos, 24b.* We should thus pray with a low voice. *Berachos, 31b.* Though for a different opinion see *Ramban, Shemos, 30:16. R. Aaron HaKohen of Lunel. Orach Chayim, Tefilah, 72. R. Yehudah HaChassid Sefer Chassidim, Os. 820.* Our prayers should be said in a low voice that only we can hear. *Rambam. Hilchos Tefilah, 5:9. Shulchan Aruch, Orach Chayim, 101:2.*

*"Voice arouses intention". *R. David Ben Shmuel Halevi Taz. Shulchan Aruch, Orach Chayim, 101:3. Rieshis Chochmah, Shar*

HaKedushah, Chap. 15. Shenei Luchos Habris, Shar Ha'osyos, 82b.

* We pray with voice to arouse our hearts and actions. *R. Yitzchak Armah. Akeidas Yitzchak, Parshas Tzav, Shar 58, p. 16b.*

* Speech is an action and thus the act of speaking prayers caus-
es a transformation of the body. *R. Schneur Zalman of Liadi. Tanya, Chap. 37, and Chap. 38. R. Shalom DovBer of Chabad. Kuntras Ha'Avodah, Chap. 1.*

* Spiritual/intellectual prayers have an effect on the spiritual and
mental realm, whereas physical/body prayers have an effect on
the physical. *Baal Shem Tov Al' HaTorah, Parshas Noach, Os 59.*
In fact, words create even higher lights, not just more tangible
vessels. See *R. Chaim Yoseph David Azulay. Shem Hagdalim, and
Rabbi Yitzchak D'min Aco. Ma'areches Gedalim.*

* The Zohar writes that the angels on high refuse to pay attention to the prayers that are not whispered. As the words of
prayer move into the supernal world there is no need or reason
for words, as this is a level that is transcendent of the spoken
word. *Zohar 3, p. 210b.*

* According to Halacha a person must hear his own voice during
the Amidah. *Tur, Orach Chayim, 101.*

* R. Schneur Zalman of Liadi teaches that at this point of the
prayers there is no room for self-expression. Therefore, the
Amidah is prayed in a quiet voice. *Torah Ohr. Parshas Vayechi,*

45d.

* Prayer represents a level that is beyond speech. *R. Shmuel of Sochatchov. Sheim Me'Shemuel, Bereishis, p. 217 –218.*

* The Amidah will be recited with voice in the future. *Torah Ohr. Parshas Vayechi. Likutei Sichos, 35, p.197.*

CHAP. 5.

The Four Descending Steps in the Morning Prayers

* Four stages after the Amidah. *Shar Hakavanos, Tefilas Hashachar, p. 78.* These are four stages within Atzilus itself: 1) Atzilus of Atzilus. 2) Beriah of Atzilus. 3) Yetzirah of Atzilus. 4) Asiyah of Atzilus.
* Between each world a Kaddish is said, but not before the Amidah so as to not separate redemption with prayer. The Kadish of Aleinu is called Kadish of the Orphan as it exists within the world of Asiyah, the world of death. The Kadish is said to elevate the souls of those who are no longer alive.

* Tapping the heart, as the root of an Aveira is an emotional desire. *Magen Avraham, Siman 607.*

* The *Avudraham* writes that chapter 20 in Psalms is appropriate

to recite when a women is in labor.

* With regards to the 9 verses and 70 words see *Zohar 3, 249b. Tikunei Zohar, Tikun 22. Torah Ohr, Parshas Shemos.*

* According to the Geonic tradition, in the name of R. Hai Gaon, Yehoshua composed the Aleinu upon entering the land of Israel. After the destruction of the second Temple, *R. Yochanan Ben Zakai* established that Alienu be recited every day. *Chidah, Machzik Bracha, Siman 132:2.* The prayer Aleinu is not mentioned in the Rambam in the order of prayers, the *Avudraham* also does not mention it. Yet, the *Tur* in *Orach Chayim, 133,* and the *Ramah 133:2,* do mention it. The *Magen Avraham (ad loc.)* writes in the name of the *AriZal* to recite Aleinu after all three prayers.

* The AriZal teaches that the Alienu is part of the sealing of the prayers. We need to make sure that awe does not become anger, and love of Hashem does not morph into lust. *Rabbi Moshe Chaim Ephraim of Sudylkov. Degel Machanah Ephraim, Parshas Ki Tisa, p. 119b.* For this reason the Degel suggests we study Torah immediately following praying.

*Aleinu is the act of bowing out. *Levush, Siman 133.* We say the Aleinu after prayers to demonstrate that we are 'waiting' and settling before we leave the world of prayer. *Taz, Siman 132:2.* Aleinu is said to assist us in integrating our prayers with the reality of this world. *Bach, Siman 133.*

CHAP. 1.

Praying as a Child with no Doubt or Worry, Anytime and for Anything

* Even after Rabbi Nachunya ben Hakana, a famous first century Rabbi, had mastered all the mystical intentions connected with prayer he would still pray like a little child. *Ketones Posim, p. 43b.* Perhaps there was a mix-up in the name of the sage, and this statement is from *R. Shamshin of Kinon.* See *Teshuvas Marshal, Siman 98.* For earlier sources see *R. Yitzchak Ben Sheishes. Teshuvas HaRivash, Siman 157. Ramak, Elimah Rabbasi, Eyn Kol, 1:2. R. Yoseph Ergas. Shomer Emunim, 2:65.*

CHAP. 2.

Praying with Love, Awe, Joy & Awe

* Pray with joy. *Medrash Shocher Tov, Tehilim, Chap. 100.*

* The Arizal writes that one should not pray in a state of depression and if he does so his soul will not be able to absorb the heavenly light that descends through prayer. *Shulchan Aruch AriZal, Orach Chayim, Chap. 1:1. Pri Eitz Chayim, Shar Olam Ha'asiya, Chap. 1. Shar HaKelalim, Hakdamah.* See also; *Kaf Hachayim, Orach Chayim, 90:32).*

* Servant vs. child. *R. Klunimus Kalmish of Peasetzna. Hachsharas Ha'Avreichim, Chap. 1.* See also *R. Shalom DovBer, the Rashab. Tof Reish Samach Vav.* The teaching of the Magid is recorded in many places among them. *Shomer Emunim, Maamor Tzhali V'Roni, Chap 6.*

* Just as begetting offspring needs to be done with joy and desire, the same is true with prayer. *Ben Pores Yoseph, Parshas Noach, p. 19d.*

* Prayers of joy are answered more quickly than prayers said in sadness. *Tzivaa's HaRivash, p. 13a.*

* Joy breaks all boundaries. *Rebbe Rashab.*

* Pray with both humility and joy. *Shulchan Aruch, Orach Chayim, 93:2.*

* Love without reverence is similar to wasted seed. *Imrei Tzadikim, p. 3.*

*"Only in Avodas Hashem can love and awe be entertained simultaneously". *Sifri, Parshas Ekev,* as quoted by the *Reishis Chachmah, Shar Ahavah, Chap. 1.* This teaching is also quoted in the name of the Ramban. *Ben Peros Yoseph, p. 54d.* Joy and reverence are both important to experience during prayer. *Medrash Tehilim, 100:3.* See also; *Keser Shem Tov, 349).*

* Contemplate your human love to arouse Divine love. See *R. Zusya of Hanipoli. Menoras Zahav, p. 169-174. See also R. Klunimus Kalmish of Peasetzna. Movo H'Sharim, Chap. 3, p. 228. Also in the name of the Seer of Lublin. Zikhron Zos.*

* The story of the princes is also recorded by *R. Eliyahu Di Vidas. Reishis Chochmah, Shar Ha'ahavah, Shar 4, p. 63a.*

* The AriZal teaches that we need to declare. *Pri Eitz Chayim, Shar Ha'Karbonos, 2. And Shar Hakavanos, Shar 6, Hakdamah.*

* With regards to the custom to turn around. See *R. Yoseph Chaim of Bagdad. Ben Ish Chai, Shana 1, Parshas Beshalach, 2.*

* Rabbi Yehudah Ha'Chassid writes that whether prayers are answered or not depends on whether those who are praying are concerned with the pain and suffering of others or not. *Sefer Chassidim, Os. 553.*

* *R. Mich'ael of Zlotshov. Likutim Yekarim, 129a.*

* Medrash about making blessings. *Tanchumah, Parshas V'zos Habracha, Chap. 7.*

* *Rabbeinu Bachya on the Torah* explains that tears are to prayers as the Nisuch Ha'Mayim, the "Lubrication of the Altar with Water", is to Karbanos, the "Offerings". *Bereishis, 1:15.*

* When a person involuntarily cries during prayer this is a sign that his prayers have been accepted on high. *R. Pinchas of Koritz. Imrei Pinchas, p. 84.*

* Tefilah comes from the word Tofel, which means to join. *Targum Onkelus, Bereishis, 30:8. Rashi, Rashbam, and Seforno ad loc. R. Mattisyohu Delecreta on Sharei Orah, Shar 2, p. 63. R. Schneur Zalman of Liadi. Torah Ohr, Parshas Terumah, p. 79d. R. Mendel of Vitebsk. Pri Ha'aretz, Parshas Vayigash.*

* *R. Yoseph Yitzchak of Chabad. Sefer Ha'ma'amorim, 5709, p. 79.*

* Prayer reveals our inner most desire to be one with Hashem, as well as Hashem's desire to be with us. See *R. Klunimus Kalmish of Peasetzna. Derech HaMelech, p. 9.*
* *The Maggid of Mezritch. Likutei Yekarim, p. 1b. See also; Os. 44.*

* *The Magid of Koznitz. Avodas Yisroel, Parshas Metzorah, p. 159.*

* Do not despair. *Movo H'Sharim, Chap. 3, p. 228.*

CHAP. 3.

Yesh & Ayin: Attachment/Non-attachment- demanding/surrendering

* We learn many of the laws and customs of praying from Chana. *Berachos, 31a.*

* Inwardly, Ayin is Histavus, "Equanimity". In the language of the Gemrah this is called, "overcoming one's tendencies". The Gemarah speaks of a person's prayers being answered quickly because that person is able to "overcome his tendencies". *Taanis, 25a.*

* The value of prayer is the praying itself. *R. Yaakov Moshe Charlap. Mei Marom, Vol. 1, Hakdamah, p. 5.*

* The human being is a being who prays. *Rashi, Baba Kama, 2a.*

* *Rabbi Moshe Chaim Luzzato. Derech Hashem, Part 4; 5:1.*

* Nahama DeKisufa, "Shameful Bread". *Yerushalmi. Orlah, Chap 1, Halacha 3.* See *Bavli. Kedushin, 36b, Tosefos.* See also; *R. Yoseph Caro. Magid Mesharim, Parshas Bereishis, p. 10. R. Schneur Zalman of Liadi. Likutei Torah, Parshas Tzav, p. 7d. Ramchal. Da'as Tevunos, and, KaLaCh Pischei Chochmah, 4.*

* Hashem's "delight" in giving is greater than our delight in receiving. *Maggid DeVarav L'Yaakov, p. 85.*

* Hashem's "desire" is fulfilled when our prayers are answered. This is a teaching of the Baal Shem Tov as recorded by *R. Moshe Yechial Epshtein. Rispei Eish Das, Shar HaTefilah, p. 92.*

* Prayers are not intended to take the place of action. We are asked to do both. Pray that you have the clarity to do what

needs to be done, but not to pray for something miraculous to occur when you can do something about it. *R. Moshe Metrani. Beis Elokim, Shar HaTefilah, Chap 1, p. 6.*

* One should not think: "I am praying with such Kavanah certainly my prayers will be answered", and thus wait for the answer. *Rosh Hashanah, 16b.* This is called negative Iyyun Tefila according to Rashi and Tosefos.

* Moshe prayed for a "gift" to be given to him as a kindness from Above, even though he could have prayed from a place of feeling deserving and entitled due to his spiritual status and accomplishments. In general a person should not ask because for something in prayer due to their own merit. *Berachos, 10b. Medrash Rabba, Devarim, Parsha 2, Chap. 1. Medrash Tanchuma, Parsha Vaetchanan, Chap. 3.* Yet, see also *Berachos, 17b,* regarding those who are sustained by their own virtue.

* Blessings do no attach themselves to curse. See *Rashi, Bereishis, 24:39.*

APPENDIX I

Ten Sounds, One Source

* Ten Vowels and Ten Sefiros. *R. Moshe Cordevero, the Ramak. Pardas Rimonim, Shar 19, Shar 28, Shar Kavanos.*

* *R. Bachya* writes that Kamatz is "above and high" and Patach is "below" the Kamatz sound. *Parshas Vayeira, 18:3.*

* It appears that according to many commentaries there is a possibility that Patach is actually a Kamatz sound. *Haskamas R. Yehudah Leib Me'yanavitch.* See also; *Siddur Torah Ohr.* See also *Rashi Berachos, 47a. Ha'gaas Yavatz, ad loc.*

* "To Hashem and not to Hashem's attributes". *Medrash Sifri as quoted in the Pardess Rimonim, Shar 32:2.* See also *Rambam. Pirush HaMishnayos, Sanhedrin, Chap. 10, the fifth principle.* In the words of the Yerushalmi "to G-d alone you cry out, but you do not cry out to the angel Michael nor Gabriel". *Berachos, Chap 9.*

* Praising for our own benefit and to change ourselves in the process. *R. Meir Aldavie. Shevilei Emunah, Nosive 1. p. 28. R. Moshe Metrani. Beis Elokim. Shar Hatefila. Chap 2. p 7.* The praise/prayer elevates the person. *Maharal. Nesivos Olam. Nosiv Ha'avodah.* Chap 2. Praising Hashem brings a sense of closeness between us and Hashem. *Reishis Chochmah. Shar Ha'ahavah. Chap 10.*

APPENDIX II

Yichud Zah V'Malchus – Unification between Zah and Malchus

* The act of prayer is to elevate Malchus, which is, before the prayers, in a condition of lack, into Zah- completion. *Shar HaKavanos, Shar 6, Hakdamah*. Before there is the Yichud in the Amidah between Zah and Malchus we read the Shema. The Shema represents Mochin, "mind" or intellect. With the Shema there is an assimilation of Mochin into the emotions, Zah. Once Zah is filled with Mind, Zah can have a Yichud with Malchus and produce "children", i.e. positive results.

* The early Chassidim would spend nine hours a day involved in prayer. *Berachos, 32b*. Prayer is Malchus, the Tenth Sefira. When prayer is "complete", it contains the full structure of all ten Sefiros, thus the nine hours in prayer. *Siddur Pirush Ma'harid*.

* During the hours of the day, the hours of Zah, Tefilah is obligatory. Whereas at night, the time of Malchus, the evening prayer, Ma'ariv, was not (originally) obligatory. The Yichud of Zah and Malchus is more accessible during the day. Nighttime is a harsher and a more judgment oriented quality of time.

* The question is asked by the Kisse Melech and is cited by the *Bnei Yissachar. Chodesh Tishrei, Maamor 9:2*.

* Hashem will bless you according to your speech. *Likutie Hala-chos, Nachlos 4:3.*

OTHER BOOKS
BY RAV DOVBER PINSON

REINCARNATION AND JUDAISM
The Journey of the Soul

A fascinating analysis of the concept of reincarnation as it appears in the works of the Kabbalistic masters, as well as how it is discussed by the great thinkers throughout history. Dipping into the fountain of ancient wisdom and modern understanding, the book addresses and answers such basic questions as: What is reincarnation? Why does it occur? And how does it affect us personally?

INNER RHYTHMS
The Kabbalah of Music

Exploring the inner dimension of sound and music, and particularly, how music permeates all aspects of life. The topics range from Deveikus/ Unity, Yichudim/ Unifications, to the more personal issues, such as Simcha/Happiness, and Marirus/ sadness.

MEDITATION AND JUDAISM
Exploring the Jewish Meditative Paths

A comprehensive work on Jewish meditation, encompassing the entire spectrum of Jewish thought--from the early Kabbalists to the modern Chassidic and Mussar masters, the sages of the Talmud to the modern philosophers. The book is both a scholarly, in-depth study of meditative practices, and a practical, easy to follow guide for any person interested in meditating the Jewish way. In addition, the book broadens our view of meditation, demonstrating that in addition to the traditional methods of meditation ,meditation is prevalent within so many of the common Jewish practices.

TOWARD THE INFINITE
The Way of Kabbalistic Meditation

A book focusing exclusively on the Kabbalistic – Chassidic, Hisbonenus approach to meditation. Encompassing the entire meditative experience, it takes the reader on a comprehensive and engaging journey through meditation. The book explores the various states of consciousness that a person encounters in the course of the meditation, beginning at a level of extreme self-awareness and concluding with a total state of non-awareness.

JEWISH WISDOM OF THE AFTERLIFE
The Myths, the Mysteries & Meanings

What happens to us after we physically die? What is consciousness? And can it survive without a physical brain? What is a soul? Can we remember our past lives? Do near-death-experiences prove the immortality of the soul?

Drawing from the fountain of ancient Jewish wisdom and modern understanding of what consciousness is, this book explores the possibilities of surviving death, the near-death-experience, and a possible glimpse of the peace and unconditional love that awaits, empowering the reader to live their day-to-day life with these great spiritual truths.

UPSHERIN
Exploring the Laws, Customs & Meanings of a Boy's First Haircut

What is the meaning of Upsherin, the traditional celebration of a boy's first haircut at the age of three? This in-depth answer to that question explores as well the questions: Why is a boy's hair allowed to grow freely for his first three years? What is the kabbalistic import of hair in all its lengths and varieties? What is the mystical meaning of hair coverings? Rav Pinson answers these questions with his trademark deep learning and spiritual sensitivity. Includes a guide to conducting an Upsherin ceremony.

THIRTY - TWO GATES OF WISDOM
Awakening through Kabbalah

Kabbalah holds the secrets to a path of conscious awareness. In this compact book, Rav Pinson presents 32 key concepts of Kabbalah and shows their value in opening the gates of perception.

THE PURIM READER
The Holiday of Purim Explored

With a Persian name, a costuming dress code and a woman as the heroine, Purim is certainly unusual amongst the Jewish holidays. Most people are very familiar with the costumes, Megilah and revelry, but are mystified by their significance. Rav Pinson offers a glimpse into the unknown world of Purim, uncovering the mysteries and offering a deeper understanding of this unique holiday.

EIGHT LIGHTS
8 Meditations for Chanukah

What is the meaning and message of Chanukah? What is the spiritual significance of the Lights of the Menorah? What are the Lights telling us? What is the deeper dimension of the Dreidel? Rav Pinson, with his trademark deep learning and spiritual sensitivity guides us through eight meditations relating to the Lights of the Menorah and the eight days of Chanukah, and a deeper exploration of the Dreidel.

Includes a detailed how-to guide for lighting the Chanukah Menorah

THE IYYUN HAGADAH
An Introduction to the Haggadah

In this beautifully written introduction to Passover and the Haggadah, Rav DovBer Pinson, guides us through the major themes of Passover and the Seder night. Rav Pinson addresses the important questions, such as; What is the big deal of Chametz? What are we trying to achieve through conducting a Seder? What's with all that stuff on the Seder Plate? And most importantly, how is this all related to freedom? His answers will surprise even those who think they already know the answers to these questions.

THE MYSTERY OF KADDISH
Understanding the Mourner's Kaddish

The Mystery of Kaddish is an in-depth and Kabbalistic exploration into the Mourner's Prayer. Throughout Jewish history, there have been many rites and rituals associated with loss and mourn-ing, yet none have prevailed quite like the Mourner's Kaddish Prayer - which has become the definitive ritual of mourning. The book explores the source of this prayer and deconstructs the meaning to better understand the grieving process and how the Kaddish prayer supports and uplifts the bereaved through their own personal journey to healing.

RECLAIMING THE SELF
The Way of Teshuvah

Teshuvah is one of the great gifts of life. It speaks of a hope for a better today and empowers us to choose a brighter tomorrow. But what exactly is Teshuvah? And how does it work? How can we undo our past and how do we deal with guilt? And what is healthy regret without eroding our self-esteem? In this fas-cinating and empowering book, world-renowned teacher and thinker, Rav DovBer Pinson lays out a path for genuine trans-formation and a way to include all of our past in the powerful moment of the now.

PASSPORT TO KABBALAH
A Journey of Inner Transformation

Life is a journey full of ups and downs, inside-outs, and unexpected detours. There are times when we think we know exactly where we want to be headed, and other times when we are so lost we don't even know where we are. Rooted in the teachings of Kabbalah, this book provides readers with a passport of sorts to help them through any obstacles along their path of self-refinement, reflection, and self-transformation.

————————

THE FOUR SPECIES
The Symbolism of the Lulav & Esrog

The Four Species, have inspired countless commentaries and traditions and intrigued scholars and mystics alike. In this little masterpiece of wisdom both profound and practical - Rav DovBer Pinson explores the deep symbolic roots and nature of the Four Species. The Na'anuim, or ritual of the Lulav movement, is meticulously detailed and Kavanos, or meditations, are offered for use with the practice. Includes an illustrated guide to the Lulav Movements.

————————

A BOND FOR ETERNITY
Understanding the Bris Milah

What is the Bris Milah – the covenant through circumcision? What does it represent, symbolize and signify? An in depth and sensitive review of this fundamental Mitzvah. In this little masterpiece of wisdom ¬–profound yet accessible, Rav Pinson reveals the deeper meaning of this essential rite of passage and its eternal link to the Jewish people.

THE GARDEN OF PARADOX
The Essence of Non Dual Kabbalah

This book is a Primer on the Essential Philosophy of Kabbalah, presented as a series of 3 conversations, revealing the mysteries of Creator, Creation and Consciousness. With three representational students, embodying respectively, the philosopher, the activist and the mystic, Rav Pinson tackles the larger questions of life. Who is G-d? Who am I? Why do I exist? What is my purpose in this life? Written in clear and concise prose, Rav Pinson gently guides the reader towards making sense of life's paradoxes and living meaningfully.

BREATING & QUIETING THE MIND
The Jewish Meditation Series

Achieving a sense of self-mastery and inner freedom, demands that we gain a measure of hegemony over our thoughts. We learn to choose out thoughts so that we are not at the mercy of whatever burps up to the mind. Through quieting the mind and conscious breathing, we can slow the onrush of anxious, scattered thinking and come to a deeper awareness of the interconnectedness of all of life.

This is book on of the series. In this illuminating series, Rav Pinson transitions theory to practice, complex information into authentic techniques for transformation. The series seeks to uncover the transformational and experiential aspects of these teachings, through exploring the lives and persons of those who taught these practices. Nor merely interested in what they taught, rather, what it was that enabled them to reach their place of wisdom and spiritual greatness.

Source texts are included in translation, with how-to-guides of the various practices.

WRAPPED IN MAJESTY
Tefillin- Exploring the Mystery

Tefillin, the black boxes and leather straps that are worn during prayer, are curiously powerful and mysterious. Within the inky black boxes lie untold secrets. In this profound, passionate and thought-provoking text, Rav Pinson explores and reveals the multi-dimensional perspectives of Tefillin. Magically weaving together all dimensions of Torah; Peshat, literal observation, to Remez, the allegorical; Derush, the homiletic, to Sod, hidden Kabbalistic, into one wonderful tapestry. Inspirational and instructive, Wrapped in Majesty: Tefillin, will make putting on the Tefillin more meaningful and deepen the experience.

ABOUT THE AUTHOR

Rav DovBer Pinson is a world-renowned Torah scholar, prolific author and beloved spiritual teacher. He is widely recognized as one of the world's foremost authorities on authentic Kabbalah and Jewish philosophy.

Through his books, lectures and seminars he has touched and inspired the lives of thousands the world over, and serves as a mentor to many across the globe.

He has authored over 25 books, many of which have been translated into various languages, such as Hebrew, German, Spanish, Russian and Portuguese.

He is the Rosh Yeshivah of the IYYUN Yeshiva and Dean of the IYYUN Center in Brownstone Brooklyn, NY.

CPSIA information can be obtained
at www.ICGtesting.com
Printed in the USA
BVHW071632020920
587907BV00001B/72/J

9 780989 007221